CONNECT FEATURES

Animated Concepts

Brand new animations with updated content on relevant computing topics including cloud computing, mobile apps and systems, social networking, and maintaining safety and security online. These animations are assignable with comprehension assessments, and also combined with a media rich e-book to appeal to all learning styles.

Interactive Applications

Interactive Applications offer a variety of automatically graded exercises that require students to **apply** key concepts. Available with Video cases complete with multiple choice questions and key term drag and drop questions, these applications provide instant feedback and progress tracking for students and detailed results for the instructor.

EASY TO USE

Learning Management System Integration

McGraw-Hill Campus is a one-stop teaching and learning experience available to use with any learning management system. McGraw-Hill Campus provides single sign-on to faculty and students for all McGraw-Hill material and technology from within the school website. McGraw-Hill Campus also allows instructors instant access to all supplements and teaching materials for all McGraw-Hill products.

Blackboard users also benefit from McGraw-Hill's industry-leading integration, providing single sign-on to access all Connect assignments and automatic feeding of assignment results to the Blackboard grade book.

The **Best** of Both Worlds

POWERFUL REPORTING

Connect generates comprehensive reports and graphs that provide instructors with an instant view of the performance of individual students, a specific section, or multiple sections. Since all content is mapped to learning objectives, Connect reporting is ideal for accreditation or other administrative documentation.

At a Glance Insights | Assignment Results & Statistics Reports | Student Performance Reports | Item Analysis Reports | Category Analysis Reports | At-Risk Student Reports | LearnSmart Reports

TECHNOLOGY
AT YOUR SERVICE
Ralph De Arazoza

Mc
Graw
Hill
Education

TECHNOLOGY: AT YOUR SERVICE

Published by McGraw-Hill Education, 2 Penn Plaza, New York, NY 10121. Copyright © 2015 by McGraw-Hill Education. All rights reserved. Printed in the United States of America. No part of this publication may be reproduced or distributed in any form or by any means, or stored in a database or retrieval system, without the prior written consent of McGraw-Hill Education, including, but not limited to, in any network or other electronic storage or transmission, or broadcast for distance learning.

Some ancillaries, including electronic and print components, may not be available to customers outside the United States.

This book is printed on acid-free paper.

4 5 6 7 8 9 QVS/QVS 20 19 18 17 16

ISBN 978-0-07-351687-5
MHID 0-07-351687-2

Senior Vice President, Products & Markets: *Kurt L. Strand*
Vice President, General Manager, Products & Markets: *Michael Ryan*
Vice President, Content Design & Delivery: *Kimberly Meriwether David*
Managing Director: *Scott Davidson*
Brand Manager: *Wyatt Morris*
Director, Product Development: *Meghan Campbell*
Product Developer: *Allison McCabe*
Executive Marketing Manager: *Debbie Clare*
Senior Marketing Manager: *Tiffany Russell*
Digital Product Developer: *Kevin White*
Digital Product Analyst: *Thuan Vinh*
Director, Content Design & Delivery: *Terri Schiesl*
Program Manager: *Mary Conzachi*
Content Project Managers: *Mary E. Powers, Danielle Clement*
Buyer: *Debra R. Sylvester*
Design: *Srdjan Savanovic*
Content Licensing Specialist: *Keri Johnson*
Cover Image: © *VLADGRIN/Getty Images*
Compositor: *Laserwords Private Limited*
Printer: *Quad/Graphics*

All credits appearing on page or at the end of the book are considered to be an extension of the copyright page.

Library of Congress Cataloging-in-Publication Data

De Arazoza, Ralph.
    Technology : at your service / Ralph De Arazoza.—First edition.
        pages cm
    ISBN 978-0-07-351687-5 (alk. paper)
    1. Information technology—Juvenile literature. I. Title.
    T58.5.D426 2015
    004—dc23
                            2014023638

The Internet addresses listed in the text were accurate at the time of publication. The inclusion of a website does not indicate an endorsement by the authors or McGraw-Hill Education, and McGraw-Hill Education does not guarantee the accuracy of the information presented at these sites.

www.mhhe.com

About the Author

Ralph De Arazoza is an Associate Professor of Technology at Miami Dade College, where he has been teaching for over 10 years. His areas of specialization include computer concepts, office applications, web development, photo editing, animation, and computer ethics. He has developed several face-to-face and online courses, including an advanced web programming course covering jQuery and mobile website development.

Prof. De Arazoza's teaching philosophy centers on the way students experience and use technology. His energetic lectures instill a passion for technology in his students, encouraging them to explore what this field has to offer. He also serves as the advisor for the MDC Computer Club, whose members hold a variety of technology workshops and compete in various local and state tournaments throughout the year.

When he is not teaching and working with students, Prof. De Arazoza prepares and writes content for publishers for various types of products such as test banks, exercises, digital presentations, instructor manuals, and chapter revisions. In his spare time he enjoys collecting (and tasting) wine, science fiction, trivia, and just about any type of comedy.

Dedication

For all the educators who have inspired me and the students who continue to motivate me.

Acknowledgments

I would first like to thank my family and friends for their support and encouragement throughout this process. I am especially grateful to my mother and brother, whose expertise on Mac systems proved to be invaluable. I would also like to thank my colleagues at Miami Dade College for their advice and assistance with various topics in this book. A final thanks goes to everyone at McGraw-Hill who continuously encouraged me and helped make this endeavor possible.

Table of Contents

CHAPTER 4
The Internet 94

CHAPTER 5
Networking & Security 132

CHAPTER 6
Changing the World 164

Preface

Before You Begin

If you are reading this textbook, it is likely that you are enrolled in an introductory computing course. Like many students in this type of course, you will soon find yourself taking notes, creating documents, and completing a variety of exercises on your computer. Before you do any of those things, there are a few tools that you should consider using to help you throughout your course.

The companion website to this book (see link below) contains information on where to find these tools. In addition, there are links that provide help on using these tools and tips on how to get the most out of them.

TEXTBOOK RESOURCES

You should become familiar with the online resources available for this textbook.

Companion website

The companion website is located at **techatyourservice .com**. It contains a variety of material that you will find interesting and useful. Here are just a few examples:

- **Before you begin.** Links and tips that cover the tools discussed in this preface.
- **More online.** Throughout the book, you will see "more online" boxes that direct you to the textbook's website. In this section of the site, you will find many useful tips and bonus material that pertain to the section of the book you are currently reading.
- **Videos.** These are links to useful videos or animations that help explain various concepts or contain step-by-step instructions for different activities.
- **Careers.** This section will have up-to-date information on various technology careers, including salary ranges.
- **LearnSmart.** This textbook will feature McGraw-Hill's innovative LearnSmart technology, which presents a study plan of questions that are tailored just for you!

Social media

Find your textbook on various social media sites to receive up-to-date technology news and updates to the book. The course website contains links to:

- Facebook.
- Google+.
- Twitter.

TAKING NOTES

Many students currently take notes in and out of class by writing them on paper or typing them into Microsoft Word. Although these methods may work just fine for you, consider the following tools and the advantages they offer.

Tools

- **Evernote.** Considered one of the premier note-taking apps, it is available on most mobile devices. There are also versions for your Windows or Mac computer. You can type a variety of notes, record reminders, and take/attach photos to your notes. Multiple notebooks can help you keep track of several classes, recipes, wish lists, and anything else you want to remember.
- **Google Docs.** Now part of Google Drive, these are web-based tools that let you create documents, spreadsheets, and presentations without installing any software. Google makes it very easy to type, format, and share notes. Apps are available for a variety of mobile devices.

Write notes, record audio, take photos, and clip websites with Evernote.

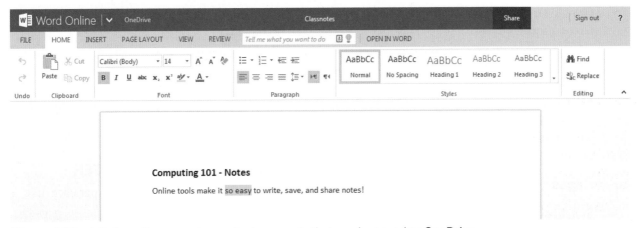

Microsoft Word Online allows you to create documents that can be saved to OneDrive.

- **Microsoft Office Online.** Microsoft now offers mini versions of Word, Excel, and PowerPoint online. These apps are similar to Google Docs, but may seem more familiar to those who have used Microsoft's Office programs before. They may also be desirable if your course includes exercises in MS Office.

Advantages

- **Instant save.** Notes are saved online as you type. If you lose power or your computer crashes, there is no need to worry . . . your notes are safe.
- **Searching.** Digital notes can be searched in the same way that you search websites. Type in a word or two and it will find any page in your notes that contains that word. This is much faster than flipping through pages in a notebook!
- **Easy access.** There is no need to copy your notes from a school's computer to yours, for example, because they are saved online. All you need to access your notes is connection to the Internet.
- **Multiple devices.** These notes are accessible on any Internet-connected device, including your tablet or smartphone.
- **Collaboration.** Share notes with classmates and work together on the same document.

SAVING YOUR WORK

If you have a computer lab or classroom at your school, it is likely that you use a small USB flash drive to save and transport your files. Although these devices are useful, there are more convenient ways

to save your work and keep the files synchronized among all the computers you use.

Tools

- **Dropbox.** This is one of the premier Internet storage and synchronization tools. Save files in a special folder in your computer and it instantly gets uploaded to your account. Manage your files on the website or on the mobile app. Free accounts start at a few gigabytes, but can increase significantly if you refer your friends.

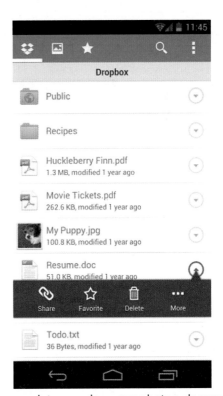

Dropbox app lets you view your photos, documents, and more from a mobile device.

- **Google Drive.** Similar to Dropbox, Google Drive offers a bit more storage because Google also includes whatever you have in Gmail and Google+ photos. It also includes Google Docs.
- **Microsoft OneDrive.** Similar to Google Drive, this new service from Microsoft offers a few gigabytes of storage and excellent integration with Office Online.

Advantages

- **Synchronization.** Each of these tools will install a special folder on your desktop/laptop computer. Anything you place in that folder is instantly uploaded to your online account so that you can access it from anywhere. Any changes you make to your files will trigger synchronization, ensuring that your files are always up-to-date in all of your computers. This is extremely useful for those who have multiple computers or are just tired of carrying around a portable storage device.
- **Access anywhere.** Your important files are accessible no matter where you are. All three of these tools have apps that can be installed on your desktop/laptop and mobile devices. In addition, they have websites that are easy to use, allowing you to open your files without the need to install the app on another computer.
- **Easy sharing.** Instead of attaching large files in emails or messages, these tools allow you to include a link to your files and photos. You control who can see your files and who cannot.

PROTECTING YOUR COMPUTER

Nothing can ruin your computing experience like a virus or spyware. Although some viruses can be deadly for your computer, many infections can slow down your system or steal valuable information from you.

It is true that Mac computers rarely get viruses; however, infections have started to rise as the Mac's popularity increases. If you have Windows, it is crucial that you have a reliable and active antivirus installed. While Windows itself offers basic protection, it simply isn't enough against today's sophisticated attacks. If you do not have an up-to-date antivirus running on your system, you can easily install one of these free tools today:

Tools

- AVG AntiVirus Free.
- Avast Free Antivirus.
- Avira Free Antivirus.

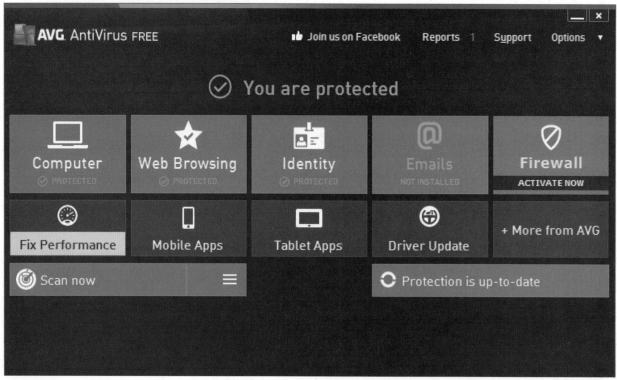

AVG AntiVirus Free.

TECHNOLOGY
AT YOUR SERVICE

Ralph De Arazoza

1

INTRODUCTION

Chapter Overview

This chapter covers the fundamentals of computing. You will discover the different types of computers that exist today and learn how they are being used in a variety of organizations. In addition, you will explore several mobile devices and wearable technology that are transforming many aspects of today's society.

PART 1:
The World of Technology

Regardless of your experience with computers, you probably have been blown away by how quickly technology progresses. This rapid change leads to amazing developments in medicine, engineering, and other fields. At the same time, it also frustrates many individuals who feel as if they are always playing "catch up" with technology. Whether it is figuring out which mobile device to purchase or how best to protect sensitive information, many individuals feel overwhelmed and confused. This book aims to ease this frustration by increasing your **digital literacy**—a broad understanding of computer and information technology, along with the ability to use it well. Once you become familiar with the world of technology, you will be ready to use it in every aspect of your life: work, education, communication, and even entertainment.

Technology Is Everywhere

Computers have drastically changed the way we do everything in our society. You could probably come up with a long list of reasons computers are important to most individuals and organizations. Many of these reasons likely have to do with information, which is something that computers allow us to create and access at very fast speeds. In addition, computers support the technology and infrastructure that allows us to communicate this information to anyone in the world.

It would be impossible to list all the ways in which computers are being used today. Therefore, this section will focus on just a few of the roles computers have in society.

HOME

Today, many American families own multiple computers, all sharing an Internet connection in their homes. While some families might share a larger computer at a desk, low prices

have made it easier for many individuals (especially students) to have their own portable computer, which they use both in and out of their home. In addition to computers, technology now allows us to manage many aspects of our home life, from controlling our TVs and sound systems to monitoring security cameras from a remote location. Let's look at some of the activities that home users can engage in with the power of technology:

- **Communication.** The power of the Internet allows computer users to communicate with people all over the world. Friends and family members can stay in touch with one another more easily than ever before. A variety of services, such as Facebook and Instagram, make it simple to share updates and special moments with everyone in your social circle.

- **Business work done at home.** Thanks to computers and Internet connections, more people are working from home than ever before. Many users connect to their employer's systems from home. Computers also are making it easier for people to start their own home-based businesses.

- **Schoolwork.** Today's students are increasingly reliant on computers, particularly for researching information online. Electronic books are replacing printed books, and easy-to-use software makes it possible for students to create polished documents and presentations. Even grade school students are using computers to learn how to read and complete basic math problems.

- **Entertainment.** Computers and video game consoles offer a variety of entertainment options, from solitaire to realistic sports and action games. People can play games alone, with a friend or family member, or go online to play with tens of thousands of others in a single, massive fantasy world. Computers can also serve as media centers, storing music, videos, and movies for on-demand playback on other computers, consoles, and televisions throughout the home.

Many students use a portable computer at home and at school.

- **Creativity.** Art, music, photography, and creative writing—these once required publishers and marketing efforts to reach a vast audience. Now, with blogs, personal web pages, and social media, people can create just about anything and share it with a large number of individuals.

- **Finances and shopping.** Computers and personal finance software can make it easy to manage your budget. Home users rely on their computers for paying bills and making investments. They also use computers to spend what they earn, shopping online for everything from cars to collectibles.

HEALTH CARE

Here are a few examples of how computers are changing the way organizations and health care providers help individuals feel better:

- **Procedures.** A variety of medical procedures now involve computers, from ultrasound and magnetic resonance imaging (MRI) to laser eye surgery and fetal monitoring. Surgeons can use robotic surgical devices to perform delicate operations and even to conduct surgeries remotely.

- **Research.** The care we all receive has been improved drastically over the years because of the research capabilities offered by computers.

Computers offer education and entertainment for many families.

Powerful systems have helped researchers discover new medications and treatments. Also, robotic technology and implantable computer chips are currently helping a variety of patients, from those who have lost a limb to individuals who suffer seizures or tremors.

- **Training.** Various technologies are being used to train students in the health sciences. One example is an automated "dummy" that simulates a real patient with a variety of conditions.

- **Medical records.** Most hospitals, doctors, and pharmacies have turned to electronic medical records. This makes it easier to search for something specific in your medical history, as well as share it with another health care provider who is also caring for you.

INDUSTRY

Today, large businesses use a variety of technologies to run their operations. Corporate headquarters are filled with employees using connected computers, while production facilities might use computer-controlled robotics to manufacture products. Here are just a few ways computers are applied to industry:

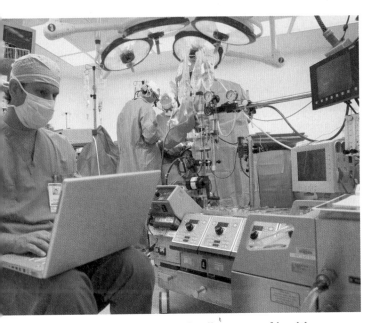

Computers help in nearly all aspects of health care, from electronic medical records to controlling machines for surgeons.

Police officers use computers to quickly access vital information.

- **Design.** Nearly any company that designs and makes products can use a computer-aided design or computer-aided manufacturing system.
- **Shipping.** Freight companies need computers to manage the thousands of ships, planes, trains, and trucks that are moving goods at any given moment. In addition to tracking vehicle locations and contents, computers can manage maintenance, driver schedules, invoices and billing, and many other activities.
- **Process control.** Modern assembly lines can be massive, complex systems, and a breakdown at one point can cause chaos throughout a company. Sophisticated process-control systems can oversee output, check the speed at which a machine runs, and analyze inventory, all with very little human interaction.
- **Administration.** Computers now help a wide range of office workers complete their tasks more quickly and efficiently. For example, accountants use sophisticated software to track income and expenses, while a human resources specialist keeps track of all employee records. Managers can use computers to oversee a variety of business operations and keep track of employee performance.

- **Marketing.** In order to compete and sell products or services, most businesses need to advertise. Computers help companies produce everything from flyers and coupons to sophisticated television commercials.

GOVERNMENT

Not only is government a big consumer of technology, but government also helps to develop it as well. As you will learn in Chapter 4, the U.S. government played a key role in developing the Internet. Today, computers play a crucial part in nearly every level of government, from federal agencies to your local police.

- **Military.** Some of today's most sophisticated technology exists because it was developed and funded by the military. A few of the earliest computers were created for combat or defense functions, such as improving radar and rocket technology. Today, the military uses computers for a variety of reasons including combat simulation, research, defense, and controlling unmanned aerial vehicles (drones).
- **Security.** Colossus, the first programmable electronic computer, was used by the British during World War II to help crack many coded messages being sent to the German army. Today, government agencies such as the CIA and NSA use large, sophisticated computer systems to gather intelligence. The United States Cyber Command is also involved with security, protecting crucial systems and networks against computer-based attacks.
- **Taxes.** The Internal Revenue Service uses computers to calculate the tax bills for millions of individuals and corporations. In addition, the IRS encourages taxpayers to file their tax returns electronically via the Internet.
- **Police.** Many police forces consider computers to be just as important as guns and ammunition. Today's police cruisers are equipped with laptop computers and wireless Internet connections that enable officers to search through millions of records instantly.

Basic Terms in Computing

Now that you are familiar with the variety of tasks that computers can be used for, it is time to learn basic terminology used in the world of computers and technology.

WHAT IS A COMPUTER?

In the simplest terms, a **computer** is a device that accepts input, processes data, and can output or store the result of its actions. All computers, regardless of their size, purpose, or type, follow this definition. Let us take a closer look at the elements in this definition:

- **Input** refers to user entries or activities that tell the computer what to do. Input can take a variety of forms, such as the text you type with your keyboard or finger movements on the touchscreen of a mobile device.

- **Processing** is the ability of a computer to perform actions based on instructions from the user or a program. As you already know, a computer can complete a variety of tasks including financial calculations and handling the graphics for a video game.

- **Output** refers to the processed results that a computer sends out to you. Typically, the results appear on the computer's screen or on a printed piece of paper.

- **Storage** is the ability of a computer to hold or remember the information it processes. Some storage is temporary, such as the data held by your computer's RAM, or memory. Most storage, however, is permanent; it will remain there until you erase it.

These four operations are part of a process called the **information processing cycle** (see Figure 1.1). In Chapter 2, you will explore a variety of devices that perform the functions in this cycle.

1) Input
2) Processing
3) Output
4) Storage

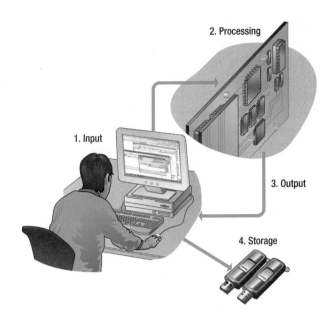

Figure 1.1   The Information Processing Cycle

HARDWARE   *Anything you can touch*

The physical devices that make up a computer system are called **hardware**. Hardware is any part of the computer you can touch. Processors, monitors, and keyboards are all examples of hardware. These parts will be discussed in more detail throughout Chapter 2.

SOFTWARE

A **computer program** is a set of instructions that directs the computer to perform a variety of tasks. These instructions are written in a computer programming language such as C++, Java, and Visual Basic. The term **software** refers to one or more of these programs that are packaged together for a unified purpose. Some software, such as the Windows or Mac OS *operating systems,* exists primarily to help the computer run and manage its resources. Other types of software known as applications or *apps* enable users to perform a variety of activities. These include creating documents, playing games, or communicating with others. A variety of software that can be purchased or downloaded (retrieved) from the Internet will be discussed throughout Chapter 3.

DATA

Data consist of individual facts or pieces of information. Suppose for a moment that you are a traffic engineer who is working on a proposal to lower the speed limit on a neighborhood street. You might collect facts (data) about the speed of each car and any accidents that you observed on that road. Choosing the right data to examine and process is a big part of making the computer an effective tool.

Hardware refers to the parts that make up a computer system.

There is a difference between information and data. Information describes concepts, facts, and ideas that people find useful. Data are raw materials that we use in the creation of information. In the example above, the individual speeds are not very useful when considered by themselves. But when we average them using computer software and give them context in our proposal, we produce useful information. Others can read the proposal and gain an understanding of what is going on in that neighborhood's street.

NETWORKS

A **network** allows users to communicate and share information between computers. A computer network is what allows multiple employees to access information about customers or products from a central computer. It also allows friends and family to have a live conversation with each other, even if they live in different parts of the world. Computers in a traditional network are connected by cables; however, more computers are now being connected via **wireless networks**, whereby communication takes place using radio waves. **Wi-Fi** is the current standard for wireless networks and Internet connectivity.

Networks allow many users to connect to a central computer to access information and communicate.

Regardless of how computers connect, networks have transformed the way in which we communicate at home and at work. We will discuss networking in more detail in Chapter 5.

THE INTERNET

The largest network in the world is known as the **Internet**, which connects billions of people and organizations throughout the world. Many of you likely go "online" every day and perhaps own a home computer or mobile device that is permanently connected to the Internet. If you have not used the Internet, you have probably heard of some of its capabilities.

Most individuals use the Internet to access web pages on the **World Wide Web (WWW)**. These pages can contain a seemingly unlimited variety of information, from news and sports to updates from your family and social circle. Another popular use of the Internet is electronic mail, or **email**, which allows messages to be sent to electronic mailboxes in an instant. The fastest-growing areas of the Internet are cloud computing and social media. **Cloud computing**, simply put, allows you to store your files and use various applications in an online account. **Social media** refers to a variety of websites and services that allow individuals to share photos, news, and thoughts on just about anything. Friends, family, and co-workers often connect by using social media. We will explore all aspects of the Internet in more detail throughout Chapter 4.

The Internet and World Wide Web offer a variety of services.

Categories of Computers

Computers, just like vehicles, come in all sorts of sizes and can serve a variety of purposes. In the same way that the automobile industry separates cars and vans into distinct categories, the computer industry also uses categories to differentiate between various types of computers. The enormous computers that fill an entire room within a large business are clearly different from those you can stick inside your pocket. As we explore all of these categories, keep in mind that the line between some categories is very thin and can change as new devices are released by manufacturers.

PERSONAL COMPUTERS

The computers that you are likely familiar with are those meant to be used by only one person at a time. Those computers have historically been known as **personal computers (PCs)** or microcomputers. However, in recent times, the term "PC" most commonly refers to personal computers that run the Windows operating system. Although Apple's line of desktop and laptop computers are technically personal computers, no one would ever refer to them as PCs. Instead, they call them "Macs." It is also important to note that the term *mobile device,* and not PC,

An all-in-one desktop computer.

is used to refer to the latest tablets and smartphones, even though they are, of course, computers that are intended for personal use. We will be exploring mobile devices in detail throughout Part 2 of this chapter. For now, let us turn our attention to desktop and laptop computers.

DESKTOP COMPUTERS

The computer that has been traditionally found on the desks in many offices and homes is the **desktop computer**. This computer received its name a few decades ago when it was originally designed to lie flat on top of your desk, with the monitor, or screen, being placed on top of it. Today, most desktop computers are in the form of towers that are usually placed below the desk. Others are available as **all-in-one computers** that have all of the hardware integrated with the monitor.

Today, the desktop is losing ground to various portable computers, which have become both powerful and affordable. However, many individuals still prefer having a desktop system that has a larger monitor and more comfortable keyboard. In addition, tower-based systems can be custom-built by anyone who knows how to purchase and connect the pieces. Various power users, such as gamers, will often take advantage of this option to get the exact configuration that best meets their needs.

LAPTOP COMPUTERS

Laptop computers are portable computers that contain all of the components of a desktop computer in a single, integrated unit. Also known as notebook computers, laptops possess a folding monitor that can rest flat against an area containing the keyboard and other hardware components. They also include wireless

Many individuals now use a laptop as their main computer.

capabilities that allow users to connect to the Internet at a variety of locations. A rechargeable battery keeps them powered for a few hours, and they can be connected directly to a power outlet when the battery runs out.

Laptops are fully functional personal computers. They can use the same software and accomplish most of the same tasks as a desktop computer. Because of this, many individuals have chosen to buy a laptop as their primary computer; they use it when they are home and when they are on the go. Let us now take a look at a few varieties of laptops that possess unique qualities:

- **Netbooks** are small and inexpensive laptops that have reduced processing power and lack a DVD drive. They are designed for budget shoppers who will use the computer primarily for browsing the web and basic office tasks, such as creating documents. These types of computers are losing popularity because the prices of regular laptops have dropped to historic lows.

This convertible laptop can be used as either a tablet or a regular laptop.

- **Ultraportable computers** are thin, lightweight laptops that possess strong processing power. They are more powerful than netbooks, but also more expensive. Many weigh less than four pounds and are often touchscreen capable in order to take advantage of the Windows 8 interface. Apple's MacBook Air competes with Intel-based Ultrabooks in this category.

- **Convertible laptops** are lightweight laptop computers that allow users to swivel or detach the touchscreen monitor. This gives users maximum flexibility, allowing them to switch between a laptop and tablet experience based on their needs. We will discuss tablet computers in more detail later in this chapter.

- **Chromebooks** are lightweight laptops that run Google's Chrome operating system. These are usually the most affordable laptops, partly because they contain very little storage inside the computer. Google encourages users to store most of their information in an online Google account, which means that an Internet connection is often needed.

More **Online:** *Do you want your laptop battery to last longer? Visit the companion website to learn the answer to this and other common laptop-related questions.*

MULTI USER COMPUTERS

Some computers, such as those that manage large retail stores or airline reservation systems, are designed to work with many people at the same time. These larger, **multi-user computers** manage a variety of services for businesses and organizations. They act as the central computer in a network, allowing personal computers to connect to them in order to access information or software stored inside of them.

Narrow blade servers are suitable for side-by-side installation in a server rack.

NETWORK SERVERS

A **network server** is a powerful computer with special software and equipment that enables it to function as the primary computer in a network. Though their exact functions are different from organization to organization, network servers all have the basic task of making files, software, and in some cases, other computer hardware available to many users at any given time. For example, a network server might run the email services accessed by all employees, while another server manages the company's website.

Often, the requests from the network grow so large and complex that a single server cannot handle the job by itself. In such cases, network server computers are linked to share the load. In some cases, dozens or even hundreds of individual servers work together to manage data processing requests. When set up in such groups—sometimes called *clusters* or *server farms*—network servers must be arranged in a space-saving manner. Each computer is reduced to a thin unit called a **blade server**, which can slide in and out of a rack that holds many of its companion servers. In these large networks, server groups are often serving different purposes or supporting a certain set of users.

MAINFRAME COMPUTERS

Mainframe computers are very large and powerful systems used in organizations where a heavy amount of processing and user requests need to be handled. A state's government, for example, might use a mainframe to store information about drivers, vehicles, and driver's licenses. Some school districts and colleges use these computers to manage records related to employees, students, and courses. Large businesses, such as international banks and airlines, might use several mainframes to handle the millions of transactions that are performed on a daily basis.

Engineer working on a mainframe computer.

NASA's supercomputer fills this entire room.

SUPERCOMPUTERS

Supercomputers are the largest and most powerful computers in the world. These enormous machines, which often fill warehouse-sized rooms, can link hundreds of thousands of processors. Supercomputers are ideal for handling large and highly complex problems that require extreme calculating power. NASA, for example, will use supercomputers to conduct modeling and simulations for upcoming missions. Others might be involved in forecasting weather, performing nuclear research, and even breaking codes on behalf of a government agency.

> More **Online:** *What is the fastest computer in the world? What does it do? Visit the companion website to find out.*

EMBEDDED SYSTEMS

All of the computers you have learned about so far are general-purpose computers—they can be used for just about anything. In contrast, **embedded systems** are limited computers because they are placed inside devices that require specific computing functions. Embedded systems manage a variety of functions inside modern cars, military equipment, medical imaging devices, and several home appliances. In this section, we will explore a few examples of these systems.

E-BOOK READERS

Electronic books (e-books) are digital books that are stored on a computing device. These books can contain a mix of text, illustrations, and photos, much like a traditional, paper-based book. Although e-books can be read on a variety of computers, several companies have created special **e-book readers**, or e-readers, to make it convenient for individuals to store many of their books. Compared to tablet computers, these devices are much lighter, affordable, and enjoy a longer battery life. They have unique screens featuring crisp black text that is capable of being read in even the brightest outdoor conditions. Because of these features, many individuals find e-book readers to be much more comfortable for extended reading than regular tablet computers. However, their limited processors prevent these devices from being used for much more than reading books. Examples of e-readers include:

- Amazon Kindle
- Barnes & Noble Nook

GAMING CONSOLES

For decades, video game systems have provided countless hours of excitement for children (and adults) in front of the TV. However, today's **gaming consoles** are complete entertainment systems, offering Internet connectivity, movie rentals, photo storage, and many other services in addition to video games. Many consoles are also Blu-ray disc players, which allow you to watch high-definition movies stored on these discs.

Sony PlayStation 4 gaming console with controller and camera.

The Amazon Kindle e-book reader offers easy reading in all lighting levels.

A variety of input devices are available for these consoles, ranging from game controllers and musical instruments to sophisticated video cameras that can capture the body's movements during an exercise routine. Example consoles include:

- Sony PlayStation 4 (PS4)
- Microsoft Xbox One
- Nintendo WiiU

SMART TVS

Many new TVs are being manufactured with the ability to use your home's Internet connection to bring you a variety of services. These **smart TVs** can connect to a variety of online services such as Netflix, Amazon, and Pandora to let you watch movies and listen to music from your accounts. Many of these TVs also offer connectivity with your home computers and mobile devices. This allows you to easily access videos, photos, and music on these devices without the need to plug in cables or storage devices to your TV.

If you are not ready to replace your current television, a variety of **streaming players** can add many of these "smart" features to almost any TV. These small, affordable devices connect to your TV and wireless home network. For those who have newer gaming consoles, it is unlikely that you will need a streaming player since these consoles include many of the same online services. Examples of streaming players include:

- Roku
- Apple TV

The small Roku streaming player can turn a TV into a smart TV.

Home automation allows individuals to remotely manage and automate their home's lighting, temperature, security systems, and various smart appliances.

HOME AUTOMATION

In addition to entertainment systems, many other areas in your home can benefit from embedded computers. We are currently seeing an increase in **home automation**, where many household activities are being automated or controlled from a distance (often using mobile devices as remote controls). The following are some examples of what home automation offers:

- **Security.** Surveillance cameras, home alarms, and door locks can now be activated or monitored from any device that has an Internet connection.

- **Temperature.** New generations of thermostats contain sophisticated programming that can manage the temperature automatically based on your schedule/routine and energy-saving goals.

- **Lighting.** The lights throughout your home can be turned on and off from a mobile device. They can also be automated with motion detectors, allowing them to turn off automatically whenever you leave a room.

- **Appliances.** Many of today's appliances have embedded systems that manage touchscreen interfaces and control a variety of internal functions. Some homeowners have also purchased automated vacuum cleaners that use advanced sensors to clean large areas and avoid obstacles.

More **Online:** Visit the companion website to learn more about the convenience and energy-saving features of the Nest thermostat.

Hands-Free Computing

The ability to communicate with a device without using your hands is known as **hands-free computing**. This technology became popular about a decade ago when individuals looked for ways to make extended cell phone conversations more comfortable. Using a short-range wireless technology known as **Bluetooth**, calls could be made with a wireless headset worn on the ear or the hands-free systems in some cars. In addition to Bluetooth, many mobile devices now support voice input as a hands-free way to issue commands and dictate messages. Hands-free computing has a couple of benefits—convenience and safety.

CONVENIENCE

Many individuals feel that it is difficult to type quickly on the small, on-screen keyboards of most mobile devices. By using your voice, you can send messages, initiate web searches, and even request a direct answer to many common questions. Apple's Siri, Microsoft's Cortana, and Google's Voice Search are three products that respond to a variety of voice commands on mobile devices. Their ability to understand you is made possible by a technology known as speech recognition, which will be discussed further in Chapter 2.

SAFETY

It can be dangerous to use mobile devices during various activities, especially when driving a car. In fact, many state governments have passed laws restricting the way you use mobile devices while driving. Instead of holding a smartphone while talking or texting, it is safer to use hands-free technology. Many new cars have buttons on the steering wheel that allow you to make and receive calls. Together with a microphone and the speakers of your car, you can have conversations while keeping your hands on the wheel. In addition, many smartphones and car dashboards include the ability to read incoming messages and driving directions out loud, thereby eliminating the need to look at the screen. Although it is best to avoid any distractions when driving, hands-free technology will let you keep your eyes on the road.

Hands-free systems allow you to keep your hands on the wheel while driving.

Safety and Courtesy

In addition to distracted driving, other risks arise from the widespread adoption of mobile devices. Furthermore, many social interactions are changing because of the constant use of these devices. Let's look at a few of these issues.

DEVICE DAMAGE

This may seem obvious, but mobile devices are not designed to handle frequent drops or crushing weight. The glass itself is surprisingly strong; however, you have probably seen a few people with cracked screens. The best way to avoid damage to your mobile device is to buy a protective case. Some of these are affordable, thin, and light, but they may not offer the best protection for those who have slippery fingers. If you want the best protection, invest in a bulkier and/or waterproof case.

One additional option to consider is an extended warranty or insurance plan. Many individuals keep their smartphones for about two years because of the way wireless contracts are structured. If your phone comes with only a one-year warranty, you will be left with a gap of one year. If you cannot afford the extra insurance, find out if your credit card comes with an extended warranty plan. Many cards come with a benefit that will extend the warranty of your purchases up to one year.

LOSS AND THEFT

Mobile devices are small and valuable. This puts them at risk of being stolen, especially because users tend

A protective case can help prevent damage from drops.

to leave them behind in restaurants, classrooms, and even restrooms. Although the monetary loss hurts, worse is having a thief go through your personal information. Imagine all the photos, emails, and personal data that can be found by looking through your apps. And if you use your mobile device for work, the organization that employs you will also be put at risk. To avoid these problems, make sure that you use both of these tools:

- **Lock screens**, which are the start screens of mobile devices, allow users to set a password, PIN, or other security measure in order to access the device. Be sure you use this feature and configure the automatic lock based on your personal habits and tendency to lose the device.

- **Remote wipe** utilities allow users to erase their mobile device if it is lost or stolen. These utilities typically require that you log into a website to issue the remote wipe command.

WIRELESS SECURITY

Many mobile users rely on wireless connections available at schools, libraries, and various businesses in their city. For maximum security, always ask an employee for the name of the wireless network that you should connect to. Once connected, be careful with the websites and apps that you use. Casual browsing is fine, but transmitting sensitive information may be risky if the wireless connection is not secure. We will cover security issues in more detail throughout Chapter 5.

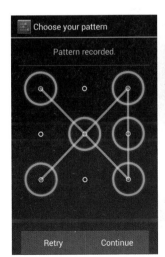

Protect your personal information by adding security on your device's lock screen.

Observe common courtesy when using mobile devices around others.

Observe Common Courtesy

RUDENESS

While personal and equipment safety are fairly straightforward concepts, the same cannot be said about courtesy to others when using mobile devices. It is true that different individuals and societies disagree on what is considered rude behavior. In addition, a behavior that may be acceptable when having lunch with co-workers will be unacceptable during a business meeting with the same people. Chapter 6 addresses computing ethics and proper online behavior. For now, a few general guidelines will help you start thinking about courteous mobile computing.

PHONE AND VOICE VOLUME

This topic is fairly straightforward. As a general rule, always put your phone on vibrate mode when in public or in the company of other individuals. When in a very quiet environment, such as a classroom or meeting, be aware that a vibrating phone on a table can still be a distraction. In addition, be aware of the volume of your voice if using your phone in a public area such as a grocery store or medical office. Don't speak any louder than you would to someone who is standing next to you. If you must speak louder, go outside.

COFFEE SHOP COURTESY

Don't make the coffee shop your new office or study center unless you've been invited to do so. If you sit down and spread your notebook computer, mobile device, and books across a four-person table, you're occupying a lot of space that the owners may have hoped could be used by more than a single person. If you plan to occupy that table for hours, consider whether that cup of coffee is adequate "rent" for the

Be mindful of both the coffee shop owner and other customers when studying for extended periods.

time and space you are using. Lastly, always be sure to check for those who are standing, waiting for a table to clear so that they can enjoy their food and drinks.

MESSAGING WHILE MAD

Mobile devices give individuals the opportunity to communicate with almost anyone in a matter of seconds. This capability can be a big problem if a person decides to send a message or post a social network comment while upset. For most individuals, it is psychologically easier to send an angry electronic message than it is to call or yell in someone's face. To spare hurt feelings and reduce your risk of losing a friend (or your job), give yourself a few minutes to think clearly before clicking "send."

DIVIDING ATTENTION

No mobile behavior is as widespread and controversial as dividing your attention between your device and those around you. Generally, using your mobile device while engaged in a face-to-face interaction signals a lack of interest in the person you are interacting with. Other times, such as when placing an order or paying for goods, your mobile device may distract you from the fact that others are waiting in line behind you. Unless you are waiting for an urgent message or phone call, it is best to put your mobile

Unfortunately, mobile devices make it a little too easy to send messages when upset.

device away during class, meetings, dinners, and many other social situations that demand your undivided attention.

Some have argued that mobile devices are slowly changing our conception of what is rude behavior. For example, many of your friends or family members may not think twice if you quickly check a notification on your smartphone. However, if you start to send messages back and forth or engage in a long conversation, your behavior will likely be deemed unacceptable. To be polite, always ask those who are close to you how they feel about mobile devices. You may find that your friends enjoy having online social interactions at the same time that you are all having conversations in person. In fact, part of the fun may be discussing a crazy photo or video that a mutual friend posted. As long as you consider the feelings and preferences of those you are with, common sense will likely help you judge when the use of your mobile device is appropriate.

Rules for using mobile devices around friends can vary from one group to another.

Computing in New Ways

Mobile and wearable technology is changing many aspects of our lives. Having an always-on Internet connection and a countless number of apps has transformed the way we communicate and stay in touch. In addition, a world of knowledge is accessible in an instant, enabling you to make better decisions as you go through your day. In this section, we look at innovative and popular activities that are made possible by the widespread adoption of mobile devices. We will continue exploring apps and online services throughout Chapters 3 and 4.

LOCATION-BASED SERVICES

If you allow it, your mobile device can identify and report your location through the use of GPS, cell phone towers, and nearby wireless access points. This allows many organizations to offer you **location-based services (LBS)** through apps installed on your mobile device. The Yelp app, for example, informs you which restaurants are close to you and how others have rated them. You can even "check in" to a variety of businesses to let your friends know where you are and receive potential discounts from those businesses. Another benefit of LBS is the ability to receive driving directions based on your current location. Through the use of apps such as Google Maps, your mobile device can perform many of the navigation functions of a stand-alone GPS unit.

Some have concerns with location-based services, especially when it comes to privacy. They worry

Check in and find nearby restaurants with the Yelp app.
Source: Yelp app

about the safety of the individuals who share their whereabouts and the data gathering being done by various companies. We will cover many of these issues in Chapter 6.

REAL-TIME INFORMATION

Real-time information refers to any information that is delivered to you immediately after it is created. Mobile devices allow individuals throughout the world to report events as they witness or experience them. They also offer a platform for opinions on just about anything, from a reality TV show to a politician's speech. The service known as Twitter has become the go-to service for real-time information. You can follow individuals and organizations that you find interesting or you can search for specific keywords related to the event that you want to know more about. Whether it is reactions to a big play in a sports game or an emergency in a location near you, Twitter will often have information before other sources.

Weather apps also offer real-time information, with radar images and weather data receiving continuous updates. The traffic reports offered by various map and navigation apps also make use of real-time data. A series of icons or colored lines indicate areas that are currently congested, allowing you to change your route before reaching the problem area.

CROWDSOURCING

Many of the companies that offer traffic data on your mobile device do not always use traditional sources such as news and police reports. Many turn to **crowdsourcing**, which is the gathering of information from a large group of people. Because many of us have location-based services on our devices, the speed of our cars can be used to determine areas where traffic is slow. In addition, apps such as Waze rely on users to report accidents, construction areas, and even gas prices. The more information that users provide, the better the app becomes for everyone.

The Waze navigation app combines location-based services, real-time data, and crowdsourcing.

MOBILE PAYMENTS

Your mobile device is now capable of becoming your digital wallet, freeing you from having to carry so many things with you at all times. Using a wireless technology known as **NFC** (near field communication), many smartphones can now be tapped on special payment devices to complete your purchase at select stores. All you need to do is save your bank or credit card information in an app such as Google Wallet. The payment device at the store will then process the transaction as if you had swiped your debit or credit card. Google Wallet can also store promotions and coupons electronically. The following are some additional ways in which mobile devices are making payments easier:

- **Sending money.** The apps of several banks now offer the capability to send anyone money, transferring a designated amount from your bank account to theirs.

- **Receiving payments.** For those who need to accept credit cards on a continuous basis, devices such as Square plug into your mobile device and allow customers to swipe their credit card like they would anywhere else. A companion app processes the payment and keeps track of all your transactions.

SOCIAL AND SHARING

For many individuals, the mobile device has become the primary tool for sharing events and

The Square credit card reader and mobile app turns a smartphone into a payment device.

communicating with friends and family. Many popular services and apps allow us to stay in touch with one another.

COMMUNICATION AND MESSAGING

Mobile communication is instantaneous: Individuals can send and receive information from others in real time. This allows mobile users to easily relay what they see and feel at the moment, as well as respond to questions quickly from wherever they are. Many users have messaging capabilities on their cell phones and smartphones that are offered by wireless providers. The **Short Message Service (SMS)** allows you to send text messages of 160 characters to any other cell phone user. The more versatile **Multimedia Messaging Service (MMS)** allows you to attach a variety of media such as photos and short videos.

There are new alternatives to these services on smartphones and tablets. Companies such as Google and Apple, along with many social media websites, offer messaging services that use your Internet connection. You no longer need to pay for a text messaging plan as long as all of the individuals that you communicate with install the same free messaging tool. Many of these services also offer free video calling capabilities that allow you to have video conversations with anyone in the world. You can message and talk as much as you wish using the following

Google's Hangouts app allows you to send messages, share photos, and make video calls.

apps, but be mindful of your data limits if you are not connecting via Wi-Fi.

- **Apple iMessage.** Exclusive to users of Apple's computers and mobile devices, this free service lets you send text messages, photos, and videos to any other user of this service.

- **WhatsApp.** Free for the first year, this messaging service has become very popular worldwide as the main substitute for SMS. Setup is easy, as it uses your current phone number and scans your contact list for other WhatsApp users. Text, photo, and video messaging are all available.

- **Videoconferencing tools.** If you prefer having a video conversation using your mobile device, several reliable services work on a variety of computers. Two of the most popular free tools are Skype and Google Hangouts, both of which provide complete messaging services in addition to video conversations. Apple offers a competing tool known as FaceTime that can be used exclusively by owners of Apple devices.

SOCIAL NETWORKING

Social networking services make it easy for friends and family to share updates and special events with each other. While messaging services target specific people, social networking allows users to post a message, photo, or video that can be viewed by anyone in their social circle. Some individuals even allow the general public to view some of their content.

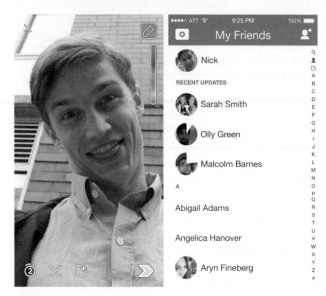

Snapchat users often share silly, casual, and private photos that are deleted after their receipt.

The following are some popular services that allow mobile users to share just about anything.

- **Full-featured social networking.** The largest social networks that offer a variety of features are Facebook and Google+. We will cover their features in more detail throughout Chapter 4.

- **Photo and video.** Instagram and Vine have become popular for making it easy to share photos and short videos with friends. Instagram also allows users to apply special effects to shared photos, adding excitement to this popular social activity.

- **Short-duration sharing.** The newcomer to the social networking market is Snapchat. This service allows users to send messages, photos, and videos to other individuals that are deleted within seconds of receipt. This has become popular for sending casual or humorous photos that users do not want to post permanently in a larger social network. It has also been the source of controversy as some individuals have used it to share illicit content. This issue, along with privacy concerns related to social networking, will be discussed in Chapter 6.

STREAMING MEDIA

Streaming media refers to music and movies that are delivered on demand from an online source. The streaming process allows you to begin enjoying your music and movies while they are still being transmitted. Although you can stream using a variety of

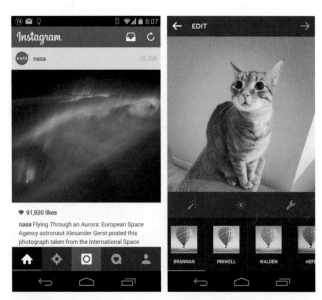

Instagram's app lets you edit photos and share them online.

devices at home, high-speed mobile networks now allow individuals to watch movies and listen to music from almost anywhere. The following are a few examples of these streaming services.

MUSIC

Mobile devices have become today's portable music players, allowing you to store and play back your purchased music files. However, if you are low on storage space or desire more variety, you should consider streaming music. There are two general ways in which to stream music. One way is to upload your purchased music files to a service that allows you to stream them back via an Internet connection. Google Play Music, Amazon Cloud Drive, and Apple iCloud are some examples of these "music locker" services. The more popular method is to subscribe to a service that offers a large collection of music. Some of these require a monthly paid subscription, while others are ad-supported. The following are examples of these services, broken down into two categories:

- **Personalized radio stations.** These services will deliver music based on your personal preferences. If you indicate which song or artist you like, they will play songs that are similar to your choice. Pandora is the most popular service in this category. Other companies, such as iHeartRadio, offer the ability to listen to thousands of actual radio stations in addition to your customized stations. Some companies, such as Songza, even use music experts (instead of automated systems) to develop playlists that match a variety of tastes, moods, and situations.

iHeartRadio allows you to listen to various radio stations or create your own based on any song or artist.

- **On-demand songs.** Instead of delivering songs that you are *likely* to enjoy, a variety of on-demand services offer you the ability to play any song you want. Companies such as Spotify offer instant access to millions of songs, allowing you to listen to whatever you want at any given moment.

MOVIES AND VIDEOS

Most individuals enjoy streaming videos and movies on their TVs. However, mobile devices are also becoming popular video and movie players, especially in areas such as airports where one might need extended entertainment. The following are a few examples of streaming video services.

- **Netflix** is by far the most popular service for streaming movies. For a low monthly fee, you can watch as many movies and shows as you desire from the company's large collection.

- **Hulu** specializes in TV shows, offering episodes that can be seen as early as the day after they air. The paid Hulu Plus service offers a large selection of TV episodes and streaming on just about every device.

- **YouTube.** The most popular video sharing site offers millions of videos that have been submitted by users. You can find a wide range of selections including music videos from your favorite artists or cooking videos that you can watch in your kitchen while preparing your next meal.

Hulu Plus lets you stream current-season TV shows on your mobile devices.

FITNESS & HEALTH

The sensors inside many mobile devices allow various apps to track your activity, such as counting the number of steps you take per day. In addition to mobile apps that make it easy to track your fitness and health, there are a variety of new devices that you can wear or use on the go.

FITNESS APPS

You can choose from various fitness apps based on your desired type and level of activity. Those that act as pedometers will count the number of steps that you take. Whether you run or walk, apps can help you keep track of your activity goals for each day. Other apps focus on providing instructions for those that use workout equipment such as machines and weights. Many apps offer cloud synchronization so that your fitness data over time is available wherever you need it. And if you need motivation and support, some apps will help you connect with your social network so that others can see your progress and cheer you on. Examples of these apps include:

- Accupedo
- RunKeeper
- Jefit

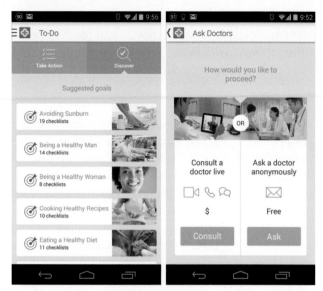

The HealthTap app offers health information and lets you connect with thousands of doctors.

HEALTH APPS

Health apps are often used to record and monitor information about your diet, vital signs, and medications. You can receive tips on improving your diet and health based on the information you enter daily. A few apps will even monitor your sleep by using the sensors in your device to measure how often you snore and move around. Many apps provide medical information at your fingertips including details on medications, symptoms, and how to treat a variety of conditions. Some even offer advice from actual physicians, allowing you to read answers to previously asked questions or engage in a virtual private consultation with a doctor for a small fee. Apps in this category include:

- HealthTap
- SleepBot
- Lose It!

FITNESS DEVICES

If you do not own a mobile device or do not want to bring it along on your daily run, you can still choose from a variety of wearable fitness devices. Some can be clipped onto your clothing while others are worn on the wrist. Like many fitness apps, these can measure the number of steps, distance traveled, and calories burned on a daily basis. Some, such as the Fitbit Flex, can even measure your sleep quality. Although many of these fitness devices offer websites and apps for tracking your activity, some can synchronize your data with existing fitness apps. Popular fitness devices include:

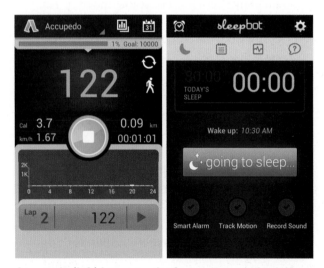

Accupedo (left) keeps track of your steps and calories burned, while SleepBot (right) monitors your sleep quality.

- Fitbit Flex
- Nike+ FuelBand

HEALTH DEVICES

Many are predicting an explosion of mobile health devices that help monitor your vital signs or make basic diagnoses. One such device, the Scanadu Scout, can measure multiple vital signs with a simple 10-second scan on your forehead. Your temperature, blood pressure, oxygen levels, and more will then be transferred to your mobile device for easy storage and tracking.

More **Online:** *Many of us sit in front of a computer for long periods and don't get enough physical activity. Visit the companion website for tips on health and fitness in a digital age.*

The Fitbit Flex wristband tracks your activity, calories burned, and sleep quality.

The Scanadu Scout is able to measure multiple vital signs with a simple 10-second scan.

Mobile Cloud Services

In the preface of this book, we discussed some useful cloud services that allow you to harness the power of the Internet to take notes and store schoolwork online. However, these services can do much more. For the mobile user, it means never having to experience the frustration of leaving a file at home or at work. In addition, these services allow anyone to take advantage of powerful online computers to complete a variety of activities from their mobile device. Although many applications and online services will be discussed in future chapters, the following sections will give you an idea of how cloud computing has transformed the way we access and create information.

ACCESS TO YOUR DATA

Many people confront the challenge of storing data that they can use in more than one place. For example, you might start working on a document at the office, but would like to finish it at home using your tablet. Perhaps you have music, photos, or other files on your home computer that you would like to access on your smartphone when you are away from home. All this is now possible through various **cloud storage** services, whereby your files can be stored online and accessed from any Internet-connected device. If you desire, these files can even be synchronized on all of your computers for offline access. The following services, which were discussed in the preface, all offer free apps on mobile devices and include several gigabytes of free storage.

- Dropbox
- Google Drive
- Microsoft OneDrive
- Apple iCloud

CLOUD APPLICATIONS

The preface also mentioned a few services that let you create a variety of notes and documents. These **cloud collaboration** tools allow individuals to view, edit, and share documents. These services help employees work on business documents, seeing each other's edits in real-time. They also allow families to share grocery lists, vacation documents, and much more. The following services are recommended:

- Evernote
- Google Docs
- Microsoft Office Online

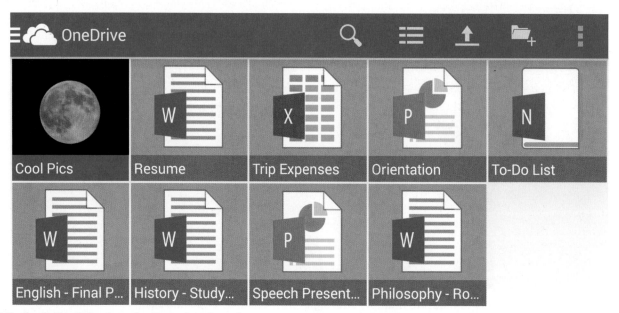

Microsoft OneDrive is a cloud service that allows you to create and store a variety of files online.

In addition to document creation, cloud computing has brought a variety of useful services to the mobile user. The following are just a few of these.

INSTANT TRANSLATION

Just a few years ago, you either needed to flip through a book or use expensive software to translate a foreign language. Today, services such as Google Translate can convert typed or spoken words into almost any foreign language. If you travel to another country, you can use this app to instantly translate what you hear into English words that appear on your screen.

INSTANT IDENTIFICATION

Another way to use the power of cloud computing is in photo identification. Google Goggles is a free mobile app that allows you to point your camera at just about anything—landmarks, artwork, and even bar codes—for the purpose of identifying what that object is. This is possible because of Google's large collection of images and its powerful computers. Once Google finds the object, it can help you find additional information on it or locate the stores that sell it.

> More **Online:** *Google's Goggles and Translate apps can transform the travelling experience. Visit the companion website for some tips on these and other useful travel apps.*

CLOUD GAMING

Mobile games have become extremely popular over the years. However, most of these games are installed and played on your device; they have nothing to do

Google's Goggles app will identify almost anything you view with your camera, from artwork to a textbook's barcode.

with the cloud. Several companies, such as OnLive, are changing this by storing the games on their servers and allowing you to play over the cloud. Whether it is on your laptop or mobile device, all you need is the OnLive software to get started. After installing it, you can choose from hundreds of games that can be played using your Internet connection.

THE POWER OF THE CLOUD

These three services clearly demonstrate the power of cloud computing. Any user with a simple smartphone and an Internet connection can use the power of large computers to accomplish a variety of tasks. Cloud computing has truly transformed many aspects of our lives—and many argue this is just the beginning. We will continue discussing software and cloud services throughout the textbook.

Review Questions

MULTIPLE CHOICE

1. Someone who possesses _____ has a broad understanding of computer technology and is able to use it well.

   a. augmented reality
   b. data
   c. digital literacy
   d. real-time information

2. Which of the following are thin, lightweight laptops that possess strong processing power and are more expensive than typical laptops?

   a. Ultraportable computers
   b. Netbooks
   c. Blade servers
   d. All-in-one computers

3. Which of the following allows users to switch between a laptop and tablet experience?

   a. Netbook
   b. All-in-one computer
   c. Convertible laptop
   d. Phablet

4. Which types of computers are ideal for handling highly complex problems that require extreme calculating power?

   a. Network servers
   b. Supercomputers
   c. Desktop computers
   d. Embedded systems

Review Questions (continued)

5. Which of the following is an e-book reader?

   a. Chromebook

   b. Roku

   c. Samsung Galaxy Note

   (d.) Amazon Kindle

6. Which of the following is a popular streaming service that specializes in TV shows, especially those that have been aired recently?

   a. Yelp

   b. Twitter

   (c.) Netflix

   d. Hulu

7. The most popular _____ is the iPad from Apple.

   a. smartphone

   (b.) tablet

   c. ultraportable computer

   d. gaming console

8. The gathering of information from a large group of people is known as:

   a. real-time information

   b. location-based services

   (c.) crowdsourcing

   d. augmented reality

9. Because of a technology known as _____, many smartphones can now be tapped on special payment devices to complete a purchase at select stores.

   a. Bluetooth

   b. streaming

   c. MMS

   (d.) NFC

10. Which of the following is NOT a cloud storage service?

    (a.) OnLive

    b. Google Drive

    c. Dropbox

    d. Microsoft OneDrive

FILL IN THE BLANK

Quiz ✓

11. _____*mainframe*_____ computers are very large and powerful systems used in organizations where a heavy amount of processing and user requests need to be handled.

12. A _____*Data*_____ consist of individual facts or pieces of information.

13. A(n) *smartphone* is a combination mobile phone and handheld computer.

14. Although it is best to avoid any distractions when driving, *bluetooth* technology will at least let you keep your eyes on the road.

15. A(n) *Network* allows users to communicate and share information between computers.

16. *all in one* computers are personal computers that have all of the hardware integrated with the monitor.

17. Many network servers come in the form of thin units known as *narrow blade* servers, which can slide in and out of a rack that holds many of its companion servers.

18. *location based services* allow various apps to recommend nearby restaurants or let you check-in at the establishment where you are currently located.

19. When using *cloud storage*, your files can be stored online and accessed from any Internet-connected device.

20. Google's Glass provides a basic _____ experience, where the real world is supplemented with computer-generated information. *augmented reality*

21. The physical devices that make up a computer system are known as software.

22. Chromebooks have very little internal storage, relying mainly on cloud storage.

23. If you do not have a smart TV, a streaming player can bring a variety of online services to your TV.

24. The app known as Spotify is used by small businesses to accept mobile payments.

25. Google Goggles is a service that will identify many of the objects and barcodes that you point your mobile device's camera at.

SHORT ANSWER

26. Name and define the four fundamental operations that all computers must be able to do.

27. List and briefly describe four ways in which computers are used in health care.

28. Describe four ways in which to automate your home.

29. List and briefly describe four ways in which computers are used by various parts of the government.

30. Describe at least three ways in which you can safeguard your mobile device and the information contained inside of it.

31. Name at least two apps that allow you to send messages to other users without the need to use your phone's SMS service.

32. Name at least two apps that allow you to upload photos and share them with your social networks.

33. List and briefly describe at least two apps that let you stream music.

34. List and briefly describe two apps and two devices that help you stay healthy and fit.

35. Name three services that allow you to create notes or documents online to collaborate with others.

Research Exercises

INSTRUCTIONS

Go beyond the book by performing research online to complete the exercises below.

1. Millions of individuals are "cutting the cord," cancelling their cable service in favor of streaming services such as Netflix and Hulu. What are some of the advantages of doing this? What are the disadvantages? Would you do it? Defend your answers and be sure to provide pricing evidence.

2. What sort of video surveillance products are available for individuals who wish to monitor their home using the Internet or a mobile device? Provide examples of solutions that are sold in stores as well as those that are installed by professional home security/alarm companies.

3. What are some of the advantages of using a Chromebook? What are some disadvantages? Would you buy one? Defend your answers.

Research Exercises (continued)

4. A variety of medical devices can be swallowed or implanted to treat various conditions. Name at least two of these and describe the technology behind them.

5. The dashboards in many modern cars are starting to look and feel like mobile devices. Find two cars from different automobile companies that have app-like interfaces and describe some of their features. How do they connect to the Internet? What type of hands-free services do they offer?

    Tesela & Nissan Sutra

6. Google Glass is an extremely innovative technology, but it is raising some privacy concerns. What are these concerns? Do you agree with them? Defend your answers.

7. The U.S. military isn't the only organization using drones. Many local police departments have started to use them. What are some of their applications? Do you support their use over the United States? Would you be in favor of companies and individuals using drones? Defend your answers.

8. What is wireless charging? How does it work? Which devices can currently be charged using this technology (list three examples)? In the future, could an entire home be charged without wires or power cables?

Search & Research use infer Red

x use drone polits to scare drone to scare birds f rum way for pla

FAA laws for Prof & Rec usuage

laws can change at any time and current decussion are ongoing.

2

HARDWARE

Chapter Overview

The various categories of computers share many fundamental components that allow them to process and store information, receive input, and deliver output. In this chapter, you will learn not just how computers work, but also how to choose the best devices to meet your personal or business needs.

PART 1:
Inside the Computer

The system unit contains various internal devices.

As a user, you likely see computers as mere tools that help you accomplish a variety of tasks. Few people have the time to stop and wonder what makes these amazing machines work. The only time most people concern themselves with what is inside the computer is when something goes wrong.

Like any machine, a computer is a collection of parts. What may surprise you is that a personal computer has only about a dozen parts. Learning about these computer components and their basic functions will improve your ability to both purchase the right computer and understand the cause of various problems when they arise.

System Unit and Motherboard

We will begin our tour of the computer with the two parts that comprise the bulk of the machine: the system unit and the motherboard. Although all computers (even your smartphone) have circuit boards and some sort of outer shell/casing, we will be focusing on desktop computers for this section.

SYSTEM UNIT

The main component of a desktop computer is the **system unit**, which is the case that houses the

The system unit of all-in-one computers are integrated with the screen.

computer's critical parts, such as the processing and storage devices. This part has historically been available in two forms: a horizontal desktop and a vertical tower. There are also all-in-one systems, such as the iMac, where the system unit is integrated with the monitor (screen).

Tower cases, which have been predominant for over a decade, are available in a variety of sizes, colors, and styles. Some have unique designs and colorful lighting that make them popular with gaming and multimedia enthusiasts.

If you were to purchase a system unit by itself, you would find that it is mostly empty on the inside. However, a few components either included or commonly purchased with the system unit are:

- **Drive bays.** Tower-based system units include several drive bays that hold the internal storage devices of your computer, such as the hard drive and the DVD drive.
- **Power supply.** This component is responsible for providing power to all the parts inside the system unit. When you plug a power cable into the back of your tower, you are essentially connecting it to the power supply. If you purchase a power supply separately, be sure to note the number of watts, which determines how many devices it can provide power to.

- **Cooling fans.** You may find one or more cooling fans responsible for cooling the inside of your computer. Many of the components inside a computer generate a great deal of heat. Without proper cooling, a computer could overheat and malfunction. Dust is an enemy of both electronic components and fans, so if necessary, use a can of compressed air to clean your computer periodically.

All parts of a computer connect to the motherboard.

MOTHERBOARD

The **motherboard** is the largest circuit board in a personal computer. It contains a variety of slots, connectors, and plugs for hooking up all the other parts of a computer, from the storage devices on the inside to the keyboard and monitor on the outside. All data travels through wires located throughout the motherboard's surface, and several **chipsets** act as traffic directors for all this data. Today's motherboards also contain specialized microchips that handle tasks such as video and sound output, as well as network communication. Nevertheless, some users may still choose to purchase add-on circuit boards known as **expansion cards** in order to improve the performance of their system's video or sound.

PORTS

At the back of your system unit, you will likely find a variety of plugs, or **ports**. These ports are typically part of the motherboard, located on the side that faces the back of the case. You may also find ports on the front of your system unit or on the sides of laptop computers. The most popular of these plugs

Ports are used to connect external devices.

is the small, rectangular **USB port**, which is used to connect almost all of today's external devices. This port has undergone a variety of improvements over the years (current version is 3.0) to increase the speed at which information can be transferred to external storage devices. Although the USB port is the most predominant, we will be looking at other specialty ports in upcoming sections of this chapter.

CPU and Memory

Most of the "action" inside any computer occurs between the main processor and the various types of memory. These components are the primary factors in the overall speed and performance of your computer.

CPU

The **central processing unit (CPU)**, or microprocessor, is the main processor of a computer. It is responsible for organizing and carrying out instructions to produce a desired output. It can perform a diverse number of operations, from finding a name in your smartphone's contacts to handling the complex calculations required by today's engineers. For this reason, it is often nicknamed "the brain" of the computer.

The CPU is plugged into a special socket on the computer's motherboard. Because modern CPUs generate a great deal of heat when they operate, they require their own cooling units. These consist of large blocks of heat-conducting metal that are pressed tightly against the CPU and cooling fans to whisk the heat from the metal. All this makes the CPU look like a very large unit inside your computer, yet the chip itself is just a thin wafer that is a fraction of an inch across.

When you shop for a new computer, the CPU will often be one of the first components listed in the specifications. Because it has such an impact on performance, you are likely to see several pieces of information about the processor. Here are a few:

- **Brand and model.** Intel and AMD dominate the market for desktop and laptop computers. Next to these manufacturers' names you will find a series and model, such as Intel's i7-3630QM or AMD's A8-4500M. Don't let all of this intimidate you. It is no different from understanding the various models of a car, such as BMW's X5 xDRIVE35i. For mobile devices, you will find companies such as Apple, Qualcomm, and Texas Instruments producing ARM-based processors. These types of chips generally produce less heat and use less power—characteristics that are crucial for mobile devices.

- **Multiple cores.** Most of today's microprocessors have several processors, or **cores**, inside a single chip. A dual-core processor can be twice as efficient as a traditional processor, given that it can handle twice the work at any given moment. Many of today's processors have more than two cores, with four, six, and even eight becoming common.

- **Clock rate.** A CPU's **clock rate** measures the frequency or speed at which it can process instructions. This speed is measured in *hertz,* which is equal to one instruction cycle per second. Today's processors have reached the

The processor model, such as this Intel Core i3, is often featured prominently on a computer.

gigahertz (GHz) mark, capable of processing billions of instructions per second. Although looking at the number of gigahertz is a tempting way to compare two computers or processors, it isn't always that easy. Since various factors can affect overall speed, experts depend on a series of performance tests known as benchmarks to compare processors.

More **Online:** *Visit the companion website to learn more about various benchmarks and how they can help you decide between two different devices.*

MEMORY

In a computer, **memory** is a general term for electronic chips that store data and program instructions that can be accessed quickly by the CPU. Many users confuse memory and storage, especially now that we have storage devices called "memory cards." This will all be cleared up in the next few pages as we contrast

The CPU is the green square at the bottom center, inserted into a socket on the motherboard.

the various memory and storage technologies. In this section, we will be exploring several types of memory used in personal computers, starting with the one you are likely familiar with already: RAM.

RAM

The most noticeable type of memory for a user is the temporary workspace known as **random access memory (RAM)**. Whenever you actively work on something using your computer, that work is temporarily stored in RAM. For example, right now you may have a résumé or school paper that is stored somewhere on your computer. When you open this document in Microsoft Word to work on it, both the Word program and the document will be copied into RAM. When you save the document and close Word, it is removed from RAM but remains safe on a storage device (see Figure 2.1).

RAM is considered to be volatile because its contents change often and will disappear if the computer loses power or is restarted. This is one of the fundamental differences between this temporary memory and your more permanent storage devices such as hard drives, DVDs, and SD cards. Let us now turn to a few details you should know about RAM:

- **Memory modules.** RAM consists of a set of chips mounted on a small circuit board called a memory module. These modules are then inserted into special slots on the motherboard. This is important to know when purchasing a computer as the number of available slots can affect your ability to add more RAM. Computers typically have anywhere from one to four slots.

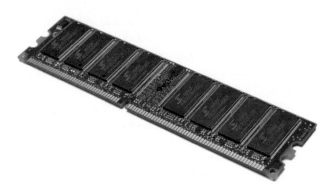

RAM modules are inserted into slots on the motherboard.

- **Type and speed.** There are a large variety of RAM types and speeds. Consider the following example: DDR3 1333. The first part, *DDR3,* indicates the type of RAM. The *1333* represents the speed at which it can transmit data to the CPU. The main reason to know these details is to ensure that you purchase the correct RAM if you are planning on upgrading your computer.

- **Capacity.** Each RAM module can hold a specific amount of information, typically one to eight gigabytes. The higher your overall capacity, the more programs and files you can open and work on at once. This allows you to have a fast and smooth experience when switching from one program or browser tab to another.

OTHER TYPES OF MEMORY

Although RAM is the most popular type of memory, a modern computer would not function properly without a few other types of memory.

- **Read-only memory (ROM)** is a small chip that contains device-specific information. The instructions on this chip are known as **firmware**, and they handle a computer's basic functions when it is powered on. On PCs, these instructions are commonly known as the *BIOS.* Currently, the "read-only" portion is a bit misleading, as most of these chips can be electronically reprogrammed via a process called *flashing.* This allows for a variety of activities, from receiving an important update from your computer manufacturer to installing a customized operating system on Android mobile devices.

- **Cache** refers to a form of high-speed memory that stores a small, frequently used set of instructions and data. It is located inside modern CPUs.

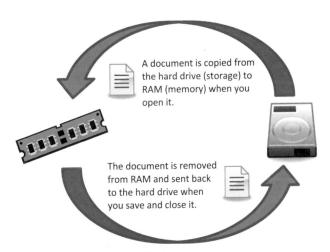

A document is copied from the hard drive (storage) to RAM (memory) when you open it.

The document is removed from RAM and sent back to the hard drive when you save and close it.

Figure 2.1   How RAM Works.

- **Virtual memory** is not actual memory, but rather a portion of your hard drive that is being used as RAM. Your operating system uses this tactic when your opened programs and files do not fit into RAM. It takes portions of them and, without you noticing, moves them onto your hard drive. The only time you may be aware of it is when you experience a tiny delay in switching from one open program to another that had been temporarily placed in virtual memory. This is because accessing RAM is much faster for a computer than accessing your storage devices.

More **Online:** *Both PCs and Macs have a tool that lets you see how much RAM and CPU your open programs are currently using. Visit the companion website to learn more about these tools.*

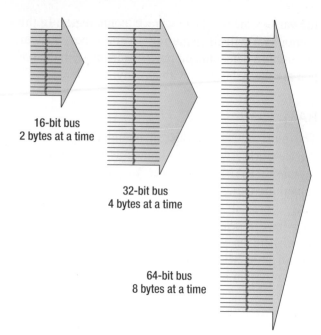

16-bit bus
2 bytes at a time

32-bit bus
4 bytes at a time

64-bit bus
8 bytes at a time

Wires (buses) carry electrical signals known as bits. Eight bits are equal to one byte.

Storage

As you have already learned, the purpose of storage is to hold programs and data permanently, even when the computer is turned off. The devices that can read, write, and erase data are called **drives**. The physical locations where things are stored are known as storage **media**. For example, your DVD discs are known as storage media, while the device that you insert them into is the drive. Let us now explore all of the various storage devices used by modern computers, as well as the units of measurement that describe their capacity.

STORAGE UNITS

The most fundamental unit of computing is the **bit**, which is typically represented as an *on* (1) or *off* (0) value. This is because digital, electrical devices can truly only "understand" the concept of being on or off. Consider for a moment that you are a wire (or *bus*) on a circuit board. Essentially, all that could possibly make sense to you is that there is electricity flowing through you at a given moment or that there isn't. It is the sequence or order of these bits that is interpreted and processed into meaningful information. Many storage devices also use this 0 and 1 system to remember all types of information, from letters to colors.

When it comes to describing a computer's storage or memory, we commonly use the unit known as the **byte**, which is simply a collection of eight bits. The eight is significant because it is the amount of space required to store a single character, such as a letter or number. In modern computing, the size of our files and programs are so large that it is helpful to use terms such as kilobyte (KB), megabyte (MB), gigabyte (GB), and terabyte (TB) to describe the

TABLE 2.1 MEMORY AND STORAGE UNITS

Unit	Approximate Value	Actual Value (bytes)
Kilobyte (KB)	1,000 Bytes	1,024
Megabyte (MB)	1,000 KB	1,048,576
Gigabyte (GB)	1,000 MB	1,073,741,824
Terabyte (TB)	1,000 GB	1,099,511,627,776

values (see Table 2.1). In a world dominated by computers, it is crucial that you memorize these storage units much like you did inches and feet when you were young.

MAGNETIC STORAGE

In the 1940s, when electronic computers were beginning to appear, researchers realized that a computer would not be able to remember or store anything if it relied solely on electrical components. With a loss of power, every component would lose its charge and all data would be lost. The development of magnetic storage allowed data to be represented by magnets, which can hold their position or pattern to represent 0's and 1's without electricity. The following are some examples of magnetic storage devices:

- The **hard drive** (also known as the hard disk), is the primary storage device of a personal computer. While most use magnetic disks, some may use solid state technology, which will be discussed later in this section. Practically all desktop and laptop computers have an internal hard drive. You can also buy an external hard drive to store additional information or make copies of your irreplaceable data. These external drives are very portable and typically connect to the USB port

Inside the hard drive are a stack of disks and a magnetic read/write head.

on a computer. Both types of hard drives are currently capable of storing a few terabytes of data.

- **Tape drives**, which use magnetic tape to store data, are popular for organizations that have large quantities of information to back up or archive. You might find these drives organized into giant tape libraries that can hold thousands of terabytes of archived information.

OPTICAL STORAGE

In addition to the hard drive, most personal computers sold today include at least one form of optical storage. These devices use lasers to read data from or write data to the reflective surface of an optical disc. Bits are represented by changing the reflectivity of small areas on the disc.

TYPES OF OPTICAL DISCS

The primary difference between the various optical discs is the amount of data that they can store. Over the years, researchers have been able to increase the capacity of optical discs while keeping their physical size the same. This allows you to insert old discs, such as CDs, in the newer DVD or Blu-ray drives. You are likely familiar with many of the following optical discs:

- **Compact discs (CDs)** are capable of storing up to 700 MB of data. Although most commercial music is still sold as CDs, this type of disc is not used much in today's computers.

- **Digital versatile discs (DVDs)** can store either 4.7 or 8.5 GB of data. The larger amount is possible because DVDs allow data to be recorded on two layers within the disc. Most of today's software and standard-definition movies are sold as DVDs.

The Blu-ray drive reads various types of optical discs.

- The latest optical technology is the **Blu-ray disc (BD)**, which typically stores 25 or 50 GB of data. This is enough to hold an entire high-definition movie, as well as the video games used in the newest PlayStation and Xbox consoles. A new type of disc, the BD-XL, can store over 100 GB of data by using three or four layers per disc.

RECORDING TECHNOLOGY

All three types of discs, along with the drives they are inserted into, have a series of designations that let you know about their read, write, and erase capabilities. If you see the word ROM after any of them, it means they are read only. A designation of −R or +R means the blank disc can only be recorded to once. However, the initials −RW, +RW, or −RE indicate that the disc can be recorded and erased. The process of recording to a blank disc is known as *burning*.

SOLID STATE STORAGE

The future of data storage may well be solid state storage, which relies on a special kind of flash memory chip to permanently store data. Since this technology uses memory chips for storage, it has no moving parts like hard drives or optical drives. Consequently, the devices can perform read, write, and erase operations at much quicker speeds. Their lack of mechanical parts also results in a much smaller size and less power consumption, which makes them ideal for ultraportable computers, mobile devices, and a variety of gadgets. Although this type of storage is the most expensive (cost per gigabyte), prices are falling at a quick

Solid state memory cards come in a variety of sizes.

pace while storage capacities increase to hundreds of gigabytes. The following devices use this new type of technology:

- A **USB flash drive** is the small storage stick that plugs into a USB port. You have likely used one of these to transfer files between computers or store copies of important files.

A USB flash drive plugs into a USB port.

- The tiny and flat **memory cards** are used to store data in tablets, smartphones, and devices such as digital cameras and digital photo frames. The most common format currently in use for these devices is Secure Digital (SD), available in various speeds and storage capacities. Smaller versions of SD are known as mini and micro SD. All of these cards can be easily removed from a device and inserted into a memory card reader, which is usually a small slot on your computer or printer.

- Many hard drives now use flash memory instead of the more traditional magnetic technology. These are known as **solid state drives (SSDs)**, and they can be found as both internal and external drives. Ultraportable computers will often use this technology exclusively, even though the storage capacity is only a fraction of what a traditional hard drive offers. Many desktop and laptop computers use a different approach, whereby they include a large traditional hard drive and a small SSD that only stores the operating system. This allows Windows, for example, to load and operate much faster than if it ran off a magnetic hard drive.

This smartphone has a slot for a micro SD card.

PART 2:
Input and Output

As you remember from Chapter 1, input refers to user entries or activities that tell the computer what to do, while output refers to the processed data that a computer sends out. Input and output devices are evolving in variety and sophistication just as rapidly as the computer itself. In this section, you'll explore some of these devices.

Input

Computers are data processing marvels, but they first need to receive information from the outside world. Sights, sounds, words, and commands are received by input devices and then converted into a digital format that can be processed by the computer. In this section, you will explore the latest versions of input devices that help computers gather information from a variety of sources.

THE KEYBOARD

For most individuals, the keyboard is still the primary input device for entering text and numbers. Nearly all computers come with some sort of keyboard. Your desktop computer likely came with a wired keyboard that is connected via a USB cable. Laptop computers have an integrated keyboard, while tablets and smartphones include a touchscreen keyboard. Alternative keyboards include:

Ergonomic keyboards are designed to ease the strain of typing for long periods.

This wireless keyboard also functions as a protective cover for the tablet.

- **Wireless keyboards.** These keyboards do not require a physical connection and can communicate with your computer via Bluetooth wireless technology. These keyboards come in a variety of sizes and can connect to all types of computers, from desktops and smart TVs to a wide range of mobile devices.

- **Ergonomic keyboards.** Individuals who type for extended periods often suffer from hand and wrist strain. **Ergonomic keyboards**, which are designed to be comfortable and tailored for the human body, have angled keys and a palm rest at the base to keep your wrists straight.

- **Keyboard covers.** These keyboards snap directly onto a tablet and can serve as a protective cover as well. They are very thin and can communicate with your tablet via wireless technology. They are very useful to those that type extensively on this mobile device.

CATEGORIES OF KEYS

The quantity, types, and location of keys vary greatly among keyboards. The traditional, 104-key arrangement for Windows-based desktops is different from the ones used with Macs, laptop computers, and mobile devices. This section will explore the most common categories of keys used today.

- **Alphanumeric keys.** These refer to the main set of keys that allow you to input letters, numbers, and punctuation. The most common arrangement of these keys is referred to as the QWERTY (pronounced KWER-tee) layout because of the first six letters near the top left.

- **Modifier keys.** These keys, such as SHIFT, modify the input of other keys when held down. The CTRL, ALT, FN, and WINDOWS keys are commonly used for **keyboard shortcuts**, which are keystrokes that can quickly perform an operation within software. Mac computers have similar keys, which are labeled as CONTROL, OPTION, and COMMAND.

Mac wireless keyboard.

More **Online:** *Visit the companion website to learn a variety of keyboard shortcuts for Windows and Mac.*

- **Function keys.** These keys, which are labeled F1, F2, and so on, are used to perform an action within a program. Each function key's purpose depends on the program you are using. For example, in many programs, F1 is the help key.

- **Cursor control keys.** These navigation keys, such as the four arrows near the bottom right, let you move around the screen without using a mouse. In many programs that display what you type, a mark on the screen indicates where the characters you type will be entered. This mark, called the **cursor** (or insertion point), appears on the screen as a blinking vertical line, a small box, or some other symbol to show your place in a document or command line.

- **Numeric keypad.** This area is very useful for numeric entry and calculations, as it contains the numbers 0 to 9 and four basic mathematical operators (+, −, *, and /). The numeric keypad is typically located on the right side of a standard desktop keyboard or larger laptop computers. It is often absent on computers with smaller keyboards.

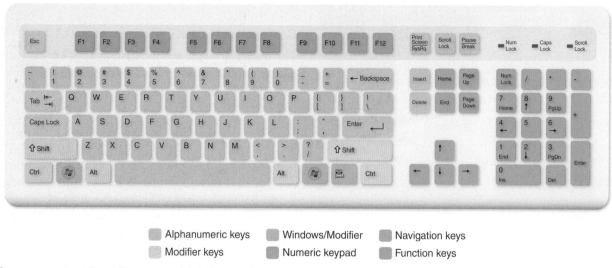

Common categories of keys on a PC (Windows) keyboard.

POINTING DEVICES

As a user, you interact with most computer software via an on-screen pointer, which is typically in the form of an arrow. Several types of pointing devices can be used to move the pointer and issue commands at the pointer's location. Commands are issued by using the following basic operations:

- **Clicking.** Pressing and releasing the left mouse button. This is often used to select an object or option on the screen.

- **Double-clicking.** Pressing and releasing the left mouse button twice in rapid succession. This is typically done to desktop icons.

- **Right-clicking.** Pressing and releasing the right mouse button. In Windows, this operation will bring up a shortcut menu.

- **Dragging.** Holding down a button while moving the mouse. This is usually used to move objects.

- **Scrolling.** Most pointing devices have a scroll wheel, which can be used to scroll, or move, information up or down on your screen.

- **Gestures.** Many new devices support the use of various **gestures**, or finger movements, to accomplish various tasks. For example, bringing your thumb and index together in a pinching motion can be used to zoom in and out.

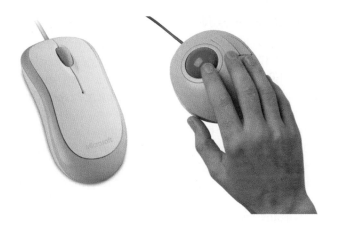

Optical mouse (left) and trackball (right) are both similar pointing devices.

MOUSE

The **optical mouse** is the most common pointing device for desktop computers. For PCs, an optical mouse will include a left and right button, a scroll wheel in the middle, and a light-emitting mechanism at the bottom to sense movement. Some mice include additional, programmable buttons, while others allow special gestures to be performed directly on their curved surface. Like keyboards, a mouse can be connected using a USB cable or via wireless technology.

TRACKBALL

A **trackball** is a pointing device that works like an upside-down mouse. You rest your index finger or thumb on an exposed ball, then place your other fingers on the buttons. To move the pointer around the screen, you roll the ball with your finger. Because you move this ball and not the whole device, a trackball requires less space than a mouse.

TOUCHPAD

The **touchpad** is a stationary, rectangular pointing surface that is typically found on laptop computers. The movement of a finger across the small, touch-sensitive surface is translated into pointer movement on the screen. Touchpads sometimes include two buttons that perform the same functions as mouse buttons. However, most touchpads now support various types of taps and gestures on their surface that can accomplish much more than the two traditional buttons.

Laptop touchpads support various types of taps and gestures.

TOUCHSCREEN TECHNOLOGY

Touchscreens accept input by allowing the user to place a fingertip directly on the computer screen. Your fingers can be used to perform a variety of taps and gestures to accomplish different tasks. This technology has become the primary way in which we interact with our tablets and smartphones. In addition, many newer laptop computers are including touchscreens to take advantage of the Windows 8 tiled interface. You will also find these monitors in many types of businesses where a simple interface is important, such as restaurants, retail stores, and ticketing kiosks.

Most of today's devices use *capacitive* touchscreens, which means that they detect the position of your finger by detecting the electrical current present in your body. This is why you cannot use most of these devices when you are wearing gloves. Alternatively, some monitors use *resistive* touchscreens, which detect the pressure of your touch. These work well in restaurants or outdoor environments where dirt and liquids would create problems for other types of input devices.

An airport check-in kiosk uses a touchscreen interface.

STYLUS

A **stylus** is a pen-like input tool that is used with a variety of touchscreen devices. You may have used one of these when signing for a delivered package or when paying for goods at many retail stores. Some tablets and smartphones come with a stylus that can be used for input or writing notes and annotations by hand. If desired, these devices can then use handwriting recognition to convert what you wrote into typewritten text.

Artists who draw images on a computer often use a stylus in conjunction with special **graphics tablets**, which offer extra-sensitive touch surfaces that translate an artist's motions into drawings on the computer screen. These styluses often have a variety of special features, such as the ability to erase parts of the drawing when used upside-down.

A stylus can be used on a graphics tablet.

SCANNERS

Computers may never see in the same way that humans do, but optical technologies allow computers to use light as a source of input. A **scanner** is a device that uses optical technology to convert objects that it analyzes into a digital format. Various types of scanners are used for homes and businesses:

- **Document scanners.** These scanners specialize in scanning large quantities of documents in a short amount of time. They can usually hold and process dozens of papers per minute. Businesses will often use them to go "paperless" by converting long, physical documents (such as contracts or medical records) into a digital format stored in the computer. Once scanned, a technology known as **optical character recognition (OCR)** can translate the document image into text that can be edited and formatted.

- **Flatbed scanners.** These scanners have a glass surface that allows you to scan almost any object, from a page in a textbook to an old photo album. Many of these scanners now include a **document feeder**, which is a tray that allows you to scan several sheets of paper automatically. These types of scanners are often integrated into multifunction printers (see page 53).

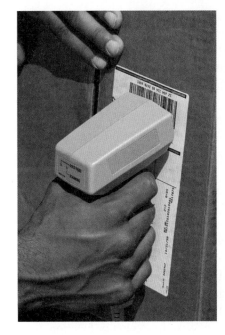

Handheld barcode scanner.

QR code.

- **Barcode scanners.** These scanners are used to scan the barcode labels that uniquely identify most products sold today. They are used by many businesses to maintain inventory, track packages, or speed up the purchasing process for customers. Some of these scanners are handheld while others, such as those in many grocery stores, are flatbed models.

  There are other types of product codes that do not use the traditional black bars. One of these, called **QR codes**, appears as a square filled with dots and lines. One of the most popular uses for these codes is to direct a smartphone to open a specific web address by simply pointing its camera at it.

Document scanner.

Flatbed scanner.

- **RFID scanners.** An **RFID tag** is a tiny chip or label that contains electronically stored data. Special RFID scanners use radio frequencies to read the data stored in these tags. Although a bit more expensive than paper-based barcodes, RFID tags can be scanned from longer distances and at higher speeds. For example, many of the automated toll collection systems in use today allow scanners installed throughout a highway to read the RFID tag inside vehicles. The tag stores a unique account number that allows the government's computers to find the driver's account and deduct the appropriate toll payment. RFID has many other applications that range from inventory control at large facilities to implantable chips that help identify the owner of a lost pet. It is worth noting that RFID tags are not GPS devices, and cannot therefore be used for tracking movement or location.

- **Scanner apps.** These software-based scanners use the camera on a mobile device to perform the scan. Because tablet and smartphone cameras have become very sharp, these apps can produce very clear scans of your documents. This allows you to input important documents and receipts into your mobile device in widely used formats such as Adobe PDF.

MULTIMEDIA INPUT

Practically all of today's computers are equipped with complete **multimedia** capabilities, which means that they can input and output sound, music, images, and

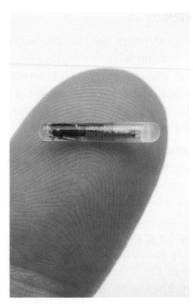

This tiny RFID tag can be implanted under the skin.

video. Let's take a look at the input devices that make this possible.

MICROPHONE

While desktop computers typically require a separate, physical microphone or headset, most laptop and mobile computers have one that is built-in. Common uses for microphones include Internet voice calling and capturing the audio portion of a video recording or conversation. A capability that is receiving increased attention is **speech recognition**, which is a computer's ability to recognize human speech. Using fast processors, sophisticated software, and an incredibly large volume of data, computers have become quite accurate in detecting exactly what we are saying. Two of the most popular speech recognition programs, Apple's Siri and Google's Search app, are enabling individuals to use their voice, rather than a keyboard, to issue commands and search for information on their mobile devices. Various professionals, such as doctors, are also using speech recognition to dictate information in locations or environments where typing on a keyboard would be difficult or obtrusive.

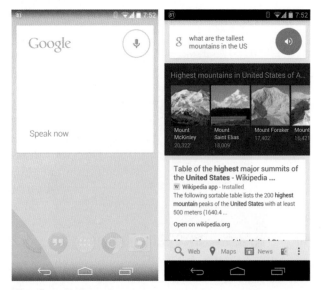

The Google Search app uses speech recognition.

More **Online:** *Are you using all the capabilities of speech recognition on your mobile device? Visit the companion website to learn more about voice commands and searches.*

DIGITAL CAMERA

Digital cameras are portable devices that electronically capture and store still images and video. They come in all shapes and sizes, from ultra-slim models that fit in your pocket to larger DSLR cameras that capture professional-quality images. In addition, most mobile devices now include one or two integrated cameras. They have become so sophisticated in the last few years, many individuals use their smartphone or tablet as their primary camera. Just be aware that the camera in the front of your mobile device will capture images at a lower quality than the one in the back.

Most digital cameras can store hundreds or thousands of high-resolution images. This depends on both the size of the storage media used and the number of **megapixels** used for the photo. Higher megapixel cameras can capture more detail, but they will produce a larger image file on your storage media. If you are running low on storage space in your local or cloud storage account, you can try taking photos with fewer megapixels or use an application that can reduce the size of your photos.

Digital SLR cameras are used by those who desire the highest photo quality.

VIDEO CAMERAS

As you have already learned, digital cameras can capture video in addition to still images. You will also find video input capabilities in the cameras that are integrated into many laptop computers, tablets, and smartphones. For those who want to capture video on their desktop computers, a **webcam** is an affordable solution. This small video camera, which is typically attached to your monitor, is commonly used for online video chats or conversations. Businesses often use more sophisticated versions of webcams to engage in **videoconferencing**, where multiple individuals hold meetings and converse using internal networks or the Internet.

Some video cameras are used by homes and businesses for security and surveillance. If they are connected to a computer with Internet access, video can be recorded and even viewed from a remote location. Other video cameras, commonly known as camcorders, allow individuals and professionals to record high-quality video that can be played or edited on a computer. These cameras usually possess large viewing screens and excellent zoom capabilities. Recently, many gaming consoles have started to include video cameras that can capture the body's movement and even detect facial expressions.

Videoconferencing uses sophisticated versions of webcams.

TV TUNERS

A **TV tuner** is a device that can capture television signals for viewing on a computer. Some TV tuners are in the form of internal cards for your desktop computer, while others are small, external USB devices. They usually have a coaxial port where you connect a cable from your home's antenna or a cable box. Many individuals are using TV tuners as **digital video recorders (DVR)** to record television shows for future playback. Although many cable companies include DVR capabilities with their cable boxes, individuals who do not have cable subscriptions can still record local television stations in HD by using afford-able antennas and TV tuners.

OTHER INPUT DEVICES

Individuals and businesses use countless specialty devices to get information into a computer. These range from music instruments and mixers that can help musicians produce and edit songs digitally to ultrasound devices that help medical professionals see what is going on inside your body. This section will focus on just a few widely used input devices that fall into their own category.

GAME CONTROLLERS

Whether you are playing games on a computer or a gaming console, you will often use a **game controller** as your primary input device. Most modern control-lers are small, wireless devices designed to be held with both hands. They provide an array of buttons, which perform a variety of functions, and analog sticks that are used for movement. Some even include internal sensors that can detect subtle movements of the device. With the Nintendo Wii, for example, a swinging motion with the controller in your hand can simulate the swing of a golf club or tennis racket. As previously mentioned, many gaming consoles now

Xbox One works with a game controller and Kinect video camera.

combine controllers and video cameras to make your entire body into a source of input.

BIOMETRICS

Biometrics refers to the measurement of patterns or characteristics found in the human body. Various bio-metric input devices are now being used to authen-ticate, or identify, an individual when accessing a device. For most people, this technology is much more convenient than remembering a password or carrying an identification card.

- **Fingerprint scanners** detect the unique pat-terns and swirls of an individual's finger. These scanners are now integrated with many portable computers so that users can log in with a quick press or swipe of their finger.

- **Facial recognition** is a biometric technology that looks for unique measurements in an indi-vidual's face. Mobile users can often gain access to their device by looking into the front-facing camera. In secure areas, such as airports, cam-eras can scan many individuals at one time and sophisticated software can detect if one of those individuals is present in a criminal or terrorist database.

Other parts of the body are increasingly being used for identification. These include the colored part of the eyes (iris), the particular geometry of the hand, and even the unique pattern of your DNA. While many have raised legitimate concerns about biomet-rics and privacy, it is important to remember that most consumer and business systems only record measure-ments and do not actually store photos of your finger-prints, for example.

The Face Unlock feature for Android smartphones is an example of biometrics.

Output

One of the most critical things a computer can do is to provide a solution or an answer. We give computers input because we want a result, or output. In this section, we will explore the latest versions of output devices that help computers produce audio, visual, and physical information.

MONITORS

The monitor is an electronic display device, or screen, used to output text and graphics to the user. The earliest monitors could only display black and one other color, such as green or amber. Today's monitors display 16.7 million colors. Two important hardware devices determine the quality of the image you see on any monitor: the monitor itself and the video controller. Both will be explored in this section.

MONITOR TERMINOLOGY

To fully understand the different types of monitors, it is necessary to review basic display terminology. In addition, these terms will help you make a better decision when shopping for a new device.

- **Pixels.** A monitor's screen is divided into millions of tiny dots, called **pixels**. Each pixel has a unique address, which the computer uses to locate the pixel and control its appearance.

- **Size.** The size of a monitor is measured in diagonal inches. As a general rule, buy the largest monitor that fits your budget and your workspace.

- The **resolution** of a monitor refers to the number of pixels that it can display on the screen. A monitor with a maximum resolution of

2560 pixels

1440 pixels

A monitor's resolution is the number of pixels that can fit horizontally and vertically on the screen.

1920x1080 will display up to 1,920 pixels in each row (horizontally) and up to 1,080 pixels in each column (vertically). Although a higher resolution will produce a sharper image, screen elements will appear to shrink because of these tightly packed pixels. Your operating system will allow you to set an ideal resolution for both your monitor and your eyes.

- The **response time** of a monitor is the amount of time (in milliseconds) that it takes for a pixel to change from black to white. Lower values are ideal for the smooth display of fast-moving images, such as those in video games.

- The **contrast ratio** of a monitor measures how close the monitor can get to the brightest white and the darkest black. This ratio will be represented with two numbers, such as 1000:1. Monitors with a larger ratio will produce higher-quality images. Manufacturers can list figures for either the static (still images) contrast ratio or the dynamic (moving images) contrast ratio.

- **Viewing angle.** Most monitors produce the best picture when viewed from a position near the center of the screen. However, many monitors will promote their large viewing angles, which indicate how far to the sides a user can be before the picture fades or blurs.

Darker Black

Brighter White

The monitor on the right has a higher contrast ratio, resulting in a darker (deeper) black and a brighter white.

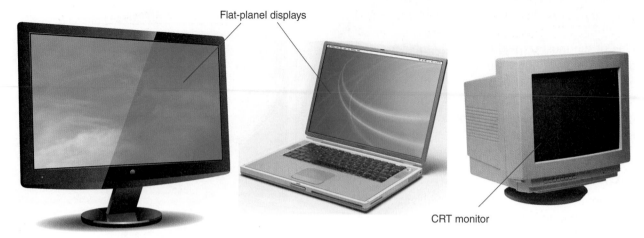

Flat-planel displays

CRT monitor

Flat-panel monitors have replaced the older CRT monitors.

TYPES OF MONITORS

Most monitors today are flat-panel monitors. They are thin, lightweight, and energy efficient. The older **CRT monitors**, which were large and bulky because they used cathode-ray tube (CRT) technology, are rarely used today. The two common types of flat-panel monitors are described below.

- **LCD.** An **LCD (liquid crystal display) monitor** contains a light source and a screen of special crystals placed in the monitor between the user and the light source. By default, the crystals do not allow light to shine through them; however, the crystals shift when electricity is applied to them, allowing light to pass through. By switching on specific pixels of crystals, patterns can be drawn on the monitor. LCD monitors use transistors to control the display of each pixel on the screen.

- **LED.** This newer technology, which also uses liquid crystals, changes the way LCD monitors are illuminated. **LED monitors** are lit by a grid of tiny electronic lights called light emitting diodes (LEDs). These lights respond to an electric current, and replace the standard backlight technology of traditional LCD monitors. This allows LED monitors to be thinner, lighter, and more energy-efficient. In addition, they tend to have better contrast ratios, response times, and viewing angles. Most monitors and mobile devices today use LED.

More **Online:** *Did you know that the improper use of monitors may cause eye and neck strain? Visit the companion website to learn how to prevent discomfort and injuries related to computer use.*

High-end video cards are purchased by individuals who use graphics-intensive software.

VIDEO CARDS

The quality of the images that a monitor can display is defined as much by the **video card** (or graphics card) as by the monitor itself. The video card is an intermediary device between the CPU and the monitor. It contains a processor, video-dedicated memory, and other circuitry necessary to process and send information to the monitor. In many newer computers, the video circuitry is built directly into the motherboard, eliminating the need for a separate card.

- The **graphics processing unit (GPU)** is the video card's microprocessor. The speed and quality of this chip, along with the RAM on the card, determines the relative power of the video card. Various applications are so graphics-intensive that they require a great deal of dedicated memory and processing power. Therefore, many individuals in the video industry, as well as those who enjoy the latest, graphics-intensive games, will shop for high-end (and expensive) video cards that have the best GPUs on them. NVIDIA and AMD are popular GPU manufacturers.

- **Connectors.** Video cards can include various types of connectors for your monitor or TV. The oldest of these is the VGA (or D-sub) connector, which contains 15 pins arranged in three rows. After this came the DVI connector, which became the standard for digital video on most computers and monitors. The newest connector is HDMI, which carries both digital video and sound. Although HDMI connectors are available on many monitors, you may be more familiar with them in HDTVs.

SOUND SYSTEMS

Today, nearly any new computer includes a complete sound system, with a microphone, speakers, and a sound card or processor. Sound systems are especially useful to people who use their computer to create or use multimedia products, watch videos, listen to music, engage in videoconferencing, or participate in online activities.

SPEAKERS

Speakers are included on practically all of today's computers. They can range from tiny ones that are integrated with your monitor or mobile device, to

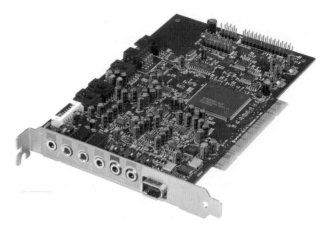

A sound card offers several connectors for surround-sound speakers.

full surround-sound systems that include a variety of speakers and subwoofers. Many computer users prefer listening to audio through headphones or a headset, rather than using speakers. Most systems include a convenient jack to accept a headset plug.

SOUND CARD

A computer's **sound card** is a circuit board that converts sound from analog to digital form, and vice versa, for recording or playback. Analog signals, such as those from your voice, are accepted from a microphone and converted into digital data for the computer to process. Inside the computer, digital data representing music can be sent to the sound card and converted to electrical current that speakers can play. Similar to video cards, many new computers provide a sound subsystem directly on the motherboard and do not require a separate sound card for audio output. Separate sound cards are primarily used in computers by users who require specialized or premium sound output.

With the appropriate software, you can do much more than simply record and play back digitized sound. Sound editing programs provide a miniature sound studio, allowing you to create, mix, and edit everything from today's electronic music to complex multi-instrumental symphonies.

PRINTERS

Over the past decade, the variety of available printing devices has exploded, serving the needs of the average home and office user, as well as those of the publishing and manufacturing industries. Choosing

A surround-sound speaker system includes speakers and a subwoofer.

the right printer requires knowledge of both printing terminology and the various categories of printers.

PRINTER TERMINOLOGY

Before exploring the different types of printers, it is important to review some basic terminology and various factors that you should consider before making your purchase.

- **Image quality.** Image quality, also known as print resolution, is usually measured in **dots per inch (dpi)**. If, for example, a printer's resolution is 600 dpi, this means it can print 600 columns of dots and 600 rows of dots in each square inch of the page. The more dots per inch a printer can produce, the higher its image quality. A school paper or business document will look good when printed at 300 dpi, but a high-quality photo may need resolutions of 1200 dpi and perhaps higher. Most modern printers can produce output with at least 1200 dpi.

- **Speed.** Printer speed is measured in the number of **pages per minute (ppm)** the device can print. Most printers have different ppm ratings for black and color printing because color graphics generally take longer to print. Be careful when comparing page-per-minute rates. Printer manufacturers and retailers often quote the speed for draft printing (a lower-quality, lower-resolution way of printing text). A printer might be able to print 35 to 40 pages per minute in draft mode but only 5 or 6 per minute at full quality.

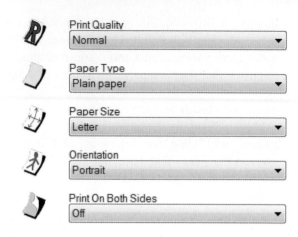

You can change various settings any time you print.

- **Duplexing.** The ability to automatically print to both sides of a piece of paper is known as **duplexing**. Various industries rely on duplexing to produce a wide range of printouts such as magazines, manuals, and catalogs.

- **Materials.** The price of new printers has fallen dramatically in recent years, while their capabilities and speed have improved just as dramatically. However, the cost of printing materials remains expensive. Consider the replacement cost of items such as ink cartridges and specialty paper, and how often you'll likely have to replace them.

More **Online:** *Visit the companion website to learn about various ways to save money on printing supplies, including information on how to recycle them.*

Recycling printer cartridges can be good for the environment and your wallet.

TYPES OF PRINTERS

Printers are divided into a variety of categories, separated by both their mechanisms and the materials used in printing.

- **Dot matrix printers** create output by striking an inked ribbon against paper using metal pins. Although they are still produced, they date to the 1970s and produce output that is inferior to other categories of modern printers. However, because of the hard impact they make on paper, they are the only printers that can produce carbon-copy or pressure-sensitive forms (think of an auto lease contract). While this need is important to a few types of businesses, these types of printers are rarely used today.

- **Inkjet printers** create an image directly on the paper by spraying ink through tiny nozzles. The nozzles are mounted on a carriage that slides back and forth across the page, applying in the desired pattern as the page is fed through the printer. Color inkjet printers have four ink nozzles: cyan (blue), magenta (red), yellow, and black. These four colors (often referred to as CMYK) are used in almost all color printing because it is possible to combine them to create any color. Inkjet printers typically use one cartridge for black, and either one cartridge for each color or a single cartridge that contains the three colored nozzles. Although these printers have become very affordable (and the standard for homes), the replacement cost of cartridges can dramatically increase their expense over time.

- **Laser printers** create output by using a laser that is aimed at a rotating drum. Toner, which is a powder composed of tiny particles of ink, then sticks to the drum in the places the laser has charged. Lastly, with pressure and heat, the

Laser printers produce sharp quality text output.

toner is transferred off the drum onto the paper. A processor and memory are built into the printer to interpret the data that it receives from the computer and to control the laser. Many laser printers are monochrome, which means that they can only print in black. Such printers meet the needs of many businesses, which is generally to produce documents. However, there are now many affordable color laser printers that produce stunning output. They work like a single-color model, except that the process is repeated four times and a different toner color (CMYK) is used for each pass. Because of their sharp quality text output and fast printing speeds, laser printers are often preferred by businesses.

- **Multifunction printers** combine either inkjet or laser printing capabilities with scanning, photocopying, and faxing capabilities. These affordable, all-in-one devices are popular in home offices and small businesses because they remove the need for several separate pieces of equipment. The only downside is that if this device malfunctions, a business will lose multiple capabilities all at once.

This multifunction printer can also scan, copy, and fax.

A dye-sub card printer (left) and a thermal label printer (right) both use heat to create images.

- **Dye-sublimation (dye-sub) printers** use a process where by colored dyes are heated and then diffuse on specialty paper or other materials. This technology is often used to create lab-quality photos, as well as the images found on plastic ID cards.

- **Thermal printers** apply heat to special thermal paper, turning select areas black to produce text and basic graphics. They are often used to create receipts and labels.

- **3D printers** are unique in that they can create a three-dimensional object made of various materials. Although several technologies exist for accomplishing this, the rapid growth is in commercially available printers that use several types of polymers, or plastics. Initially, a 3D model is created on a computer using special software. When it is transferred to the printer, a nozzle will heat special plastic material until it melts. This nozzle will expel the liquid in a series of layers, which quickly hardens into solid form. There are countless applications for 3D printing that range from the creation of plastic toys at home to producing equipment and parts for astronauts that are stationed on another planet.

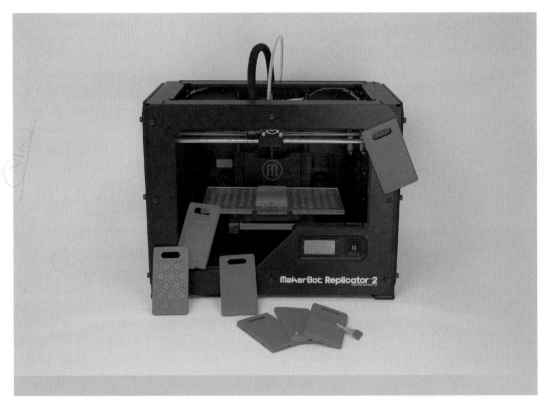

This 3D printer can create almost any plastic object, such as these custom cases for smartphones.

OTHER OUTPUT TECHNOLOGY

Monitors, speakers, and printers are by far the most common devices used to deliver computer output to a user. Many other devices, however, can provide output for more specialized applications.

PROJECTORS

Digital projectors are used to project digital images and video onto a large screen where they can be viewed by an audience. Projectors can be placed on a table or permanently mounted on a wall or ceiling. They can accept data to output directly from a computer, a local network, or even a USB flash drive. Some projectors are often used with **interactive whiteboards**, whereby a user can interact with the images projected on a screen or whiteboard.

HAPTIC TECHNOLOGY

The communication of vibration, motion, or physical resistance to a user is called **haptics** or **haptic feedback**. Haptic technology can enhance audio or video output from computers to make them more relevant or noticeable. One of the most common devices using haptic technology is the smartphone, which can buzz for incoming calls or be triggered by a specific action within an app. Game controllers for consoles and PCs commonly use haptic feedback to increase the sense of immersion for users who are driving, flying, or

Interactive whiteboard combines with a digital projector.

shooting things on the screen. In modern flight simulators, haptics are sometimes used in the handheld control systems to provide feedback to pilots. Robotic control systems can also employ haptic feedback. For example, the controls for a robotic arm that handles radioactive or toxic materials might use haptic technology to let operators feel resistance as they move the controls to twist, squeeze, and lift with the robotic arm.

Flight simulators often use haptic feedback in the pilot's controls.

KEY TERMS

3D printer, 54
biometrics, 48
bit, 38
Blu-ray disc (BD), 40
byte, 38
cache, 37
central processing unit
   (CPU), 35
chipset, 35
clock rate, 36
compact disc (CD), 39
contrast ratio, 49
core, 36
CRT monitor, 50
cursor, 42
digital camera, 47
digital projector, 55
digital versatile disc
   (DVD), 39
digital video recorder
   (DVR), 47
document feeder, 45
dot matrix printer, 52
dots per inch (DPI), 52
drive, 38
duplexing, 52
dye-sublimation printer, 54
ergonomic keyboard, 41

expansion card, 35
facial recognition, 48
fingerprint scanner, 48
firmware, 37
game controller, 48
gesture, 43
graphics processing unit
   (GPU), 50
graphics tablet, 44
haptic feedback, 55
hard drive, 39
inkjet printer, 53
interactive whiteboard, 55
keyboard shortcut, 42
laser printer, 53
LCD monitor, 50
LED monitor, 50
media, 38
megapixel, 47
memory, 36
memory card, 40
motherboard, 35
multifunction printer, 53
multimedia, 46
optical character recognition
   (OCR), 45
optical mouse, 43
pages per minute (PPM), 52

pixel, 49
port, 35
QR code, 45
random access memory
   (RAM), 37
read-only memory
   (ROM), 37
response time, 49
resolution, 49
RFID tag, 46
scanner, 45
solid state drive (SSD), 40
sound card, 51
speech recognition, 46
stylus, 44
system unit, 34
tape drive, 39
thermal printer, 54
touchpad, 43
touchscreen, 44
trackball, 43
TV tuner, 47
USB flash drive, 40
USB port, 35
video card, 50
videoconferencing, 47
virtual memory, 38
webcam, 47

Review Questions

MULTIPLE CHOICE

1. Which of the following is a pointing
   device that can be useful if you have very
   limited space on your desk?

   a. Trackball
   b. Stylus
   c. GPU
   d. Controller

2. Which type of printer should you purchase
   if your company needs to print employee
   ID cards?

   a. Dot matrix
   b. Laser
   c. Dye-sub
   d. Thermal

Review Questions (continued)

3. Which type of memory is nothing more than the use of your hard drive when you are running out of RAM?

   a. ROM

   b. Cache

   c. BIOS

   (d.) Virtual memory

4. You are shopping for a new computer online. The description lists the following: "Intel i7 3630QM." What part of the computer does that refer to?

   a. RAM

   (b.) CPU

   c. Solid state drive

   d. Monitor

5. If you want to know the maximum number of pixels that a monitor can display on the screen, you would look at its:

   a. contrast ratio

   b. response time

   (c.) resolution

   d. size

6. Both fingerprint scanners and facial recognition are examples of:

   (a.) biometrics

   b. haptics

   c. firmware

   d. ergonomics

7. _____ is the primary storage device of a personal computer.

   a. RAM

   b. ROM

   c. The DVD drive

   (d.) The hard drive

8. The quality of a printer's output is measured in:

   (a.) PPM

   b. DPI

   c. OCR

   d. CRT

9. Which optical disc typically holds 25 GB or 50 GB of data?

   a. DVD

   (b.) Blu-ray

   c. CD

   d. SD card

10. Which type of keyboard is designed to be comfortable and help reduce the chance of hand and wrist strain?

    a. Multimedia

    b. Biometric

    c. Interactive

    (d.) Ergonomic

FILL IN THE BLANK

11. The _System unit_ of a desktop computer is the case that houses the computer's critical parts, such as the processing and storage devices.

12. The _motherboard_ is the largest circuit board in a personal computer.

13. The ability to automatically print to both sides of a piece of paper is known as _duplexing_

14. _3-D Printers_ are unique in that they can create a three-dimensional object made of various materials.

15. The most fundamental unit of computing is the _bit_, which is typically represented as a 1 or a 0.

16. _RAM_ is the temporary workspace of a computer. It stores the content you are currently working on.

Random access memory

17. A(n) _TV Tuner_ is a device that can capture television signals for viewing on a computer.

18. The USB _Flash Drive_ is the most popular type of plug found on desktop and laptop computers.

19. _Multifunction Printers_ combine either inkjet or laser printing capabilities with scanning, photocopying, and faxing capabilities.

20. A technology known as _____ can translate the image of a scanned document into text that can be edited and formatted.

TRUE / FALSE

21. One gigabyte is larger than one terabyte.

22. Without proper cooling, a computer could overheat and malfunction.

23. Modern ROM chips can be electronically reprogrammed.

24. Because of their high speeds and the sharp-looking text they produce, dot matrix printers are preferred by modern businesses.

25. With speech recognition, it is possible to issue commands and search for information by speaking into your mobile device.

SHORT ANSWER

Quiz

26. Other than in video games, where might you find haptic technology being used?

27. Why are LED monitors replacing the more traditional LCD monitors?

28. List five modifier keys that you would find on a laptop computer running Windows.

29. Why do some computers include a small, solid state hard drive in addition to the large, magnetic hard drive?

30. What is the difference between RAM and storage? Use an example to support your answer.

31. Describe a product that can protect your tablet computer and help you type on a surface that is more comfortable than the screen.

32. What are gestures? Give one example of a gesture commonly used on touchpads or touchscreens.

33. Other than gestures, list and briefly describe five operations that can be performed with pointing devices such as the mouse.

34. Which expansion card do gamers and individuals in the video industry normally purchase to improve their graphics? What types of components are found on this card?

35. What is the difference between a document scanner and a flatbed scanner? Why would a business choose a document scanner?

Research Exercises

Go beyond the book by performing research online to complete the exercises below.

1. Experts are claiming that 3D printers are going to change a variety of industries. Name at least two of these industries and provide a few examples of the products that will be 3D printed.

2. Several types of LED technology are used in monitors, TVs, and mobile devices. Name these technologies and briefly describe the differences.

3. List the required steps for changing the resolution on your desktop or laptop computer. If you do not own these types of computers, find the steps for a machine that runs Windows 8.

4. List the required steps for changing your printing options to consume less ink. If you do not own a printer, find the steps for Windows 8 and a printer of your choice.

5. Why is it important to recycle printer cartridges? Find a store near you that is willing to accept empty cartridges and offer discounts on the purchase of new cartridges.

6. Many large organizations and cloud providers use enormous data centers for their storage needs. Find at least one of these large data centers and describe their processing and storage needs.

7. List the steps for identifying the RAM and storage capacities of your computer. Record the type of computer you have along with these capacities.

8. Gaming consoles are not the only systems that can accept input through the movement of your body. Find at least three other devices that can track the movement of your hands, eyes, or other body parts without the need to touch the input device.

3

SOFTWARE

Chapter Overview

This chapter provides an overview of the software that operates today's computers. You will also learn about a variety of software that individuals use for productivity, education, and entertainment. You'll also gain an understanding of how the computer can help you manage and organize your important files, such as documents, photos, and music.

PART 1:
System Software

As you learned in Chapter 1, software contains computer programs that instruct the computer to complete a variety of tasks. Without software, a computer would not know what to do after you power it on. Furthermore, we would find little use for a computer if it weren't for the wide range of software that exists today. Two broad categories of software will be discussed in this chapter:

- **Application software** is any type of software that is made for you, the user. It allows individuals to complete a variety of work and school-related tasks. In addition, the software that you use for entertainment—managing music, editing photos, playing games, and so on—also falls under application software.

- **System software** refers to any software that is created for the operation, maintenance, and security of a computer. Most users take this software for granted, especially if it was included with their computer. However, it is crucial for the proper operation and well-being of your system. In this section, we will explore the various categories of system software.

Operating Systems

The purpose of an **operating system (OS)** is to manage the flow of data between hardware components and allow the user to communicate with the computer. It also supports all the other software that is installed in that computer. This is why the operating system must be loaded before any other software during the computer's start-up or **boot process**.

To better illustrate the function of an operating system, imagine a situation where you need to copy an image from a web page and save it in your hard drive. Typically, this operation only requires one or two simple clicks of your pointing device. However, behind the scenes, the operating system has to manage many components and resources. First, it has to manage your connection to the Internet. Next, it must support the software that we use to browse websites. Lastly, it has to interpret your clicks and ensure that it creates a perfect copy of the image on the hard drive. It doesn't always get noticed, but the operating system is performing countless services in the background that allow users and applications to complete their tasks. Let us now look at some key concepts and features related to operating systems.

- **Compatibility.** Because all software runs on top of the operating system, each has to be programmed to work with a specific operating

Operating systems perform a variety of functions such as managing your Internet connection and saving image files on your storage devices.

system. If, for example, you buy accounting software for your Windows-based Dell laptop, it is unlikely to work on your Mac computer. However, it will work just fine on your HP desktop computer because it too runs Windows. Computers that have the same operating system are said to be **compatible** with each other because they can support the same software.

- **GUI.** You generally interact with a computer using various mouse operations or hand gestures. This is because modern operating systems have a **graphical user interface (GUI)**, allowing users to communicate via graphical elements on the screen. GUI elements include objects such as windows, icons, menus, and buttons. This is in contrast to computers that use a **command-line interface**, which requires users to memorize and type a series of commands. For home users, this older type of interface was phased out over 20 years ago.

- **Multitasking.** The ability to run multiple programs at the same time is known as **multitasking**. A modern operating system will, for example, allow you to work on a document in one window while researching information online in another. This is in contrast to older operating systems such as Microsoft DOS (1980s) in which you could only use one program at a time.

- **32 vs. 64-bit.** You may encounter two versions of the same operating system that differ only in their bit numbers. If you recall from Chapter 2, a bit refers to the 0s and 1s that represent data in its most fundamental form. A 32-bit operating system is intended to work with older 32-bit processors, which can only handle 4 GB of RAM. The newer processors are 64-bit, making them more powerful and capable of supporting much more RAM. The 64-bit operating systems are created to work with these types of processors, which are quite prevalent in today's computers.

- **Device drivers.** Operating systems com-municate with most hardware components using **device drivers**. These programs, which are usually downloaded and installed automatically, instruct the operating system how to use or "drive" a newly installed device.

"Tux" the penguin is the logo most often associated with the Linux operating system.
Source: Linux

Unix uses a command-line interface.

SERVER OPERATING SYSTEMS

The operating systems for desktops, laptops, and mobile devices are generally intended for a single user at any given time. Because of this, they are not well suited to be installed on powerful servers, which manage a variety of functions and resources for many organizations today. Server operating systems must have the capability to handle the connections and requests of large numbers of users at the same time. They must also be very stable as they manage many critical aspects of organizations such as banks, universities, and airlines. You may not have worked directly with the following operating systems, but you have definitely used the resources they support.

UNIX

Unix (or UNIX), which dates to 1969, runs many of the world's most powerful servers. Although Unix may not be as easy to use or configure as Windows, for example, it is very powerful and extremely stable. Since its development, Unix has been operated by a command-line interface. Although there are several GUIs that can now be added to Unix, many system administrators prefer to use it by typing quick commands. Today, you will find many variants of Unix, with Oracle's Solaris being one of the most popular.

LINUX

Linux is an open source, Unix-like operating system that was created by Linus Torvalds in 1991. It is considered to be **open source** because it can be freely distributed and modified. Its popularity has exploded and thousands of users participate in the global community that has built up around this OS. This community invites Linux users and developers to contribute modifications and enhancements, and it freely shares information about Linux-related issues.

Even though Linux is free, companies may choose to sell their own versions of Linux. These companies, such as Red Hat, typically include customer service and support as part of the price, which is desired by most businesses that use Linux. Currently hundreds of Linux variants, or *distributions,* are available commercially or as a free download. Linux has grown at a very rapid pace and can be found in millions of servers worldwide. There are also desktop versions, which will be discussed later in this section.

> More **Online:** *Visit the companion website to learn more about Linux and its various distributions.*

WINDOWS SERVER

Although Microsoft has been making operating systems since the early 1980s, it wasn't until the mid to late 1990s that its server products gained any significant popularity. Today, Microsoft's Windows Server operating system is widely used in businesses of all sizes to manage users and a variety of services. It employs a GUI that is very similar to the desktop version of Windows. The newest version, Windows Server 2012, matches the style of Microsoft's other operating systems such as Windows 8 and Windows Phone.

DESKTOP OPERATING SYSTEMS

The operating systems used on desktop and laptop computers are likely the ones that you know best. Although Windows and Mac OS are dominant for these types of computers, we will explore a few others that are starting to get noticed.

MICROSOFT WINDOWS

Windows is Microsoft's operating system for personal computers. It has the largest market share of any competitor, with one version or another appearing on roughly 90 percent of the world's personal computers. Hundreds of PC manufacturers sell Windows-based computers. In addition, anyone can build a desktop computer using the same parts as those found in popular brands of PCs. As long as you install Windows on your machine, it will be compatible with any other PC.

Windows has undergone dramatic transformations since its introduction in the mid-1980s. The latest version is Windows 8, which is intended to unify the desktop/laptop experience with those of Microsoft's tablets and smartphones. It can run mobile-style apps in the area known as the **Start screen**, while running traditional Windows software in the more familiar **desktop**. The Start screen has replaced the older icons on the desktop with new **live tiles** that can display real-time information such as the current weather, news, or social media updates.

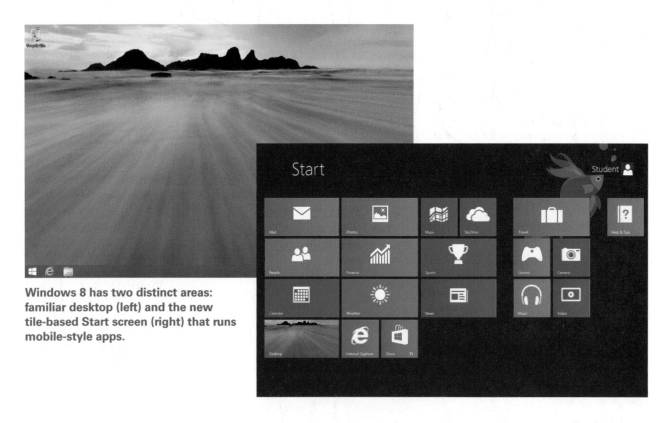

Windows 8 has two distinct areas: familiar desktop (left) and the new tile-based Start screen (right) that runs mobile-style apps.

MAC OS

Mac OS is the operating system used for computers sold by Apple. "Mac" refers to the Macintosh brand name of computer, introduced by Apple in 1984. At the time, Apple's GUI was revolutionary. Macs were quickly adopted by many schools and individuals in the graphics, music, and design industries. However, most businesses never switched to Macs, opting to keep their IBM PCs. This, along with Apple's reluctance to allow any other manufacturer to build Mac-compatible computers, partially explains why PC usage spread quickly and became the computers used by most individuals and businesses today. Some also cite cost as a factor, with Macs generally being more expensive than similarly equipped PCs.

The current Mac operating system, OS X, has gone through multiple versions over the years, each with its own nickname such as "Mountain Lion" or "Yosemite." Recent versions have increased the Mac's integration with Apple's other products, which is especially beneficial to individuals who own an iPhone and/or iPad. Though OS X and Windows share similar features and functions, they each have a distinctly different style and operation. Although most computer owners stick with Windows, users who purchase a Mac cite some key advantages of owning these types of computers:

- **Stability.** Mac computers seem to be more stable and suffer from fewer issues than PCs. This is partly due to the programming that lies at the heart of OS X. Another reason has to do with Apple being in control of both the hardware and software powering their computers. This is in contrast with Windows, which can end up on hundreds of different systems, including ones that individuals build for themselves.

- **Fewer viruses.** Macs rarely get infected by computer viruses and other malicious programs. This is because viruses can only target one operating system. Since Windows is found on many more machines, individuals who want to create chaos will generally write malicious programs for Windows-based computers.

- **Included software.** OS X includes various applications that a wide range of individuals find very useful. These include iPhoto, iMovie, and GarageBand, which allow users to create and edit photos, videos, and music.

Apple's OS X has a distinctive "dock" at the bottom and menu bar at the top.

- **Unified ecosystem.** Apple manufactures popular smartphones, tablets, and laptops. If you own at least two of these devices, you can experience a unified "ecosystem." Your devices work well with each other and all of your data is seamlessly synchronized to the cloud using Apple's iCloud service. Apple controls its ecosystem tightly to ensure a comfortable, worry-free experience for its users. Both Microsoft and Google are building competing ecosystems for their devices.

- **Support.** Many users argue that Apple's customer service is second to none. One of the reasons for this claim is that you can simply walk into an Apple store and get help from various experts that work at the "Genius Bar."

- **It runs Windows.** This fact surprises many people, including some Mac users. Because Macs are now powered by Intel processors, it is possible to purchase and install Windows on a Mac computer. Using the Boot Camp program, users can decide whether to boot up their Mac using Windows or OS X. By running Windows, a user no longer has issues when switching to Mac—all existing Windows software will work!

If you want to learn more about the various Mac devices, turn to the buying guide in the appendix of this book.

DESKTOP LINUX

Although Linux is widely used on servers, many distributions have been aimed at desktop computers. Various companies, such as Ubuntu, are trying to lure Windows and Mac users with their friendly interfaces and familiar features. It also doesn't hurt that the operating system is free. If you want to try Linux before replacing your current OS, many versions can be run directly off a USB drive. If you do decide to make the switch, you will find a surprisingly good operating system and many free, open source applications waiting for you.

Ubuntu Linux for desktops has familiar GUI elements.

CHROME OS

The newest member of this group of operating systems is Google's Chrome OS. In essence, the Chrome web browser will be running your computer. Therefore, an Internet connection is required to get the most out of this operating system. All of the available apps are those that work with the Chrome browser. Your services, from file storage to document creation, are those offered by Google. With this operating system, you will be fully immersed in Google's ecosystem.

At the moment, Chrome OS is available on a few small, ultraportable computers. Their prices are lower than Windows or Mac laptops, and Google even offers 100 GB of free cloud storage for those who purchase these systems. Overall, Chrome OS–based laptops are attractive options for individuals (such as students) who enjoy Google's various services and find themselves near a wireless access point at all times.

MOBILE OPERATING SYSTEMS

Various operating systems are made solely to operate tablets and smartphones. Most of their features revolve around the needs of mobile users, who require quick access to information and notifications of incoming messages and daily reminders. These operating systems support mobile apps, which are

Chrome OS, with its Google apps at the bottom left, is included in this Samsung Chromebook.

generally fast, touch friendly, and require little storage space. The following are the four most popular operating systems for mobile devices.

iOS

The iOS operating system powers Apple's iPhone and iPad. It is considered to be a very friendly and stable operating system, largely due to Apple's tight control of the hardware and software ecosystem. Apple practically set the standards for a user-friendly interface with the debut of the iPhone in 2007. Since then, Apple has added a variety of features including messaging, videoconferencing, and cloud storage that are exclusively available for Apple users. More recently, the Siri speech recognition system has made a big impact on the way many users interact with their mobile device. In addition to these built-in features, you can download over a million apps from the App Store to extend your device's functionality.

ANDROID

Like Linux, Android is an open source operating system. Although Google owns Android and manages the Google Play Store for apps, it allows any manufacturer to use and modify this operating system for their devices. This is why you see Android-based smartphones and tablets from companies such as Samsung, Motorola, and HTC. Google also has its own line of "Nexus" Android devices that many individuals seek because they contain the pure, unaltered versions of this operating system. Android versions use numbers (e.g., 4.2.2), but they are popularly referred to by the names of various sweets, such as "Jelly Bean" and "Ice Cream Sandwich." Each version brings a wide range of improvements, some of which rival or even

The "BlinkFeed" home screen of the HTC One demonstrates how much Android can be customized.

exceed the features of iOS. One unique feature is the ability to add **widgets**, which are much larger than icons and provide automatically updating information without the need to open an app.

The open source nature of Android allows any programmer to alter it and add innovative features. Many individuals and groups even release their own Android versions, or *ROMs,* that can replace the one you have on your device. To allow this, your phone must be *rooted,* which involves a series of steps that give you full access and control over your device. This type of access is necessary for *flashing* a custom ROM as your new operating system. Although this will void the phone's warranty, many individuals are willing to take the risk in order to replace their inferior version of Android with a more useful one.

More **Online:** *Visit the companion website to learn more about Android customization and flashing ROMs.*

BLACKBERRY

The BlackBerry operating system can be found on a variety of BlackBerry smartphones. These phones achieved tremendous popularity a few years ago with the small, physical keyboards that were integrated into these devices. Since then, iOS and Android devices have come to dominate the market. Nevertheless, BlackBerry devices are still enjoyed by those who became accustomed to sending messages and email on those keyboards.

WINDOWS RT AND WINDOWS PHONE

Although Microsoft waited several years to create a mobile OS that could compete with iOS and Android, its recent efforts have received significant attention. Microsoft uses two operating systems for its mobile devices: Windows Phone and Windows RT. Windows Phone, as the name implies, powers smartphones created by several manufacturers such as Nokia. This OS features frequently updating live tiles on the home screen that are similar to those in the new Windows 8 Start screen. Microsoft also incorporated these tiles in Windows RT, which is used in its new Surface tablets.

Microsoft has received praise for giving users a unified experience on Windows-based smartphones, tablets, laptops, and desktops. At the same time, it has also received some criticism. Since Windows RT looks the same as the Start screen of Windows 8, some users have become confused. In a nutshell, Windows RT is made to compete with iOS and Android. Devices running Windows RT, such as the Microsoft Surface RT, are limited to running mobile-style apps much like their competitors' tablets. However, computers running Windows 8 can run both Windows RT apps and traditional Windows software, including those made for older versions of Windows such as 7 and XP. Windows 8 is what powers Microsoft's Surface Pro devices and most of the laptops and desktops sold today.

Microsoft's "Live Tiles" are present on Windows smartphones (right), Surface tablets (left), and Windows 8 computers.

Utilities

As you just learned, operating systems are responsible for managing your hardware and allowing you to easily communicate with your computer. Historically, desktop operating systems included only the most fundamental programming, allowing users to complete basic tasks such as managing files and opening programs. Little by little, programmers began to create a variety of **utilities** that enhanced or extended the operating system's capabilities. In some cases, these utilities offered features not provided by the operating system. Among these were utilities that protect your computer from viruses and increase your storage space through compression. As operating systems were improved and updated, the functionality of popular utilities started to be included with subsequent releases of the OS. Although today's operating systems include many of the utilities covered in this section, some users still choose to install third-party utility software.

SECURITY UTILITIES

The purpose of **security software** is to keep you, your computer, and your personal information safe from a variety of threats. With millions of infections and intrusions yearly, home users and businesses can no longer afford to be without basic security software. Many types of security software can be purchased individually or even downloaded for free from several reliable companies. Others are available as a **security suite**, which is essentially a bundle of programs that accomplish a variety of security-related tasks. Many

Security suites often bundle several security utilities into one package.

individuals opt for these types of suites since one software title (with one interface) can take care of all of their security needs. We will cover all aspects of computer security throughout Chapter 5. For now, let's look at some of the software that can provide a variety of security services.

ANTIVIRUS

A virus is one of many types of computer programs that are created to harm your computer or steal valuable information. Collectively, all malicious programs are referred to as **malware**. Although recent versions of Windows include some level of malware protection, you should consider one of the following tools to protect your desktop and laptop computers from all types of malware:

- **Paid:** Norton AntiVirus, Bitdefender Antivirus Plus
- **Free:** AVG Anti-Virus Free, Avast Free Antivirus, Avira Free Antivirus

FIREWALL

A software-based **firewall** is dedicated to examining and blocking Internet traffic. Most desktop operating systems, including recent versions of Windows and Mac OS, include a firewall utility that is usually activated for you. Although several security suites will include a firewall, it is rarely necessary for you to purchase a separate one. Businesses also use firewalls, but their needs are usually more complex.

ENCRYPTION

Encryption is the process of scrambling your data or storage devices to make them unreadable by anyone who doesn't have the proper key. This key

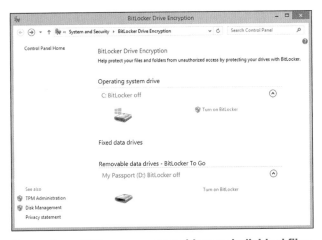

Encryption utilities can protect drives or individual files.

can be a password, PIN, or even a card. Encryption can be useful to prevent someone from gaining access to your data, such as a USB flash drive that you accidentally left at school. Both Windows 8 and Mac OS include an encryption utility for your drives.

PASSWORD MANAGEMENT

Remembering countless passwords for all of your accounts can be frustrating, but it is dangerous to reuse passwords for multiple websites and services. With information being stolen at an alarming rate, you cannot risk a thief having access to many of your accounts. Although many web browsers include a password storage utility, they are limited to services that you visit with that browser. LastPass is a secure and reliable password management utility that stores all of your passwords on each of your computers, including mobile devices. If you can remember one master password, you will have instant access to every account login and password you have ever created. In addition, this tool can also help you generate strong passwords so that you don't have to come up with your own each time.

PARENTAL CONTROL

Parental control utilities allow parents to set a variety of limits on their children's Internet usage.

Password management utilities help you remember passwords and will generate new ones as well.

Parents can set time limits, block adult content, and even receive reports on their child's activity. Both Windows and Mac OS have a variety of parental control utilities. If you desire a separate one, Net Nanny has been a popular choice for over a decade.

VIRTUAL MACHINES

A **virtual machine** is a special environment that allows you to run an operating system on top of another operating system. The operating system that runs in this virtual environment will think it is your primary OS with all the capabilities to manage hardware and run other programs. This is useful for individuals who wish to test a different operating system or for those that have software that requires an operating system other than the one that runs their computer. Earlier in the chapter you learned that you could try Linux by running it off a USB drive. An alternative way is to install and run Linux in a virtual machine, which allows it to run normally inside a window of your current operating system. The software that allows you to run a virtual machine is usually referred to as **virtualization software**. VirtualBox from Oracle (free) is a good choice for individuals, while businesses often use products from VMware.

Virtualization software (left) allows one operating system (Ubuntu Linux on the right) to run inside another.

STORAGE OPTIMIZATION

Most of what you store inside a computer is located in the hard drive. Therefore, if this component is not functioning efficiently, it can impact the speed at which the operating system stores and retrieves data. Furthermore, many of your other storage devices might need occasional troubleshooting to solve a variety of issues. Whether it is fixing an SD card that is seemingly unreadable to helping you make files smaller, these utilities are all crucial aspects of managing storage.

DISK FORMATTING

Preparing a storage device for use by an operating system is known as **formatting**. It is possible that you have never gone through this process yourself. The computers you buy at the store come preformatted with the operating system already installed for you. Furthermore, many portable storage devices come formatted in a manner that allows them to be used in a variety of computers. However, if you are setting up a new hard drive, you might have to format it before writing data to it. Additionally, devices such as SD cards and USB flash drives may become corrupted and can only be saved by formatting them. Although all data gets erased during formatting, there are times when we simply have no choice.

Formatting utilities, which are included with operating systems, are capable of performing several functions that are crucial to storage devices. The following are a few that you should become familiar with:

- **Partitioning.** Dividing a hard drive into multiple sections is known as **partitioning**. Although many hard drives just have one large partition, others might be split into two or three sections. One common reason for doing this is to create a recovery partition that allows you to restore your computer to its factory settings. Since your computer's manufacturer doesn't want you to store anything in this area, it sections it off to make it look like a separate storage device that is clearly labeled.

- **File system.** The **file system** of a storage device, which is configured after partitioning, determines how the operating system manages the space on the device. For PCs, there are two popular file systems: FAT and NTFS. Since FAT enjoys more widespread compatibility with other operating systems, it is often used on removable devices such SD cards and USB flash drives. However, your primary hard drive uses the more powerful and secure NTFS. Other operating systems, such as Mac OS, Unix, and Linux, use distinct file systems for the hard drive.

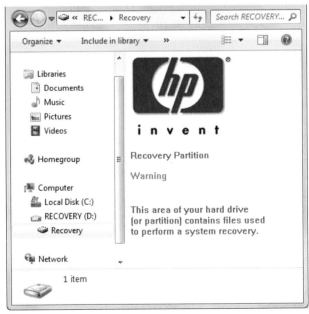

The Recovery (D:) drive on this computer is nothing more than a partition on the main hard drive.

More **Online:** *Do you have an SD card or USB flash drive that can no longer be read by your computer? Visit the companion website to learn how you can recover your precious data from these drives.*

DEFRAGMENTATION AND OPTIMIZATION

At some point, most magnetic hard drives become cluttered with thousands and thousands of file fragments to the point where there are no large areas of empty space available. If the operating system needs to write a large file, it must separate the large file into smaller parts and write them in areas scattered throughout the disk surface. Reading a file that is fragmented in that manner takes extra time because the read/write head of the drive needs to keep repositioning itself.

Operating systems typically contain a **disk defragmentation** or optimization utility, which will reorganize files and fragments to place related ones nearer to each other. Reading from the disk surface will now occur far more quickly because the file portions are all next to each other. You should always follow your operating system's recommendation to either automate or run this utility periodically. If you have a solid state drive, fragmentation is not an issue because these drives do not possess read/write heads. Nevertheless, these utilities will optimize them in a different way to ensure that they are working as efficiently as possible.

DISK CLEANUP

Operating systems and many other programs (such as web browsers) create temporary files during their operation. These files, which are necessary for a variety of reasons, take up space on your hard drive just like any other files. Operating systems generally make an effort to clean up this data. However, if you want to clear these temporary files yourself for storage, performance, or privacy reasons, you should run a **disk cleanup** utility. Most operating systems and web browsers include these utilities.

FILE COMPRESSION

The process of making a file smaller than its original size is known as **file compression**. Compression utilities use a variety of techniques that can "squeeze" one or more files into a smaller, compressed file. They are often unusable when compressed, but they

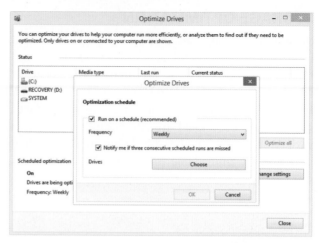

The Optimize Drives utility in Windows 8 can improve your computer's performance.

definitely occupy less space on your storage devices. Many users choose to compress several files into one for the sake of easy transport, especially when attaching them to an email message. It is better to attach one compressed file than many separate files.

Most operating systems contain a file compression utility. The most popular format for compression is known as *ZIP*. In Windows, these files are represented by an icon that looks like a folder with a zipper on it. Less popular is the compression known as *RAR*, which requires separate utility software to create and open. Regardless of the compression type, always be sure to remove or extract the files from their compressed container before using them.

BACKUP

A **backup** is a copy of one or more files (or entire storage devices) that is made in case the originals become lost or damaged. Ideally, the backup should be made to a separate storage device in case your computer is severely damaged or stolen. Creating a backup can be as simple as copying important files to a DVD or external USB drive. However, there are many backup utilities that can automate this process to make it easier for the user. Most operating systems include at least one backup utility. Windows 8 uses utilities known as System Restore and File History that can help you recover files or restore your system to a previous moment in time. Mac OS has a similar backup utility that is known as Time Machine. Regardless of which tool you use, it is *crucial* that you get into the habit of creating

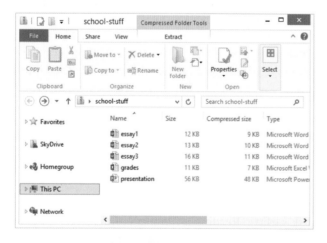

This compressed (zipped) file in Windows contains five files.

frequent backups. You never know when a disaster could strike you or your business, causing you to lose irreplaceable files.

CLOUD BACKUP

With many homes and businesses now having access to high-speed Internet connections, many users are choosing to store their backups online. **Cloud backup** providers are companies that provide utility software that creates automated backups to an online account. The advantage of creating online backups is twofold.

- **Safety.** An online account is probably the safest place for your backups. If, for example, some thieves were to enter your home, they might steal both your computer and the USB drive that contains your backups. A cloud storage account is immune from theft, fires, and other disasters that could hit your home or business.

- **Accessibility.** As you have already learned, the files that you store in the cloud can usually be accessed from any device that is connected to the Internet. This is not the case with physical backups, which are stored in your home or business.

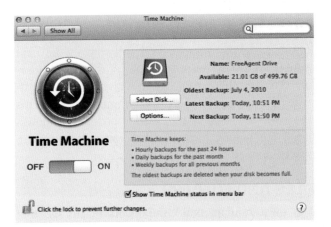

Apple's Time Machine utility backs up your Mac automatically to an external drive.

Cloud backup providers typically charge an annual fee that varies based on how much data (and how many computers) you have to back up. The types of files that are usually backed up are your irreplaceable data files—documents, music, photos, and videos. It is not necessary to back up your operating system or application software because you likely have those on DVDs or you are able to simply download them again. There are dozens of cloud backup providers, with Carbonite being one of the most popular.

DISK WIPING AND RECOVERY

Most individuals believe that the files they delete from their portable storage devices and recycle bins are gone forever. This is not entirely true, as it is possible to recover all or parts of these files using recovery utilities. While these utilities may help you bring back an important file, they can also be used by those who purchase or obtain access to used computers. For this reason, it is crucial to use disk wiping utilities to remove all traces of your files from computers you are selling or giving away (see Research Exercise 1). For mobile devices, this can often be accomplished via a *factory reset* option.

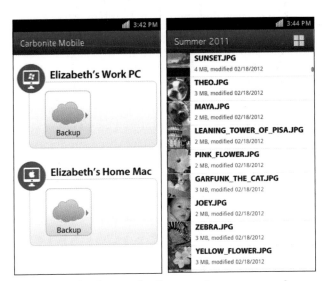

Many cloud backup tools allow you to access your home or office computer's backups from a mobile device.

File Management

Before we explore application software in the next section, let us first learn about one of the most important activities that we engage in with our system software: file management. Although many of the terms and examples used in this section are for Windows-based computers, most of what you will learn can also be applied to other operating systems.

FILES AND FOLDERS

The most fundamental components of storage that users interact with are the files. Before computers, homes and businesses used quite a bit of paper. These papers could contain almost anything—letters, financial reports, building instructions, musical notes, and even photos. In essence, papers contained information or instructions that were crucial to the individuals using them. Computer files are similar. They can contain the instructions of a computer program or the data that you care to store, from school papers to vacation photos and videos. Because of their importance, computers offer us a variety of ways to store and organize our files. This structure, known as the **file hierarchy**, consists of several components:

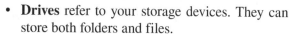

- **Drives** refer to your storage devices. They can store both folders and files.

- **Folders** are containers that can store files or other folders. When a folder is located inside another folder, it is referred to as a *subfolder*. In some operating systems, folders may be referred to as *directories*.

- **Files** can be located inside drives, folders, or subfolders. When they are located on a drive without being inside any folder, they are often said to be in the **root directory** of that drive.

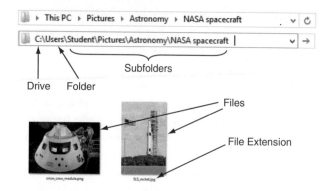

Figure 3.1 Example of a File Path Windows can display the current location, or path, in different ways, as shown in the two address bars at the top.

THE PATH

A file **path** is a complete address that describes the exact location of a file. Each operating system uses a unique path that contains words and symbols to describe drives, folders, and files. Figure 3.1 compares the address that Windows displays to the user with the actual path of that file. If the path looks a little familiar to you, it is likely because you have seen a similar notation in the address bar of your web browser. This is not a coincidence. Much of the Internet was designed by individuals using Unix-based computers, which use paths that look practically the same as the addresses for web pages.

FILE EXTENSIONS

As you have already learned, files can contain computer programs or data. If you look at a file on your storage device, you probably have discovered various ways to determine what kind of file you are looking at. One possible way is to look at its **icon**, which is a graphical representation of a file, folder, or drive.

TABLE 3.1 COMMON FILE EXTENSIONS

File Extension	Description
.exe	Windows executable file
.jpg, .png, .gif	Image files
.mp3, .m4a	Music files
.mp4, .avi, .mov	Video files
.pdf	Adobe PDF document
.docx, .xlsx .accdb, .pptx	Microsoft Word, Excel, Access, PowerPoint
.zip	Compressed ZIP file

That icon might contain a "W" indicating that it is a Word file or it might display the logo of your favorite video game. In addition, many operating systems will reveal the file type when you select the file. If the previous two options are not available (such as in an email attachment), it is useful to understand the **file extension**—a short, unique sequence of characters located after the file's name that indicate the file type. File extensions are always located after a period (dot) that follows the file's name. All files have this, even if your operating system doesn't display it at all times. Table 3.1 shows some common file extensions.

FAVORITE LOCATIONS

Most operating systems help you manage special folders that contain popular file types such as documents, music, photos, and videos. Mac OS will display these as *favorites* while Windows uses the term *libraries*. In Windows, these libraries display both your personal folders and public folders that are accessible to anyone that uses your machine. Although Windows also displays favorites, this area is used for other folders on the computer such as your downloads and your desktop (yes, the desktop is just another folder on your computer).

Every user account created on a computer will have unique folders created for that account. If other individuals use your computer, they will see document, music, and image folders that are unique to them. You don't see those folders in your favorites/library; you see your own. This helps users avoid the distraction of seeing countless files that do not belong to them. Now, if you want to share files with those who use your computer, you can place the files in a public or shared folder that is viewable by everyone.

MANAGING YOUR FILES

Now that you know what files, folders, and drives are, it is time to explore a variety of things that you can do with them. In Windows, files are managed with a tool known as *File Explorer*. On a Mac, that tool is known as *Finder*. No matter which tool you use, the basic file management operations are usually the same.

CREATING FOLDERS

File managers contain a feature that allows you to create folders and subfolders in a specific location. This is an important operation that helps keep similar files organized. If you have a folder with images, for example, you could create subfolders for categories such as birthdays, vacations, and holidays. Document folders could also be organized with subfolders for your various classes and personal files at home.

COPYING AND MOVING FILES

One of the advantages of computer files and folders is the ease with which we can copy or move them from one location to another. For example, you might choose to copy photos from a friend's USB flash drive onto your computer's hard drive. Alternatively, a teacher might choose to move a set of student documents from a parent (main) folder into a subfolder for a particular semester. Regardless of what method an individual uses for copying or moving, there are certain concepts that are important to know:

Finder (left) and File Explorer (right) are both file managers.

- **Clipboard.** In the real world, you often move an item by grabbing with your hands and then placing it in a new location. A computer also needs a temporary location for things that are being moved or copied, and that location is known as the **clipboard**. This clipboard is managed by RAM and the operating system.

- **Copy.** The **copy** command places a copy of the object (or objects) that are currently selected into the clipboard.

- **Cut.** The **cut** command removes the selected object (or objects) from their current location and places them into the clipboard.

- **Paste.** The **paste** command takes whatever is currently in the clipboard and places it in the location where this command is issued. Copy and paste will end up making a copy, while cut and paste is used to move something to a new location.

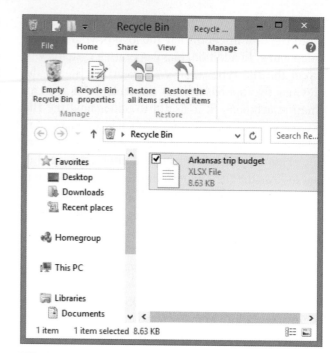

Windows 8 Recycle Bin holds deleted files.

DELETING AND RECOVERING FILES

When you no longer need a file or a folder, you can use the **delete** command to remove it from your drive. On most operating systems, files deleted from the hard drive go to a location that helps you recover those files that were erased by accident. On Windows it is known as the *Recycle Bin,* while on Mac OS it is called the *Trash.* Depending on your settings, files deleted from removable storage devices may not be sent here. Also keep in mind that while files remain in this second-chance location, you have not truly freed up any storage space on your computer. Therefore, be sure to clear these deleted files periodically.

SEARCHING FOR FILES

Most operating systems are trying to reduce the frustration of searching through countless folders or menus to find specific files. With Mac OS and Windows 8, you can type any search text and the operating system will find any files that contain this text. In addition, these operating systems will also search through programs, settings, and even the web in order to display relevant results alongside your files. In Windows, the *Smart Search* feature can be activated by typing on the Start screen, while Mac's *Spotlight* feature can be accessed from the menu bar or the Finder window.

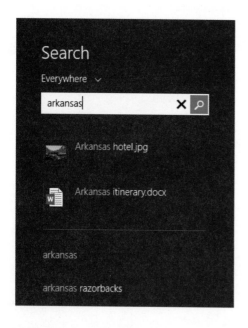

Windows 8 (left) and Mac OS (right) allow you to initiate file and web searches from just about anywhere.

PART 2:
Application Software

The software that most individuals and businesses purchase and use on a daily basis is known as application software. Tens of thousands of software titles are available for purchase and download for the various operating systems in use today. Before we cover some of the most popular categories of applications, let us first explore the various ways in which this software is sold and distributed.

Acquiring and Installing Software

All individuals and businesses have a variety of options when acquiring software. While mobile users download apps directly from their device, a business with hundreds of computer systems might sign a special contract with the software company. Home users typically purchase a DVD or an electronic download from companies such as Amazon. Once the software is acquired, it must first be **installed**—set up by the operating system—before it can be used.

Before deciding to purchase or install software, one must be aware of the license that governs the software's use. A **software license** is a contract from the software creator that specifies the rules for using this software. This is in addition to federal **copyright law**, which gives software creators a variety of rights and privileges over their creative work. There are many types of licenses, with some being customized to meet the needs of a large business. The following terminology and license categories will help you gain a better understanding of the software acquisition and installation processes.

END-USER LICENSE AGREEMENT

An **end-user license agreement (EULA)** is the typical license that a user must agree to before installing software. Most EULAs take the form of an electronic notification that appears when starting the installation process. The user then has a choice to accept or decline the terms of this agreement. Although many users ignore these agreements and accept them blindly, you should read some of the basic usage and privacy notices before proceeding with the installation.

Most of the software and apps that individuals install are intended for one user at a time. In other words, you usually cannot take that same DVD, for example, and install it on the computers of all your friends and family members. Unless the software comes with a license that permits installation on multiple devices (typical for most antivirus software), you must limit your installation to only your machine. Other licenses allow you to install the software on all the machines that you use, such as your desktop and laptop or your tablet and smartphone. All of these variations demonstrate how important it is that you familiarize yourself with the license agreement.

VOLUME LICENSE

It would be inefficient for a medium or large business to purchase or download multiple copies of software to install on each employee's computer. For this reason, software companies usually offer a **volume license**, which allows companies to install the software on multiple machines. Businesses can buy a license for a certain number of users, or they can negotiate a package that includes maintenance and support. Software companies will usually offer a discount for volume licenses.

An end-user license agreement (EULA) must be accepted before installing software.

SUBSCRIPTION MODEL

Certain types of software, such as those for professional graphics and design, can reach or exceed $1,000 per copy. To ease the burden of paying that much at one time, many software companies have started to offer subscriptions. With the **subscription model**, users pay a fixed amount of money per month to use the software. Some subscriptions are done on a month-to-month basis while others require an annual commitment. Once the user stops paying, the software will no longer work. This is enforced by having the software check the user's online account for payment verification periodically, usually once per month.

Users must evaluate whether the subscription model will save them money for the period in which they need this software. In addition, some of these subscriptions include many added benefits, from installation on multiple computers for the family to a variety of cloud services. Adobe, for example, charges students and teachers about $1,000 for its large collection of graphics and design software. However, the monthly subscription that allows you to access the same software is only $30 per month and it also includes a generous cloud storage account. If you only need to use this software for a year, then the savings are easy to see.

SHAREWARE / TRIAL SOFTWARE

Some software is free to download and install, but will stop working as intended after about 30 days. This software is known as **shareware** or trial software. To keep using the software after the trial period, you must purchase a full version or a code that can be entered into the software. This software is very popular with users, as they get to try it for free before they commit to paying for it.

FREEWARE

Freeware is software that is free to use without any specified time restrictions. Although it doesn't cost anything, it is still protected by a license and by copyright law. Many programmers that are just starting out might offer their software for free to establish a fan base. However, even large companies might offer freeware, knowing that they can make money using methods such as these:

- **Promoting the paid version.** Many free software titles, such as antiviruses, do everything possible to promote the paid version that has more features. You will often see promotions for this full version while you are installing or using the free version.

- **Viewing content.** Some free software is required to view files or content created by the paid version. For example, the free Adobe Flash Player is required to view the web-based animated content and movies created with Adobe Flash Professional. Adobe hopes that users who view these animations online will become inspired to purchase the professional tool that can create them.

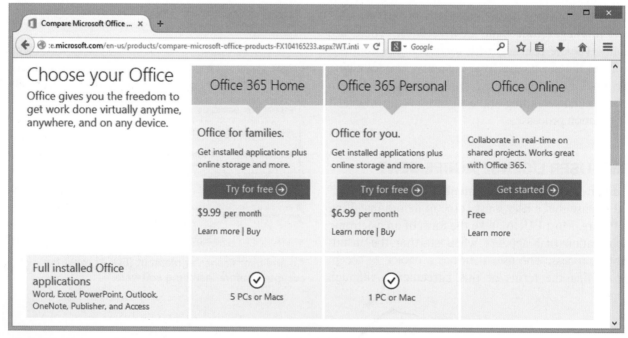

Microsoft offers various subscription plans for Office 365.

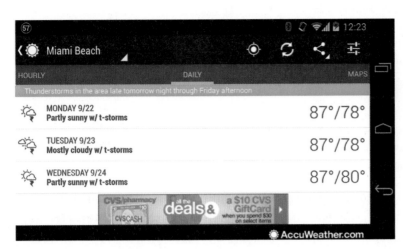
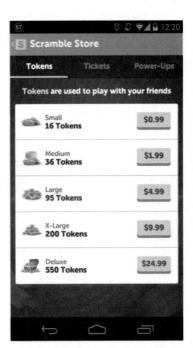

Free apps often include advertisements or offer in-app purchases.

- **Advertising.** Although some desktop software contains advertisements or third-party toolbars, this method has become most popular for mobile devices. You may have noticed that many free apps have small, rectangular advertisements at the bottom. These developers get money from the viewing and/or clicking of the ad. Many others sell a version of the app without the ads, hoping that users will pay a few dollars to get rid of that permanent advertisement.

- **In-app purchases.** The last way in which free software can make money is by offering users the chance to purchase a variety of things within the program. Games, for example, might offer desirable characters or objects with a one-time purchase.

OPEN SOURCE SOFTWARE

Earlier in this chapter, you explored a variety of open source software such as Linux and VirtualBox. Although they can be obtained legally for free, programs such as these are governed by licenses. One of the most famous open source licenses is the *GNU*

General Public License (GPL), which ensures that a particular program and any of its derivatives (modified versions) remain free to distribute. In addition, its programming code can be examined and modified by anyone. For many, open source is more than free software: It is a philosophical movement that hopes to change the way we acquire, use, and share software.

CLOUD AND WEB-BASED APPLICATIONS

Powerful web and cloud technology enables anyone to use various types of software that do not require installation. **Web-based applications** are programs that run directly on your web browser. This technology allows you to play games, edit documents, and even create basic drawings without leaving your web browser. Although you can use services such as Evernote, Google Docs, and Microsoft Office Online on your browser, it is often more convenient to install a mobile app that offers quicker and more convenient access on your mobile device. Regardless of where you use them, your settings and data are saved because they are located on remote servers.

Types of Applications

Many categories of application software are used for a wide range of purposes, from entertaining and educating children to running the day-to-day operations of a business. Although it would be impossible to cover all types of applications, this section will introduce you to those that are widely used. Unless otherwise stated, these applications are primarily for servers, desktop, and laptop computers.

OFFICE SOFTWARE

Office software includes some of the most popular programs that help businesses efficiently carry out tasks such as writing letters, analyzing sales figures, and scheduling meetings. The same software helps students create reports and presentations for class. Often, several office programs are bundled as a unit known as an **office suite**. Although these suites have traditionally been made for desktop and laptop users, many have started to offer mobile and cloud-based versions (see Chapter 1). The following are some of the most popular office suites:

- **Microsoft Office.** The popular office suite from Microsoft can be found in most homes and organizations.

- **LibreOffice.** This free and open source office suite is gaining popularity and can be used on Windows, Mac OS, and Linux.

- **iWork.** Apple's office suite allows you to create documents, spreadsheets, and presentations on Mac OS and iOS devices.

LibreOffice is a complete open source office suite.

More **Online:** *Can mobile devices open the files created with desktop office suites? Visit the companion website to learn more about file compatibility.*

WORD PROCESSING

Word processing software provides tools for creating and editing all kinds of text-based documents. In addition, this software allows you to format your document by changing the appearance of text and the layout of each page. These capabilities allow you to create anything from simple one-page letters and résumés to large reports and publications containing separate chapters, a table of contents, and an index. These programs also enable you to add photos, graphics, tables, and various other elements to each page. This makes it easy to create eye-catching documents such as newsletters, flyers, and brochures. Popular titles in this software category include:

- Microsoft Word
- Corel WordPerfect
- LibreOffice Writer
- iWork Pages

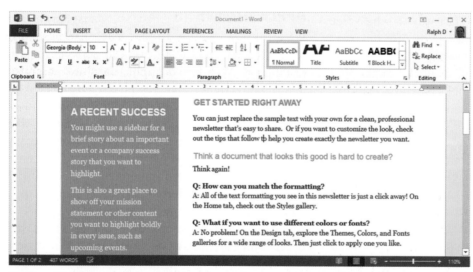

Microsoft Word includes many sample documents with attractive formatting and layouts to help you get started.

SPREADSHEET

Spreadsheet software is used for entering, calculating, and analyzing sets of numbers. These programs also create charts and graphs that are based on the selected set of numbers. Spreadsheets have a wide range of uses, from managing a teacher's grade book to performing complex analysis on a company's sales figures. One of a spreadsheet's most powerful purposes is to answer "what if" questions for a variety of scenarios. For example, a company can preview the financial consequences of changes such as price increases or rising fuel costs. This is made possible by this software's ability to instantly recalculate totals and redraw charts the moment any number is changed. Popular titles in this software category include:

Microsoft Excel allows you to create charts and perform complex calculations.

- Microsoft Excel
- LibreOffice Calc
- iWork Numbers

DATABASE MANAGEMENT

A computer **database** is simply an organized method for storing information. Practically every business and organization relies on databases for the storage and quick retrieval of information. For example, an online store selling electronics would have the need to store data about customers, suppliers, employees, inventory, sales, and shipping. Each of those categories has different types of associated data. A customer *record,* for example, might include each person's name, address, and payment information. However, the records for each product in their inventory would include different attributes such as model number, manufacturer, price, and quantity on hand. Databases have to be able to create connections, or *relationships,* between different types of data in order to create transactions and generate meaningful information for this company. To create and manage such complex databases, businesses can use software known as a **database management system (DBMS)**. The software best suited for an organization often depends on its size and needs:

- **Small businesses and individuals:** Microsoft Access or LibreOffice Base.

- **Medium to large businesses:** Microsoft SQL Server or Oracle Database.

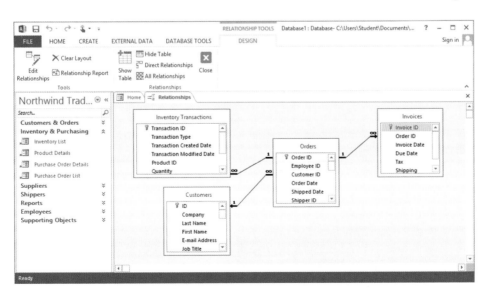

Microsoft Access creates relationships between different types of data.

PRESENTATION

Presentation software enables users to create electronic slideshows that are used to present information. Each slide in the presentation can contain a combination of text, images, charts, videos, and other elements that are arranged in an appealing layout. These slides are then shown in sequence to support the individual who is speaking in front of an audience. The content of these slides often comes from other office software. A presenter might

Microsoft PowerPoint helps you create eye-catching presentations.

copy some text from a document and a chart from a spreadsheet to create a brief summary for an upcoming meeting. The alternative, which is showing a long document or spreadsheet with small text, is not very appealing when trying to relay information to an audience using a digital projector. The most popular titles for presentation software are:

- Microsoft PowerPoint
- LibreOffice Impress
- iWork Keynote

PERSONAL INFORMATION MANAGEMENT

A **personal information manager (PIM)** is software designed to keep individuals organized. You can use

a PIM to manage your contacts, create appointments and meetings, set up reminders, and keep track of various to-do lists. A PIM also provides email capabilities that allow you to send messages to any one of your contacts. Most office workers, from employees to managers, use a PIM on a daily basis. In fact, some offices coordinate most of their activities through PIM software. It can automatically determine the best times for meetings and available rooms simply by scanning everyone's schedule. Let's take a look at a few categories and examples of PIM software.

- **Traditional.** The most popular PIM software for business is Microsoft Outlook, which often connects to a Microsoft Exchange Server that stores and manages all this information.

- **Open source.** Mozilla Thunderbird and Zimbra Desktop are popular choices.

- **Cloud based.** Google, Microsoft, and Apple all offer PIM services. These can be accessed on the web and on mobile devices. Some organizations have started to use premium versions of these cloud services, relieving their need to buy servers that manage employee or student email, calendars, contacts, and even documents.

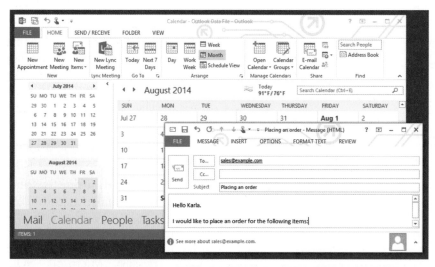

Microsoft Outlook manages email, appointments, contacts, and tasks to keep you organized.

ACCOUNTING & FINANCE

The software in this category helps businesses and individuals with a variety of finance-related tasks. With powerful reporting, this software makes it easy to see where your money is going and it helps improve the way you or your business manages both income and expenses.

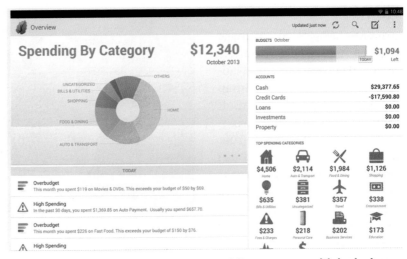

Mint can help you manage your personal finances on multiple devices.

BUSINESS ACCOUNTING

Accounting software helps businesses manage all aspects of their company's finances. It keeps records of every transaction between customers and suppliers, generating a variety of invoices and forms. The software can keep track of all business contacts and maintain your entire inventory. It also manages the employee payroll, making it easy to calculate taxes and report information to the IRS. Software in this category includes:

- Intuit QuickBooks
- Sage 50 Accounting
- Xero (cloud based)

PERSONAL FINANCE

Personal finance software helps individuals and families manage their budget. It keeps track of all your expenses and helps you create a budget that works with your income. Many programs will even connect to your financial institutions to download transactions and make sure they match your entries in the software. If you tend to have trouble with your finances, the following software can help you get out of debt and change the way you manage your money:

- **Desktop and mobile.** Intuit Quicken and YNAB both offer desktop software that synchronizes with your mobile app. You can enter transactions or view your budget from wherever you are.

- **Cloud based.** Mint is the most popular cloud-based financial application. Once you log into your financial accounts using this website, it practically does all the work for you. Both the web-based service and the mobile app are free.

TAX PREPARATION

Tax preparation software allows individuals to prepare their income taxes and file electronically (e-file) with the IRS. This type of software is usually available in several versions that vary depending on the complexity of your tax return. Some companies even offer free web-based tax preparation if your income is lower or you meet specific requirements. The following are the most popular desktop programs in this category:

- Intuit TurboTax
- H&R Block

CREATIVE AND MULTIMEDIA

As you remember, *multimedia* is a term that encompasses a variety of media such as music, graphics, photos, and video. Individuals and businesses use different types of software to create, edit, and publish these types of files. Although Macs are the preferred systems for those in these fields, PCs are capable of producing the same type of files. When it comes to multimedia software, Adobe dominates the field.

Before we explore the various categories of multimedia, it is important to note that operating systems include applications that allow you to view (and sometimes create) many of these files. **Media players** refer to applications that allow you to listen to music and play videos. In addition, you will find several image viewers that allow you to view image slideshows and manage photo galleries on desktop and mobile operating systems.

DRAWING

For those who need to create graphics from scratch, a variety of drawing programs are available. Those based on **bitmap graphics**, such as Microsoft Paint, will record your drawings on a pixel-by-pixel basis. Your bitmap or *raster* graphics can then be saved in popular formats such as JPG, GIF, and PNG. However, any attempt to make these images larger than their original size will result in blurriness and distortion.

Vector graphics, on the other hand, rely on mathematics to generate and manipulate a variety of shapes. This allows you to increase or decrease the size of your graphics without any distortion. Drawing programs based on these types of graphics are well suited for work when accuracy and flexibility are important. Practically all professional-level artwork, from company logos to animated characters, is created with vector-based drawing tools. The following are popular choices:

- Adobe Illustrator
- CorelDRAW
- Inkscape (open source)

Adobe Illustrator uses vector graphics to help you create artwork.

GRAPHICS EDITING

Graphics editing software, which is sometimes referred to as image or photo editing software, contains bitmap-based tools that are used primarily to edit images. Individuals will often use this software to remove blemishes and imperfections in photos or add special effects to any type of image. Many mobile and web-based applications allow amateurs to improve or apply cool effects to any of the photos they take with their digital cameras. However, for more professional programs, consider one of the following:

- Adobe Photoshop
- GIMP (open source)

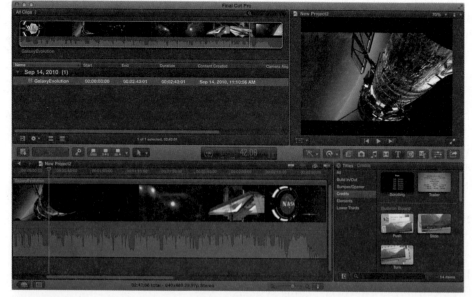

Apple's Final Cut Pro helps you edit videos, their accompanying sound, and apply special effects.

VIDEO EDITING

Video editing software is used to edit and produce a variety of videos. Amateurs can use simple (and free) applications such as Apple's iMovie and Windows Live Movie Maker to create vacation movies and fun slideshows from their photos. Professionals use more sophisticated tools to edit and export videos for use in movies, TV, and even websites. Popular video editing programs include:

- Adobe Premiere
- Apple Final Cut Pro

CAD / 3D MODELING

A variety of professionals now turn to software to create both two and three-dimensional designs. **Computer aided design (CAD)** software aids architects, engineers, and many others who need to create a digital model of an object. For example, before a city starts construction on a new bridge, a digital version will be created using CAD software that contains all the specifications for the bridge in a visual format. **3D modeling software**, on the other hand, is typically used by professional artists and animators who need to create three dimensional graphics and characters for advertisements, video games, cartoons, and movies. The following are some of the most popular software titles in these categories:

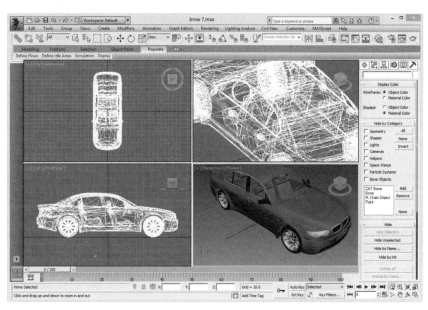

Autodesk's 3ds Max helps artists create and animate realistic 3D models.

- **CAD.** Autodesk's AutoCAD has been the industry standard CAD and drafting tool for over two decades.
- **3D modeling.** Autodesk offers two products for professional 3D modeling and animation: Maya and 3ds Max. For an open source alternative, many use Blender for their 3D needs.

AUDIO EDITING & PRODUCTION

It is likely that you have used one or more programs designed to play and organize your music collection. Software such as Apple's iTunes allows home users to manage their music and playlists, purchase new songs, or *rip* existing music from their CDs into a digital format such as MP3. This software is very different from those used by musicians and sound engineers. These professionals use audio production software to compose, edit, and mix music or sound effects. Although performers usually record their music at a professional studio, much of the editing and enhancements can now occur on the computer. Additionally, much of today's electronic music can be composed using this software. Musicians can sample pieces of other songs or create sounds that are replicas of those produced by a variety of musical instruments. Some examples of this software are:

- Avid Pro Tools (the industry standard).
- Apple GarageBand (included with Mac OS).
- Audacity (open source sound editor).

DESKTOP PUBLISHING

Desktop publishing software is used by professionals to create works that require complex layouts and contain a mix of text and graphics. Magazines, newspapers, and textbooks are all created with this type of software. Popular titles include:

- Adobe InDesign
- QuarkXPress

WEB DEVELOPMENT

Although there are now countless ways to create a website, professionals who need to manage complex sites will often use web development software. In addition to a variety of design and programming tools, these programs also help the web developer publish the site to a web server. The following are some popular tools:

- Adobe Dreamweaver
- Microsoft Visual Studio

EDUCATION & ENTERTAINMENT

Some of the most popular software titles for the home are those that either educate or entertain us. Thousands of programs teach children how to read and do basic math. Older students often purchase software that offers tutoring in a specific subject or helps prepare them for a variety of standardized exams. One of the fastest-growing categories of educational software is those that help teach a foreign language. Programs such as Rosetta Stone include a variety of advanced features such as the ability to detect whether you are pronouncing a word correctly.

For entertainment, there are many categories of games created for both desktop computers and mobile devices. These range from simple action games and puzzles to complete fantasy worlds that can be played online with millions of other individuals. Many feel that the future of gaming will involve **virtual reality**, where humans can experience realistic environments that are simulated by computers. A variety of headsets and machines have already been developed for playing games. Others can be used to train individuals such as pilots or soldiers, or even allow individuals to travel virtually to any other place in the world.

VERTICAL MARKET

Vertical market software is created for a specific industry such as health care or insurance. Unlike most of the applications you studied in this section, this software is not intended for general use. It is tailored for one specific type of company or role. For example, the software used by pharmacies needs to track inventory, process patient prescriptions, and communicate electronically with doctors and hospitals. No business would have use for such software except for pharmacies. Companies that sell this type of software generally create a license or contract that includes installation, setup, training, and support.

LARGE BUSINESS

It would be difficult to operate a large business if many of its core functions were managed by different types of software. **Enterprise resource planning (ERP)** systems bring together many types of business functions into one software solution. It can handle tasks as diverse as manufacturing and quality control to accounting and human resources. Managers can also use it for **project management** functions, where a sophisticated plan is created and tracked to achieve a variety of goals. Some ERP systems also integrate **customer relationship management (CRM)** capabilities that allow sales departments to manage call centers, support customers, and keep track of sales commissions.

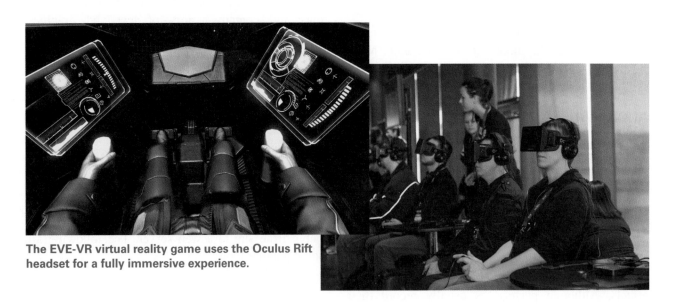

The EVE-VR virtual reality game uses the Oculus Rift headset for a fully immersive experience.

Software Development

Now that you have explored a variety of software, we will consider how it is all created. As you remember from Chapter 1, software is made from computer programs that contain detailed instructions for the computer. To create successful software, computer programmers go through a series of steps known as the **software development life cycle (SDLC)**. This cycle takes programmers from the idea and planning stages through the actual programming, testing, and maintenance of the software. In this section, we will explore some fundamental concepts in computer programming by taking a quick tour of the typical development stages.

PLANNING

Like most things you do on a daily basis, software development begins with an idea and a plan. Programmers must come up with a detailed description of the tasks they want their software to accomplish.

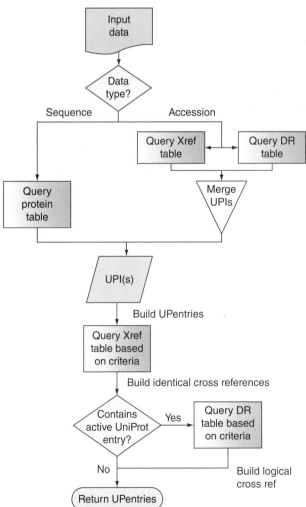

Figure 3.2 Flowchart Tracing Steps of a Program

They will come up with a series of steps, known as an **algorithm**, that describes exactly what each portion of their program is supposed to do. This algorithm is often represented visually as a **flowchart**, which uses special symbols to trace the steps of the program (see Figure 3.2). Once programmers have developed their algorithms and flowcharts, they essentially have a blueprint or guide that will allow them to start writing their program.

If you have trouble understanding this stage of development, imagine for a moment the process that you go through to cook and eat hamburgers for dinner. Not only do you need to come up with an idea of what you want to eat, you must also create a plan for successfully preparing the hamburgers. From heating the grill to cutting vegetables while the hamburgers cook, you probably have developed a series of steps that you follow to prepare this or any other meal. For more complex dishes, you likely have a recipe with detailed ingredients, notes, and steps that you must review before you start cooking. That is the sort of planning that programmers must engage in before they start to work on the actual coding of the program.

CODING

In this phase, the programmer will begin the process of converting the algorithms and flowcharts into an actual computer program, a process known as **coding**. The code created by these programmers is written in one of many computer programming languages that contain their own vocabulary and grammar (syntax), much like English, Spanish, and practically every other language. Although these programming languages use many words that you would immediately recognize, they also use complex symbols and sequences that require a great deal of training to master. The following are some of the most popular programming languages for creating computer software:

- C++
- Java
- Visual Basic
- Python

Many programmers today use an **integrated development environment (IDE)**, which is software that helps them build their computer programs. This software, such as Microsoft Visual Studio, provides a variety of tools and features that can increase the programmer's speed and accuracy. In addition, these IDEs contain a **compiler**, which is a program that translates a specific programming language into a machine language that can be processed by the CPU.

Once a computer program is compiled, the IDE will produce an **executable file** that can be run by the operating system on a user's computer.

> More **Online:** *Several websites offer fun and interactive tutorials on programming for free. Visit the companion website to learn more.*

TESTING AND MAINTENANCE

In the same way that you test and adjust a recipe to make it as perfect as possible, software must also go through a process after it is created. First, a programmer will look for errors, or **bugs**, by testing the software under a series of conditions. The process of finding and fixing these bugs is known as *debugging.* Once this phase is over, programmers might want to test the software in real-world conditions. They will release a **beta version** to a limited audience that will test it on their systems. Programmers can now collect information from these users about any errors that were encountered.

Once the software is deemed ready, it is released to the general public. However, no software is truly free of bugs. Errors and security vulnerabilities will continue to be found and programmers will "patch" them by offering **software updates** to users. It is crucial that you download and install all software updates (especially for the operating system) the moment they are released. Most software does this automatically, requiring only an occasional restart of the program or your computer. Some updates may also include improvements and new features that many users desire. Programmers will continue to update and maintain the software until the company decides to no longer support this software or one of its particular versions.

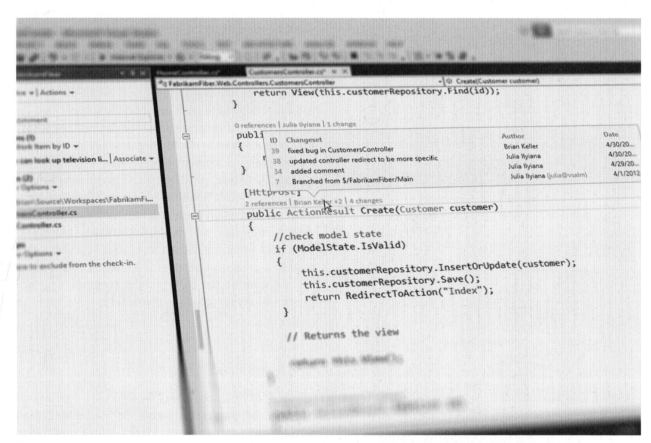

Integrated development environments, such as Visual Studio, help programmers build software and apps.

KEY TERMS

Review Questions

MULTIPLE CHOICE

1. Operating systems communicate with most hardware components using:
   a. compilers
   b. device drivers
   c. algorithms
   d. widgets

2. Collectively, all malicious programs are referred to as:
   a. malware
   b. bugs
   c. vectors
   d. CRM

3. A(n) _____ is a special environment that allows you to run an operating system on top of another operating system.

   a. file system
   b. *virtual machine*
   c. widget
   d. IDE

4. Which of the following is a DBMS that you might find a large business using?

   a. *Oracle*
   b. Excel
   c. QuickBooks
   d. AutoCAD

5. Which of the following is NOT an office suite?

   a. Microsoft Office
   b. Apple iWork
   c. *Adobe Creative*
   d. LibreOffice

6. Dividing a hard drive into multiple sections is known as:

   a. formatting
   b. defragmentation
   c. compression
   d. *partitioning*

7. Which type of software is used for entering, calculating, and analyzing sets of numbers, as well as creating graphs and charts?

   a. Word processing
   b. *Spreadsheet*
   c. Database
   d. Presentation

8. A(n) _____ is software designed to keep individuals organized.

   a. CRM
   b. ERP
   c. IDE
   d. *PIM*

9. Which of the following is NOT a popular computer programming language?

   a. *Exchange*
   b. C++
   c. Visual Basic
   d. Java

10. Which of the following products would you choose if you wanted to edit videos?

    a. *Apple Final Cut Pro*
    b. Adobe Photoshop
    c. Adobe InDesign
    d. Microsoft Visual Studio

FILL IN THE BLANK

11. The purpose of a(n) _operating system_ is to manage the flow of data between hardware components and allow the user to communicate with the computer.

12. _Encryption_ is the process of scrambling your data or storage devices to make them unreadable by anyone who doesn't have the proper key.

13. A(n) _end user license agreement_ is the typical license that a user must agree to before installing software.

14. The ability to run multiple programs at the same time is known as _multitasking_

15. A(n) _backup_ is a copy of one or more files that is made in case the originals become lost or damaged.

Review Questions (continued)

16. A file _path_ is a complete address that describes the exact location of a file.

17. A computer _____ is simply an organized method for storing information.

18. Modern operating systems have a(n) _____, allowing users to communicate via graphical elements on the screen.

19. Many feel that the future of gaming will involve _Virtual reality_, where humans can experience realistic environments that are simulated by computers.

20. _(CAD)_ software aids architects, engineers, and many others who need to create a digital model of an object.

Computer Aided design

TRUE / FALSE

21. Application software is made for the computer's proper operation, while system software aims to make users more productive.

22. The most popular format for file compression is known as CRM.

23. In some operating systems, folders may be referred to as directories.

24. With a subscription model, users pay a fixed amount of money per month in order to use software.

25. A programmer or software company will often release a beta version in order to test software in real-world conditions.

SHORT ANSWER

Quiz

26. Name four operating systems used in mobile devices. Are any of those open source?

27. List and describe at least three ways in which freeware could still make money.

28. Describe the operations used to copy and move files using a file manager.

29. List six different file extensions and describe the type of file they belong to.

30. Describe two unique features of open source software. In addition, provide at least three examples of open source software.

31. Name and describe the two distinct areas of Windows 8.

32. Name two examples of paid security suites and two examples of free ones.

33. List two reasons for using file compression.

34. Name one cloud backup provider and describe two advantages of using cloud backups.

35. What type of software do businesses use to keep track of monetary transactions? How about individuals? Provide at least two examples of each type of software.

Research Exercises

Go beyond the book by performing research online to complete the exercises below.

1. Find at least one utility that can help you recover files that you thought had been permanently deleted. Find another utility that can permanently wipe data in high-security environments.

2. Which settings or activities accelerate the draining of the battery in a mobile device? Name at least three. Find one utility (app) that claims to increase the battery life of your mobile device.

3. Find any software title or suite that offers both traditional purchasing and a subscription. Compare the two options, assuming that you will use the software for two years. Which do you feel is a better deal? Why?

4. List and describe at least three accessibility features in your operating system.

5. Discuss the philosophy of the free and open source movement. Do you agree with this philosophy? Defend your answer.

6. Compare the applications that are included with Windows and Mac OS X. Are the offerings of one operating system superior to those of the other? Provide a few examples in your response.

7. Find and list five free mobile apps, each in a different category. Why is each of them offered for free?

8. While most software is protected by a license and copyright law, others are protected by a patent. How can software qualify for patent protection? What sort of problems has this created for technology companies? Are there any proposals that aim to remedy these problems?

4

THE INTERNET

Chapter Overview

Just as the personal computer revolutionized the way the world solves problems and completes tasks, the Internet has changed how the world learns and communicates. This chapter provides basic information about the structure of the Internet and discusses an array of services that the Internet provides to its users.

PART 1:
Internet Basics

In Chapter 1, you learned that the Internet is the largest network in the world. It connects billions of people and organizations, with millions of new users joining each year. Thanks to the Internet, virtually any computer on any network can communicate with any other computer on any other network. These connections allow users to exchange messages, have live conversations, share data and programs, and access enormous amounts of information.

The Internet has become so important that its proper use is considered an essential part of computer competency. Mastering the Internet is one of the first things you should do if you want to get the most from your computing experience. In this chapter, you will learn about the Internet's history and its major components, and gain a broad overview of how we connect and what we do while we're online.

The Internet connects billions of people and organizations all over the world.

History and Structure

The following section will help you understand how the Internet came to be and which organizations are responsible for its development and maintenance.

DEFENSE DEPARTMENT RESEARCH

The seeds of the Internet were planted in 1969, when the Advanced Research Projects Agency (ARPA) of the U.S. Department of Defense began connecting computers at four universities in the western United States. The resulting network was called **ARPANET**. One goal of this early project was to create a large computer network with multiple paths—in the form of telephone lines—that allowed researchers in one location to access the computing resources at another location. This was crucial because, at that time, the number of powerful computers that could be used for advanced research was very small.

ARPANET expanded from the original four universities quite rapidly. By 1971, 18 locations had access (see Figure 4.1). The network jumped across to Europe in 1973, connecting a system in Norway to ARPANET. It kept growing through the early 1980s with continued funding from ARPA.

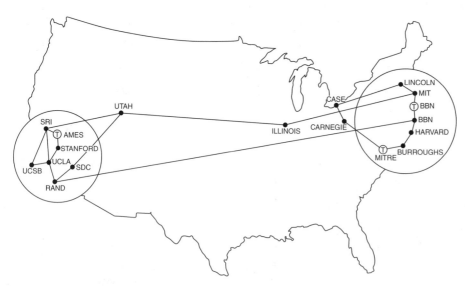

Figure 4.1   The Reach of ARPANET in 1971.

CREATING STANDARDS

We human beings set rules for almost everything we do, from playing sports to dispensing medication. We do this so that everyone knows which procedures to follow. In a similar manner, computers that communicate over a network must follow certain rules to ensure that the transmission is sent properly and understood. These rules are known as communication **protocols**.

The protocols at the heart of Internet communication are known as **TCP/IP** (Transmission Control Protocol/Internet Protocol). Developed in 1973, TCP/IP created standards for transmitting packets (units of data) to ensure that future networks would be able to communicate with existing networks such as ARPANET. TCP/IP sets rules for both the transport of these packets and the addressing system for a network. Today, every computer or device that is on the Internet needs an **IP address** that uniquely identifies it. The most widespread addressing system is known as IPv4; however, it is slowly being replaced by the newer IPv6 system, which offers many more possible addresses (see Figure 4.2).

SCIENCE RESEARCH & EDUCATION

Participation on ARPANET was limited to the handful of institutions and researchers that supported ARPA's research goals. Other U.S. government agencies and

> 192.168.1.101
>
> fe80::d14b:58c:1e50:217f

Figure 4.2 IPv6 addresses (bottom) offer many more combinations than IPv4 (top).

researchers decided to work on their own networks starting in the early 1980s. Among them was the National Science Foundation (NSF), which created **CSNET** in 1981 to bring together researchers in the field of computer science. By 1986, approximately 165 university, industrial, and government computer research groups belonged to this network.

In 1986, the NSF established connections between five supercomputing centers that were available to anyone who wanted to use them for academic research. The NSF created a new high-speed network called **NSFNET** that could transmit data at 25 times the speed of CSNET. In addition, it created connections to smaller regional networks, other agencies' networks, CSNET, and ARPANET. The young Internet was finally taking shape as this new interconnected "network of networks."

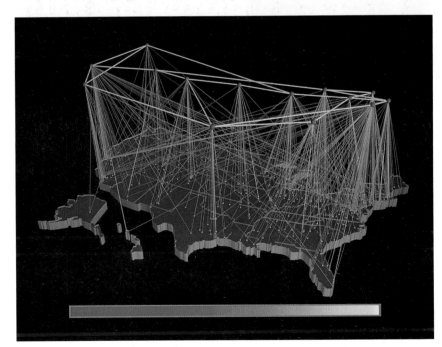

Visualization of the NSFNET T1 backbone and client networks (Sept 1991). The backbone is represented by the white lines connecting the red dots. The colored client networks represent data flow into the backbone.

COMMERCIAL USE

As NSFNET traffic grew rapidly in the late 1980s, the organization realized that it would need help from the private sector to upgrade the network. Various companies, including IBM, provided equipment and established new telecommunications networks to help improve the Internet. As years went by, these companies continued to upgrade existing networks and create new **backbones**, which refer to the connections that carry most of the Internet's traffic. By 1995, there were about 100,000 connected networks throughout the United States, with several backbones operated by private telecommunication companies. Based on this success, the NSF decided to stop funding NSFNET and leave the Internet in the hands of the private sector.

Interest in the Internet exploded in the mid to late 1990s. A network that had been started by the Department of Defense had now found its way into millions of businesses and homes. Expansion continued through the rest of the world, eventually becoming the standard way in which individuals communicated and shared information. The most recent growth has been in the mobile sector, where many companies compete to become your provider for the "always on" Internet connection in your pocket.

WHO OWNS THE INTERNET?

Today, the Internet connects multiple networks and over 2 billion users around the world. It is a huge, decentralized, and cooperative community; no single person or group controls the network. Many telecommunications companies provide the infrastructure in a particular region, and these companies connect with each other at various points to ensure their users have a global reach. It is up to each country's government to determine whether it will regulate or censor the content that ends up reaching the businesses and homes within its boundaries. If the government decides to censor, it typically will ask the regional telecommunication company to filter the incoming content before sending it out to the rest of the country.

FREEDOM AND OPENNESS

The concepts of free expression and censorship are hot topics around the world. Many have argued that it is the Internet's independence and free flow of information that makes it the universally powerful tool it has become. If you can use a computer and if the computer is connected to the Internet, you are not only free to use the resources posted by others but also free to create information of your own. Although several organizations (such as The Internet Society and the W3C) propose standards for Internet-related technologies and appropriate use, these organizations almost universally support the Internet's openness and lack of centralized control.

Overview of Internet Services

The Internet acts as a carrier for several different services, each with its own distinct features and purposes. Think of the Internet as the road upon which many different types of vehicles travel. The roads in your city allow various services to reach you, from UPS and FedEx deliveries to emergency vehicles that can save your life. In a similar manner, you can enjoy services such as websites, email, and online games because the Internet provides the infrastructure that can carry this type of information. Let's look at some of the popular services that exist because of the Internet.

THE WORLD WIDE WEB (WWW)

The **World Wide Web** (also known as the web or WWW) is a global system of linked, hypertext documents. The hypertext in these documents refers to text that is capable of acting as a **hyperlink**, or connector, to another piece of text or document. While these

The Internet is decentralized. Small networks connect to larger networks, which in turn connect to each other.

hyperlinks were originally limited to specially coded text, it eventually became possible to use images and videos as hyperlinks. Web-based documents are normally referred to as **web pages**. Several related pages that connect to each other are referred to as a **website**. These sites are typically located, or hosted, on servers known as **web servers**. It is these servers that deliver a requested web page to your computer using a protocol known as **HTTP** (hypertext transfer protocol).

The web traces its origin to a proposal made by Tim Berners-Lee in 1989. He envisioned a large collection of documents, all stored in different places but all linked in some manner. These linked documents would create a sort of "web" of interconnected information. If you extend that collection of documents and their links to cover the entire globe, you would have a "world wide web" of information. In 1990, this proposal was realized when the first web page was created and placed on the first web server. It was a simple document, containing only black text and hyperlinks. The language used by this first page, **HTML** (hypertext markup language), is still used in pages today along with newer languages such as CSS and JavaScript.

As with all computer technology, the web has continued to evolve since its creation. The web pages you see today can contain music, photos, videos, and even games. In the second half of this chapter, we will take a closer look at all the activities we engage in on the World Wide Web.

More **Online:** *Visit the companion website to see the first web page created by Tim Berners-Lee while he was working at CERN.*

PARTS OF A URL

Home and business addresses throughout the world must follow certain standards (house number, postal code, etc.) to make physical visits and deliveries easier. Web pages also have a standard addressing system known as a **URL** (uniform resource locator), which allows them to be located on the Internet. Most users arrive at a specific address by clicking a link that connects them there. Other times, users can type it directly into a web browser if they know the full URL. It is important to pay attention to URLs, as they can often reveal a great deal about the site that you are on. Use Figure 4.3 and the following list to gain a better understanding of a URL's components.

The HTML and CSS code (below) are converted by the web browser into an attractive web page (above).

Figure 4.3 The parts of a URL.

- **Protocol.** The http:// portion of a URL represents the standard web protocol. If you see **HTTPS** instead, it means that a secure, encrypted connection has been established, such as when shopping or logging in to your bank.

- **Domain.** The **domain name** uniquely identifies a site and a brand on the web. Examples include *apple.com*, *whitehouse.gov*, and *redcross.org*. The first part indicates the unique domain name, while the second half, known as a top-level domain (TLD), indicates the type of site. "Com," for example, is commercial, while "gov" represents a site from the government. Although a few rules are strictly enforced, organizations are generally allowed to use any domain and TLD they want. In fact, anyone can purchase a domain for less than $20 a year.

- **Subdomain.** The **subdomain** of a URL is located just before the domain. It usually indicates a specific subdivision or server within a large site. While "www" is the most popular, sites such as yahoo.com have subdomains for each of their services. When you see *sports.yahoo.com*, for example, you know that you are in the sports section of that site. Many scammers take advantage of the subdomain to trick users into thinking that a site is legitimate. For example, if you accidently land on a

site whose URL is *microsoft.example.com*, do not believe that you are on a Microsoft-related site because of the subdomain. Whoever owns *example.com* is allowed to add subdomains with any name, including those that could trick users.

- **Folders and file.** The last part of a URL will list the folders and subfolders (or directories) where the web page file is located. Remember that a web page is nothing more than a file that contains code for the web browser. Like all files on a computer, they are stored on a disk and possibly located within a folder/subfolder structure.

ELECTRONIC MAIL SERVICES

Electronic mail, more commonly called **email**, is a system for exchanging messages through a computer network. People often use email to send and receive messages containing only text. However, email can also contain images, and practically any type of file can be attached to a message. Because of its versatility, email has become an important and widely used form of communication, particularly in the workplace.

Email started to gain popularity a few years after the launch of ARPANET. Its growth has continued, with practically every employee and Internet user having an email account. Unfortunately, that growth has also come with an increase in **spam**, which is unsolicited email that is sent in bulk. This "junk" mail is not only a nuisance and a waste of network resources, but it also can contain links to dangerous

1&1 DOMAINS

Got a great idea? Get a great domain!

.com $14.99 first year $7.99*

.us $14.99 first year $7.99*

.info $14.99 first year $0.99*

Companies compete to become your domain name registrar.

websites. Fortunately, many companies have become quite good at filtering out spam so that you don't see it while going through your inbox. Nevertheless, if you don't recognize the sender or if the content of the message is suspicious (even from someone you know), you should delete the email immediately.

More **Online:** *Is it "e-mail" or "email"? Do I capitalize "internet" and "web"? Visit the companion website to discover the answers and the reasons behind them.*

WEB-BASED EMAIL

It is typical for individuals to have an email account at work and one that is issued by their Internet service provider. However, many choose to create additional, free accounts on the websites of companies such as Google, Microsoft, or Yahoo. These companies offer free web-based email services that are usually supported by advertisements. You can check this email from just about anywhere, including your mobile device.

It is often useful to create at least two of these free accounts. One should be given out to a limited number of people, such as friends and family. This one will have all of your important messages and very little spam. The other can be given out to just about anyone, including businesses that want to send you newsletters and special offers via email. You can check this one when you have extra time or want to look for a particular coupon.

Many web-based email services, such as Gmail, offer mobile apps.

EMAIL COMPONENTS AND ACTIONS

Although you likely have used email, you may not be familiar with certain aspects of it. Understanding all parts of an email will help you communicate more effectively and ensure that you don't make a mistake when sending messages at work. The following are the parts of every email message:

- **To.** This contains the email address of the primary recipient(s) of your message. This address typically contains the name of an individual and the organization that provides the email, separated by the "@" symbol (e.g., liz_williams@example.com).

- **Cc.** The section known as **Cc**, or carbon copy, is used to send a copy of your message to individuals other than your primary recipient. For example, suppose that you are part of a four-member committee. If you want to send some ideas for the next meeting to the chair of the committee, you would place her email address in the "To" area. However, since you want to offer other committee members the chance to comment on your ideas, but they are not the primary target of your message, you would place their email addresses in the "Cc" section. Another popular use of "Cc" is when you want another individual, such as a supervisor, to be notified, or "copied," on an email message that you are sending to someone else.

- **Bcc.** Any email address placed in the **Bcc**, or blind carbon copy, will be invisible to the recipients of your message. It is common to use Bcc when sending email to a large group of people, especially if you want to protect the privacy of the recipients' email address. It also prevents individuals from having to scroll through a very long list of recipients when reading the message.

- **Subject.** The subject of an email indicates the topic or purpose of your message. Be sure to always fill this box, as it makes it easy for individuals to know what a message is about before opening it. If the subject contains the letters "re," it indicates that the message is a **reply**, or response. If it contains "fw," it means that the message has been **forwarded**, or re-sent, after its initial transmission. Be sure to use good judgment when forwarding email or replying to a group of individuals. Always consider the privacy of the original sender and be considerate with other people's time. They may not appreciate

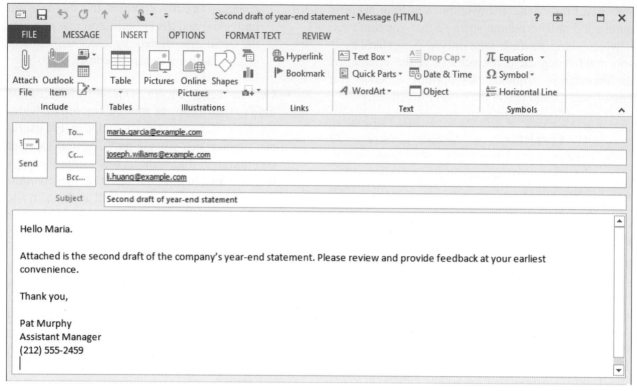

The parts of an effectively written email message.

receiving a large number of messages that are not relevant to them.

- **Body.** The body of an email message contains the text that you want your recipient to read. Most email accounts also support the placing of images alongside your text. At the bottom of the message, most individuals add a *signature,* which typically contains their name, title, and contact information.

- **Attachments.** If you want to include a file with your message, you must place it in the **attachments** area. Always try to attach small files, as the recipient may have an email account that has size limits and restrictions. Whenever possible, place your files in a cloud storage account so that you can simply send a link to those files in the message area of your email.

USING EMAIL PROPERLY & EFFECTIVELY

The previous section introduced the parts of an email and some tips on how to use them effectively. In addition, other guidelines and best practices should be followed to communicate properly and effectively with others, especially in business. Although many of these guidelines are not official, some general rules of conduct are expected by those who use email.

One of the most important rules to observe with respect to email is the proper use of your account. Never use your work or school email for anything other than their respective purposes. Not following this could violate policies set forth by that organization. Furthermore, you don't know how long you will be at that particular institution, so if you start using that email for personal activities, you could eventually lose access to those messages. Besides this major rule, there are other guidelines that you should follow for good email etiquette:

- **Language.** Use traditional spelling and grammar in most, if not all, workplace and school communication. Unless your message is for a friend or family member, avoid using the type of abbreviations and casual tone you might use in text messages.

- **Tone.** It is often difficult to sense sarcasm and other emotions in a written email. Although you can use **emoticons** (symbols representing emotions) in casual messages, you should be careful with the tone of your writing when sending email at school or work. It is also important to note that writing in ALL CAPITAL LETTERS indicates to the reader that you are shouting.

- **Be brief.** Always be mindful of how busy the recipient of your email might be. Make your messages brief, yet clear enough to convey your thoughts. If you have quite a bit to say, a conversation may be better than an email message.

REAL-TIME COMMUNICATION

Generally, an email message arrives at its destination just a few seconds after you send it. However, you must wait an indefinite amount of time until the recipient decides to check email, open your message, and write a reply. This is acceptable when communicating with your supervisor or professor, but it may not be best when trying to converse with a friend. For this reason, many individuals today prefer various forms of **real-time communication**, where messages and conversations between two or more people occur instantaneously. This section will cover some of the most popular tools that individuals use to converse in real time.

INSTANT MESSAGING

Instant messaging is the act of having an online, text-based conversation with one or more individuals. Unlike an email, which can be read by the recipient at any time, instant messengers engage individuals in a

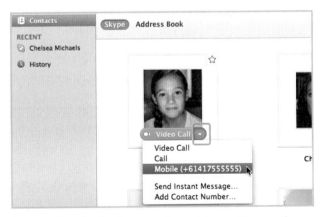

Skype offers instant messaging, video calling, and VoIP services.

live conversation. During conversations, you will see some sort of icon showing that the other person is typing. And before starting a conversation, an icon or status message will notify you of the person's availability to chat. Some of the earliest forms of this communication were the instant messengers and chat rooms of America Online (AOL). Today, instant messaging is built into many web-based email and social networking sites. Companies such as Google, Facebook, and Microsoft (Skype) all have popular instant messaging services. Some require that you go to a particular website while others offer a downloadable program that lets you chat without going to the web. There are also many instant messaging apps for mobile devices, some of which were discussed in Chapter 1.

VIDEO CALLING AND CONFERENCING

If you prefer to have a conversation using voice and video, then a video calling or videoconferencing service would meet your needs. This is quite useful for having conversations with friends and family that do not live near you, or having a meeting with employees located in a different office. Like instant messaging, these conversations occur in real time much like a face-to-face conversation. If both you and the other individual have an account with the same service, such as Google Hangouts or Skype, you can usually talk for as long as you want, regardless of where you both live. Much like instant messaging tools, these services are often available directly through your web browser, as desktop software, or as a mobile app. Most of these services are free; however, many business users pay for videoconferencing services that offer more features and support for a larger number of participants.

VOICE OVER IP (VOIP)

Voice over Internet Protocol (VoIP) translates analog voice signals into digital data and uses the Internet to transport the data. VoIP systems can connect to the telephone network, allowing you to place a call to another individual's phone from your computer or Internet-connected phone. Companies such as Vonage and MagicJack allow you to use your existing Internet connection and home telephones to make calls. However, many users are opting to pay for a package from their Internet provider that includes VoIP. Other companies, such as Skype, offer affordable calling packages (local and long distance) in addition to free video calling. Regardless of which option you choose, VoIP allows many individuals to cancel their traditional phone service and make all calls using their Internet connection. Just be sure to consider all the advantages and disadvantages, including the possibility of being without a home phone if you lose power or Internet connectivity.

BROADCASTS & STREAMING MEDIA

As you learned in Chapter 1, streaming media refers to music and movies that are delivered on demand from an online source. Netflix is the most popular streaming service, delivering movies and TV shows to your computer, entertainment system, or mobile device. Various reports have indicated that Netflix often accounts for over 30 percent of all Internet traffic in North America.

Other types of content take advantage of streaming. A **webcast** is the broadcast of various types of media over the web. Many stations, from radio to TV, will broadcast music, news, sports, and other content live on the web for anyone who wishes to listen or watch. In addition, many individuals and organizations create original content on the web since it is affordable and accessible. You can find many *channels* on YouTube, for example, that contain web-only content. Some of them are very high quality and intend to compete with many of the shows and videos you watch on TV.

Some types of broadcasts are referred to as **podcasts**. Many of these are typically prerecorded and can be downloaded from a variety of sources, including Apple's iTunes. Because you can subscribe

The White House offers a variety of podcasts.

to a podcast, future episodes will be downloaded automatically by your system.

FILE SHARING

An important service offered by the Internet is the ability to transfer files anywhere in the world. The most popular method for file transfer today is known as **peer-to-peer (P2P)** file sharing. This method uses a distributed network of individual users instead of a central server to transfer files. Specialty software allows an individual's computer to identify other computers in the distributed network and access their shared files directly and independently. Requesters seeking a specific file may find multiple copies within the peer-to-peer network and request a copy from a participating computer with the most efficient connection.

The BitTorrent protocol has recently become very popular for sharing large files, such as software or full-length videos and movies. BitTorrent uses a P2P design that makes large numbers of user connections and requests small pieces of the desired file from each of them. This allows a large amount of data to be **downloaded**, or received, by the requesting machine without relying on just one connection to one sender. It also allows requesters to become senders. As soon as a data piece has been downloaded to the requester's computer, that piece is made available to be **uploaded**, or sent, to others who need it.

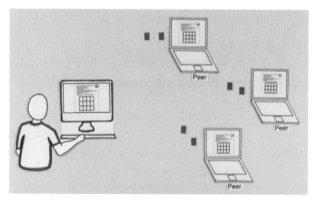

A BitTorrent user downloads parts of a file from other users. After receiving a piece, this user can then provide it to others.

Many companies have adopted P2P technology as a quick means of transporting files. This is true for a large number of software companies that distribute software and updates to millions of users at a time. Instead of overwhelming their servers on any given day, they use BitTorrent networks to allow the file to be distributed more efficiently from users to users. In addition, many amateur artists and musicians can also use this service to quickly share their work with anyone in the network. Unfortunately, P2P networks are also used for illegally sharing copyrighted works such as movies, books, music, and software. We will discuss illegal sharing and violation of copyright law in the first half of Chapter 6.

ONLINE CLASSES

The Internet makes it easy to send video and other multimedia content anywhere in the world. Because of this, it is possible to deliver educational content such as classroom broadcasts or complete online courses. Some of these classes are designed to supplement classroom education. For example, if a professor wants students to hear a specific lecture from the professor at another school, videoconferencing equipment can be set up to watch the lesson live in the classroom. Other classes are completely available online, allowing students to be anywhere in the world while they learn. While this may seem desirable, online classes generally require students to be self-motivated and not fall victim to the distractions at the location where they log into the course.

Some universities even offer entire accredited degree programs online. Students learn via online lecture notes or presentations using a **learning management system (LMS)** such as Blackboard Learn. They use this system to complete exams, turn in work, and communicate with their instructor and classmates. Some traditional universities offer degrees that use a combination of face-to-face and online classes, while others offer their services exclusively over the Internet. Universities are also experimenting with blending classroom and online components, where you meet with your class in person on one day, but meet online for the other.

Students who simply want to learn and do not require course credit can now enroll in a **massive open online course (MOOC)**. These are huge online courses offered for free by a variety of universities, including prestigious ones such as Princeton, Harvard, and MIT. Their aim is to offer high-quality content to millions of individuals throughout the world who do not have the opportunity to attend select classes at these universities. If you enroll in one of these classes, you might discover that tens of thousands of students are registered along with you.

ONLINE GAMES

The Internet offers more than the games you download to your mobile device or play on websites. For many years, it has been possible to connect gaming consoles such as the PlayStation and Xbox to the Internet in order to play with (or against) other players. For PCs, a category of games known as **MMORPGs** (massively multiplayer online role-playing games) has experienced rapid growth. In these games, millions of players connect to various servers to team up with other players in very large virtual worlds. While some games can be played using a web browser, most require the purchase and installation of software.

Coursera offers hundreds of noncredit MOOCs from a variety of universities.

Connecting to the Internet

Now that you know many of the services that the Internet has to offer, it is time to explore the ways in which users connect to this global network. We will begin with some basic terms related to data communication and Internet connectivity.

Every type of Internet service requires a connection and monthly payment to an **Internet service provider (ISP)**. These are usually telecommunications companies that offer homes and businesses access to the Internet. These companies have connections to an Internet backbone or a higher-level ISP (see Figure 4.4). When choosing an ISP, you will often be given a choice of various speeds. The speed at which data travels to and from the ISP is measured in **bits per seconds (bps)**. As speeds have increased, so have the units. A kilobit is a thousand bits, while a megabit is a million bits. Keep these units in mind as we compare the various types of Internet connections.

DIAL-UP

The first way in which most users connected to the Internet was using a **dial-up** connection with their phone line. Back then, many computers would include a **modem**, which is a device that can convert digital information from a computer into the analog sound waves that could be transmitted over the phone lines. The computer was essentially making a phone call to another computer that would then convert the sound waves back into digital form. The most popular dial-up service was America Online (AOL). Not only did the service connect most users in the 1990s, but it also offered software and services to make things easier for first-time Internet users.

Only a minority of users in North America continue to use dial-up. One of the biggest drawbacks was the maximum speed of 56 Kbps (kilobits per second), which made it difficult to download larger files and load pages with many images. Additionally, a dial-up user will essentially tie up the phone line for the house, making it impossible for family members to make or receive phone calls.

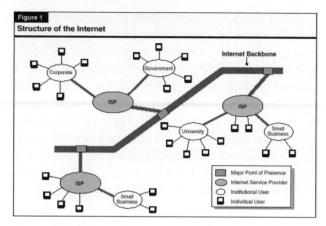

Figure 4.4   ISPs connect users to the Internet.

BROADBAND

The term **broadband** is used to describe any digital data connection that can transmit information faster than standard dial-up by using a wider band of frequencies. For homes, the ISP will usually provide a router or **residential gateway**, which is a device that connects your home's network to the Internet. The following are the most common types of broadband:

- **DSL.** With a digital subscriber line, or DSL, companies use the same telephone lines already present in your home. Telecommunication companies simply upgraded their networks to handle digital data instead of analog voice signals.

- **Cable.** If you already subscribe to a cable TV package in your home, you can add Internet connectivity to that package. The same technology that carries hundreds of TV channels can also transmit Internet signals.

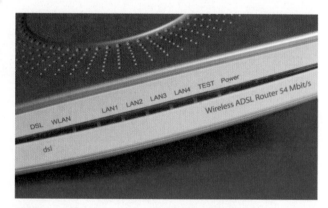

A DSL router acts as a residential gateway.

Max Turbo	Max Plus	Max	Elite	Pro
DOWNSTREAM SPEEDS UP TO **24** MBPS	DOWNSTREAM SPEEDS UP TO **18** MBPS	DOWNSTREAM SPEEDS UP TO **12** MBPS	DOWNSTREAM SPEEDS UP TO **6** MBPS	DOWNSTREAM SPEEDS UP TO **3** MBPS
$66/mo.*	$56/mo.*	$51/mo.*	$46/mo.*	$41/mo.*

ISPs usually offer various home packages at different speeds.

- **Satellite.** If you live in an area where companies do not offer DSL or cable, you can purchase a special dish and connect to the Internet via satellite. This same dish can also give you access to hundreds of TV channels.

- **Fiber-optic communication.** Several companies, such as Verizon and Google, have begun to promote fiber-optic technology for the home. This means that data travels using light pulses through an optical fiber instead of through the traditional copper wires. Most telecommunication companies use the better-performing fiber-optic technology throughout their networks, but the extension of this technology directly to homes and businesses is fairly new. That is what makes services such as Verizon's FiOS unique and very desirable.

> More **Online:** Visit the companion website to learn how to test your Internet connection speed at home or on your mobile device.

Many individuals wonder which of the various services they should use for Internet access. In most cases, it comes down to pricing and special offers. Ask what sort of discount is available if you bundle services such as TV, Internet, and a wireless plan for your mobile device. For many users, speed is the biggest factor. Depending on the area in which you live, one broadband technology might offer a faster connection than the other. While 1.5 to 3 Mbps might be sufficient for most Internet activities, those who desire high-definition video or engage in heavy downloading will likely want 6 to 12 Mbps speeds.

MOBILE

The use of mobile devices for Internet connectivity is increasing daily. If you are at home, you will typically use your existing wireless network to access the Internet from a tablet or smartphone. However, when you are on the go, you will need a mobile **data plan** that allows you to connect to the Internet using a cellular network. These data plans, which often limit the amount of data you can send and receive per month, are measured in megabytes (MB) or gigabytes (GB). If you go over your limit during any month, you will be required to pay an additional charge for the extra data usage.

Many terms are used to describe the type and speed of mobile networks. The general terms are 3G and 4G, which simply represent a generation number. The one you connect to is determined by your mobile device, your area, and the wireless carrier (company) that you choose. Although it is obvious that 4G is an improvement over 3G, the various subcategories of 4G (e.g., LTE and WiMAX) make it difficult to define a specific speed range.

MOBILE HOTSPOTS

A **mobile hotspot** refers to a device that can connect to a mobile network and offer Internet access to multiple devices near it. This device can be either a smartphone or a stand-alone hotspot device such as the MiFi. If your smartphone is the device, all you need to do is pay for a data plan as described in the previous section. Then, use the **tethering** feature to make your phone act as a wireless access point. Any computer that is near it, from a laptop to a tablet, can now connect to your smartphone and use its Internet access. Although many smartphones are capable of doing this, most carriers charge an extra fee for this service.

If you do not own a smartphone or do not wish to use it for tethering, you can purchase a mobile hotspot device from most wireless companies. This small device, which requires a mobile data plan, can be taken almost anywhere to provide wireless Internet access to a group of people. This is useful if you and a group of friends or family members frequently find yourselves in locations that do not offer free wireless Internet. It is worth noting that the term "hotspot" is also used to refer to a location or business that offers wireless Internet access. We will discuss wireless technology further in Chapter 5.

Web Browsers

To view web pages, you need special software known as a **web browser**. Web browsers are so important that practically all desktop and mobile operating systems now include one. In this section, you will discover some of the features and settings of popular web browsers.

INTRODUCTION

A web browser has two fundamental purposes. First, it helps you find and retrieve a web page that you are interested in viewing. Second, when the page arrives at your computer, the browser translates the code that web pages are made of into the attractive layouts you see today. Although all browsers can handle today's web programming languages, it is possible for a page to look slightly different from one browser to the next. The following are some of the popular (and free) web browsers used today:

- Apple Safari
- Google Chrome
- Microsoft Internet Explorer
- Mozilla Firefox

AT&T mobile hotspot device.

BROWSER BASICS

Each web browser may offer unique features and capabilities. However, all of them have several components in common. These are important for the understanding and effective use of a web browser. Observe Figure 4.5 as you review the following components.

ADDRESS BAR

The address bar of a web browser displays the URL of the web page you are currently looking at. Users can enter a new URL into this area to navigate to a new page. Newer browsers also use this area to allow users to initiate a web search.

NAVIGATION BUTTONS

Browsers contain various navigation buttons that let you easily move between web pages. Here are a few examples:

- **Back.** This button takes you to the previous web page that you were viewing.
- **Forward.** This button returns you to the page you were on before clicking the *back* button.
- **Stop.** If a page is taking too long to load, you can click the *stop* button to give up the attempt to load it.
- **Refresh.** This is often used immediately after clicking the *stop* button. It will ask the browser to make another attempt to retrieve and display that page. Another popular use for the *refresh* button is to request the most current information (such as news or weather) for the page you are currently on.
- **Home.** You are allowed to configure the **home page**, or starting page, for each browser. Clicking this button will return you to this specific page.

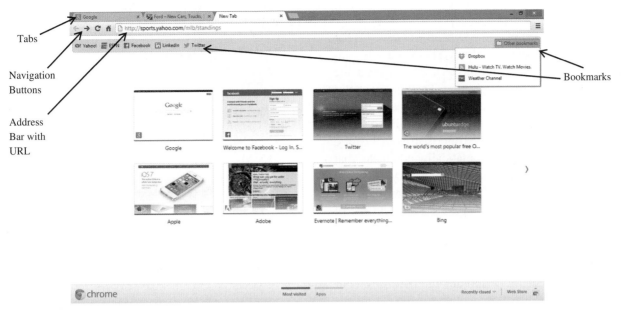

Tabs

Navigation
Buttons

Address
Bar with
URL

Bookmarks

Figure 4.5 **Google's Chrome web browser showing frequently visited pages.**
Source: Google Plus

TABS

Several years ago, web browsers would open an additional window if you wanted to view a second web page on your computer. As you can imagine, this got a bit messy if you wanted to open many web pages at a time, such as when performing research for a school project. All newer browsers use a **tabbed browsing** interface, which allows you to have multiple web pages open in one browser window. You can navigate between these pages by clicking its tab at the top of the browser window.

It is not uncommon for users to have a dozen or more tabs open at any given time. If your browser or computer malfunctions, browsers such as Google Chrome will remember every one of the tabs you had open and will restore them immediately when the browser is reopened. Furthermore, Chrome will allow you to access these tabs from a remote location as long as you log into the browser with your unique user ID and password.

> More **Online:** *Visit the companion website to learn useful shortcuts for tabs and other common browser operations.*

CONVENIENCE AND PRIVACY

There are various features and settings in web browsers that offer many conveniences to users. However, these same features could also be seen as a privacy threat by some users. Although Internet-related privacy issues will be discussed in Chapter 6, this section will offer a brief introduction to these browser features.

BOOKMARKS/FAVORITES

If you visit a website or page that you would like to remember for the future, you can add it to your browser's **bookmarks** or favorites. This area will remember the exact URL of any page and offers you easy one-click access to it. Browsers let you organize related bookmarks into various folders. In addition, you can also add your most important bookmarks to a special toolbar near the top of the browser window. The main privacy issue with bookmarks occurs when someone borrows your computer or watches you while you use it. For example, if you are married and you added a bookmark for a specific piece of jewelry at a famous store, it may spoil the surprise if your spouse sees it when opening the bookmarks area of the browser.

HISTORY

Browsers keep a list of every website you have visited in an area known as the **history**. This feature is convenient in cases where you forgot to bookmark a site that you visited several weeks ago. The history shows you the name and URL of every site you have visited. It also comes in handy when typing the URL of a site in the address bar. If that website is in your history, then the browser will automatically complete that URL for you. The privacy issue here is very similar to that of bookmarks. The difference is that anyone who accesses your computer will have a complete list of every site you have been to recently.

CACHE

The browser **cache**, or temporary Internet files, contains every single page, image, and video for all the web pages you have recently retrieved. Recall that the history only remembers the name and URL of the site. The cache, which is usually stored for a few weeks on your hard drive, contains the actual files. Browsers keep these files so that frequently visited pages can be loaded faster. This occurs because many of the larger files, such as images, can be loaded locally from your hard drive instead of having to be retrieved from the Internet. Law enforcement agencies typically look at the cache to see what content a suspect has been looking at online.

COOKIES

The small data files known as **cookies** are one of the most misunderstood features of the web. Most websites ask the browser to create and keep these files so that they can remember users and their preferences the next time they visit the site.
If all websites behaved ethically, everyone would likely welcome these cookies. However, many companies use cookies to track users' habits as they go from one site to the next. To better understand cookies, it is important to distinguish between the two fundamental types:

- **First-party cookies.** These cookies can only be created and read by the actual website you are visiting.

History

11:59 PM	TWC	National and Local Weather Forecast,
11:59 PM		ESPN: The Worldwide Leader In Sports
11:58 PM		Apple www.apple.com
11:58 PM		Evernote	Remember everything with
11:57 PM		Yahoo! ☆ www.yahoo.com
11:57 PM		Sign In login.live.com
11:57 PM		Twitter ☆ twitter.com
11:57 PM		World's Largest Professional Network
11:56 PM		Welcome to Facebook - Log In, Sign L
11:56 PM		Bing www.bing.com
11:56 PM		Google www.google.com

A browser's history shows the name and URL of every site visited.

Companies such as Amazon often request that the browser make cookies that allow the company to remember your name and ID when you return to the site. Other companies, such as UPS, use cookies to remember the selections you made when first visiting the site. It would be annoying to users if they had to select their country every time they navigated to the UPS site. With cookies, UPS can read that preference and immediately direct users to the site tailored for the country they are from.

- **Third-party cookies.** These cookies are typically created by marketing and advertising companies that work with the website you are visiting. For example, suppose that you visit the websites of two different car manufacturers who happen to employ the same advertising company. Besides receiving first-party cookies from the car companies, you will also receive third-party cookies from the advertising companies.

UPS uses cookies to store your selected location.

While the second car company is not allowed to read the cookie from the first car company, the advertising company can read the cookies issued from both sites! This allows the company to effectively track you because it knows which of its partner's websites you have visited. Gathering general information about your online activity allows advertisers to generate ads that better target your interests. This sort of tracking makes many individuals uncomfortable, even though personal or secure information is not being collected.

PLUG-INS AND EXTENSIONS

A browser **plug-in** is a separate program that allows your web browser to play several types of multimedia content. The most popular plug-in is Adobe Flash Player, which is required to watch many videos and play games in the browser. Most plug-ins are offered as free downloads.

A browser **extension** is also a separate program, but its purpose is to add a variety of useful features to the web browser. These include activities such as sending instant messages or playing mobile-style games from your browser window. Many of the programs discussed in this book, from Evernote to Google Hangouts, also create browser extensions to make their programs more convenient to use.

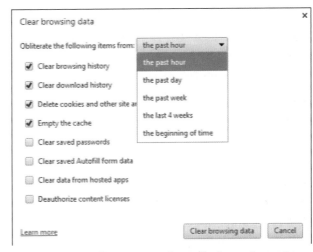

Web browsers allow you to clear all of your browsing history, cache, and cookies.

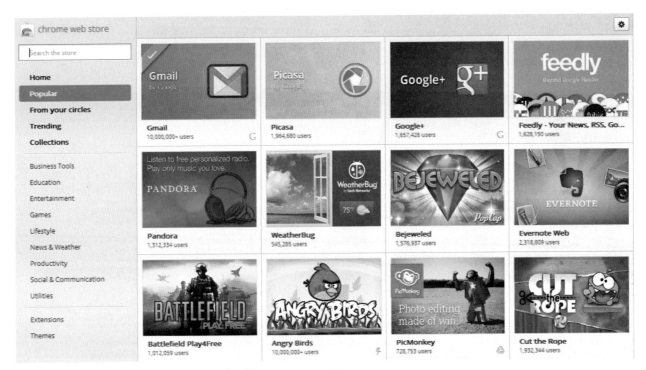

The Chrome Web Store offers thousands of browser extensions.

PART 2:
Exploring the Web

You have just learned about a variety of services that exist because of the Internet. In this section, we will focus mostly on activities that individuals engage in on the World Wide Web.

Finding Information

One of the most important reasons individuals use the web is to find information. This ranges from today's news and weather to school or work-related research. This section will cover the most common ways in which we search for information and the websites that help us find what we are looking for.

SEARCH ENGINES

Search engines are sophisticated services that store the URLs of millions of web pages and most of the content on those pages. When users type specific keywords into the search engine, they will receive an organized list of matching sites, images, and news articles that contain those keywords. The order of the search results can be based on a variety of factors including the relevance of your keywords and the website's popularity. Recently, search engines have begun to personalize the results for users, taking into account your current location, social networks, and previous searches. You will learn more about effective online searches and research later in this chapter.

Search engines continuously index, or *crawl*, the web's contents, finding new sites and revisiting existing ones in order to update their database of sites. In some cases, search engines can identify new information (for example, news stories) within a few minutes of it being published. There are several search engines, but two currently dominate the market. Google has firmly established itself as the leader, but Microsoft's Bing is a worthy alternative for finding what you need on the web.

> More **Online:** *Microsoft offers rewards for using its Bing search engine. Visit the companion website to learn more.*

WEB PORTALS

A **web portal** is a website that provides a variety of useful information and services to visitors. Yahoo and MSN are both popular web portals that many users have as their browser's home page. When you load Yahoo, for example, you will have today's headlines,

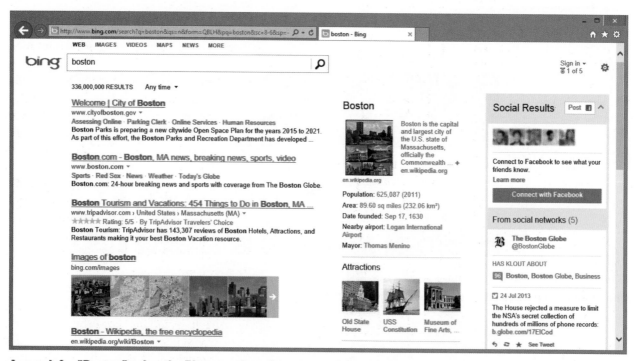

A search for "Boston" using the Bing search engine returns these results.

local weather, sports scores, and financial data all on the home page of that site. In addition, you can access a general search engine, web-based email, free online games, and the Flickr photo-sharing site with just one click. Companies invest millions of dollars to run a portal, hoping that one large website will provide most of a user's information-based needs. Their motivation is essentially the same as that of any TV network: If they keep you from turning the channel (or leaving the site), you will see more advertisements.

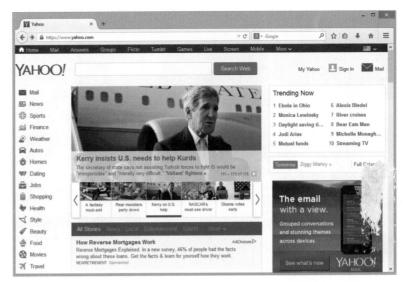

Yahoo is a web portal that offers useful information and a variety of services.

NEWS

The web has changed the way we learn about current events. All the major news organizations, from CNN and Fox to *The Wall Street Journal* and *Time* magazine, now place many of their articles, photos, and videos on the web. This makes it easy to scroll through a large number of headlines, stopping to read the ones you find most interesting. Most news websites are supported by advertisements; however, a few premium news sources may charge a monthly or annual fee to access some of their content. You can also use a search engine to browse a variety of news sources that contain the keywords you entered.

Many users are finding creative ways to read today's news. The first is by using a mobile app known as a **news aggregator**. These tools, such as Flipboard and the Windows 8 News app, allow you to pick a variety of news sources in different categories. It will then present them to you in a magazine-style interface for easy reading. In essence, you are designing your own magazine that delivers the exact types of news and topics that you want to read each day. The other creative way to get news is to simply follow popular news sources on social networks. That way, you will see an occasional headline or breaking news mixed in with updates from your friends and family.

More **Online:** *RSS feeds also allow users to gather news from multiple sources. Visit the companion website to learn more.*

MAPS & BUSINESS INFORMATION

Many individuals use the web to learn more about a business. By typing the name of the business in most search engines, you can quickly retrieve that organization's website, contact information, operating hours, a detailed map, and even user reviews. Bing, for example, will show you reviews from Yelp, which is one of the most popular review sites in the world. Alternatively, you can go directly to Yelp's website or app whenever you need any type of business information. Like search engines, Yelp can detect your general location to give you results that are nearby.

Internet-based map tools have been incredibly powerful in the last few years. Google's map service, for example, will show you detailed road

Flipboard's app displays news from various sources in a magazine-style format.

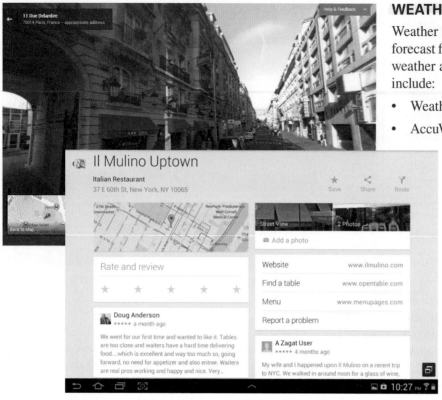

WEATHER

Weather services now provide a detailed forecast for several days along with severe weather alerts and radar maps. Examples include:

- Weather Channel (weather.com)
- AccuWeather (accuweather.com)

JOBS

If you are looking for a job, several websites can help you search through large listings. In addition, they will help you prepare and upload your résumé for employers that want to browse for candidates. Two popular sites are

- Monster (monster.com)
- Indeed.com

Google Maps offers traffic information and business details (below), and Street View (above) lets you drive virtually through many cities in the world.

TRAVEL

One type of travel site contains tips and reviews that help guide you while planning your trip. Some of these offer expert reviews and recommendations (e.g., frommers.com and fodors.com), while others allow individual travelers to rate their experiences (e.g., tripadvisor.com). Both can be crucial for helping you avoid bad hotels and attractions. In addition to review sites, travelers also use online travel agencies as part of their travel research. These services help you find and book flights, hotels, and cars.

- Expedia (expedia.com)
- Orbitz (orbitz.com)
- Priceline (priceline.com)

and satellite maps for any address in the world. It also offers turn-by-turn driving directions, traffic information, and details on any business on the map. One of its most powerful features is *Street View,* which shows you almost any part of the map as if you were driving through that street. This was made possible by Google sending out hundreds of specially equipped vehicles that contained a 360-degree camera. This has become useful for individuals who wish to see an unfamiliar business on the outside in order to find it easier when they drive to it. Others use Street View to learn more about cities they have never been to, essentially taking a virtual drive through it from the comfort of their home!

OTHER USEFUL INFORMATION

Although search engines can often provide or lead you to useful information with a simple search, it is often more efficient to search within reliable websites that specialize in one area or category. The following sections will briefly describe these areas and then list a few popular websites that also have mobile apps.

ENTERTAINMENT, SPORTS, AND LEISURE

Many sites specialize in providing information for a variety of leisure activities, including following every major sport or reading the latest celebrity gossip. The following are three examples of these types of sites:

- **Sports.** ESPN.com or Yahoo Sports (sports.yahoo.com).
- **Movies.** IMDB.com or RottenTomatoes.com.
- **Recipes and food guides.** Foodnetwork.com or Allrecipes.com.

FORUMS

Many companies and specialty websites offer **forums**, or discussion boards, where individuals can ask questions and reply to each other. This is often a great place to find solutions to specific issues or learn what everyday users think about a product or service. Many forums are moderated, or supervised, by a company's employees or experts in a particular subject.

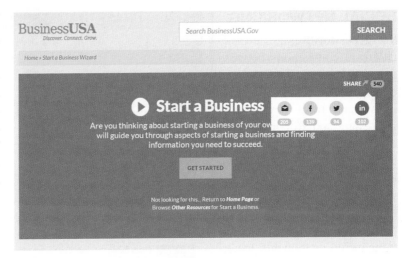

Social share buttons such as "Like" help websites gauge the popularity of their content.

The Social Web

The popularity of using the Internet for sharing personal thoughts, opinions, and details on events in one's life has skyrocketed in recent years. The term **social media** refers to the tools and services on the Internet that allow anyone to create and share different types of information. This can include text, photographs, music, and even videos. In addition to sharing, individuals also use social media to interact, collaborate, and build (or strengthen) relationships with others.

The desire people have to share information, along with the Internet's ability to connect people around the world, led to both the development of social media and the phenomenon commonly known as **Web 2.0**. In the early years of the web, only larger organizations and tech-savvy individuals created web pages that users simply viewed. Web 2.0 refers to a new way to use the web, whereby any user can create and share content, as well as provide opinions on existing content. These user contributions and opinions have dramatically changed and personalized large portions of the content available on the web. This section will explore some of those changes by providing an overview of a few social media categories.

COMMENTING AND RATING

Social media websites are not the only ones that encourage the creation of user-generated content. A variety of companies, from news organizations to retailers, now allow users to write comments on practically every page of the site. This allows individuals to provide their opinion or review on any article or product. In addition, there is usually a way for other users to rate any one of those comments. This will elevate opinions and reviews that are popular, while lowering or hiding those that are not. In many cases,

you will find company representatives or site owners engaging users through these comments, answering some of their questions or even addressing concerns and complaints.

Websites use a variety of methods to gauge user interest and opinion. Facebook uses the now-famous "like" system, while Google+ uses a "+1" button. Others may use a star-rating system, such as music review sites and Yelp. Twitter popularized a system that uses the **hashtag** symbol (#) to mark keywords or topics in a message. As more people use hashtags, such as #election or #cats, it increases the likelihood that the keyword becomes a trending topic. In addition to ratings, many services also pay attention to how many times an item has been shared by its users. Funny or fascinating content, for example, is said to go **viral** when it is shared again and again over a short period. This usually causes it to be noticed by a large number of Internet users and even reported by news organizations. Some content can become so popular and widespread over time that it ends up becoming an **Internet meme**. These popular, cultural items can range from a funny phrase or expression, to an activity that many photograph or record themselves doing.

More **Online:** *Both social media and instant messaging have popularized many abbreviations and Internet slang. Visit the companion website to learn more about these.*

SOCIAL NETWORKING

Social networking sites are used to create connections between friends, family members, and organizations. They also help individuals meet new people who share some of their interests. Social networking allows users to keep up-to-date with events happening around the world and in the lives of those they care about. Any user can post, or submit, just about anything including thoughts, hyperlinks, and photos. They do so with the intention of sharing them with one or more individuals. For example, if you have photos of a major event, such as your graduation, nothing beats social networking's ability to share those photos with all the people in your life and allow them to provide their thoughts on this important event.

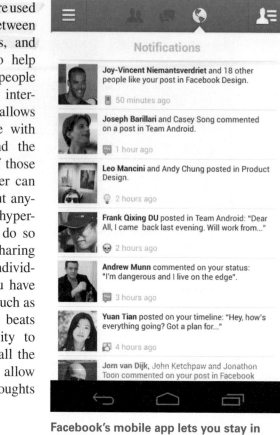

Facebook's mobile app lets you stay in touch.

FACEBOOK AND GOOGLE+

Facebook and Google+ are two examples of large-scale social networking services that invite users to share any type of information with others. New users create a free account and are then prompted to provide a wide range of personal data and preferences. This includes information such as their name, contact information, relationship status, college attended, as well as their favorite movies, books and music. Along

with personal data, these sites encourage users to invite people they know and add them to their list (or circle) of friends. Essentially, everything these services do is aimed at collecting as much data from as many users as possible. The goal is to look for trends and preferences that can be used to provide you with targeted advertisements. As you remember, many applications and services that you use for free are powered by advertising money.

FRIENDS AND CIRCLES

Facebook calls connected people friends and refers to the group of friends as a user's friends list. Google+ uses a similar system, except it refers to connections as people in your "circles." Both allow users to control who can read a particular post. For example, if you post photos from a family gathering, you may only want to share those with your family members. Conversely, a general thought you may have about a current event might be OK to share with all of your friends or even the general public.

Users can make new connections by searching the system for names of people or organizations that they wish to connect with. Social networks also provide their users with suggestions for new connections based on your existing contacts, preferences, and interests. In Facebook, a friend link is established only by mutual consent: Both users must accept. However, Google+ allows you to follow any person you want, making only that person's public posts available for you to read. Both treat the pages of businesses and celebrities in a similar manner, allowing users to follow or "like" these pages in order to keep track of their posts. Once you have set up a network of friends and chosen a few pages to follow, all of their posts will show up in a single feed on your account.

Google+ organizes your connections into various social circles.
Source: Google Plus

PROFESSIONAL NETWORKING

LinkedIn is similar to other social networks, but it is designed with a strictly business-oriented focus. Most of a user's profile is related to education, professional experience, and other items that one might find on a résumé. Your connections might be co-workers or professionals that you met at a seminar. When recommending new connections, LinkedIn considers several factors such as present and past employers, types of employment, region, and the user's existing network of connections. When posting on LinkedIn, items such as vacation photos, links to funny or controversial websites, and details about relationship problems are largely considered inappropriate by the user community. Instead, you might see individuals posting notifications of upcoming events such as conferences and online seminars.

LinkedIn encourages participants to provide endorsements and recommendations for others in their network. Recommendations are free-form notes that identify something exceptional about the individual based on the writer's experience as a co-worker, employee, or manager of this individual. These recommendations can serve as a significant set of professional references for job seekers looking within their online network for new employment.

BLOGGING

A **blog** (web log) is a web page or small website that contains a series of chronological posts and comments. These posts can contain just about anything, from the thoughts of an individual to updates from the executives of a large organization. It can be a work that stands on its own or a portion of a large corporate website. Blogs tend to have a sort of personal tone that would be inappropriate in more formal areas of a business website. In most cases, the Internet community is encouraged to comment on the posts of the blog's writer, or *blogger*.

WordPress has become the most popular blogging tool. Individuals can create a free account, choose the site's theme, and start writing within minutes. A blog's purpose can cover a wide range of topics such as politics, sports, movies, video games, music, creative writing, and much more. Besides creating their own work, bloggers can follow other bloggers that they find interesting. Some bloggers have gone on to become quite famous, moving on to careers in journalism or expanding their small blog to a popular news or entertainment destination. These large blogs, such as Engadget or The Huffington Post, are often difficult to distinguish from standard news websites.

Tumblr is a popular microblogging service.

More **Online:** *Visit the companion website to learn more about WordPress and other services that allow you to create your own blog or website.*

MICROBLOGGING

A **microblogging** service, which is essentially a short-form blog, is one where users share brief thoughts, links, and multimedia. Much like regular blogs, individuals can follow their favorite blogs and write comments or responses to any post they read. One of the leading microblogging services is Tumblr. It takes seconds to make an account and start posting. A typical Tumblr blog might be about sharing art, funny photos, or creative recipes. If you visit Tumblr, you will notice that a photo is at the center of most posts, with links or brief comments written underneath.

TWITTER

No microblogging service has become as popular or as important as Twitter. This service is specifically designed to encourage people to make short, frequent posts about news, thoughts, and events. The service restricts posts, referred to as *tweets,* to a maximum of 140 characters, requiring people to become more concise in expressing themselves. In addition to text, Twitter allows posts to contain photos and links. The company also owns a mobile video app known as Vine that allows users to record six-second clips that can be posted to their Twitter account.

Although a Twitter account can be set to private, the majority of users post messages with the intent of making them public. Much like other social networks, you can follow any other Twitter user so that their tweets appear on the home page of your account. Many celebrities and politicians use Twitter to send messages to their fans, while news columnists and bloggers use the service to express thoughts on current events in between longer pieces they publish on

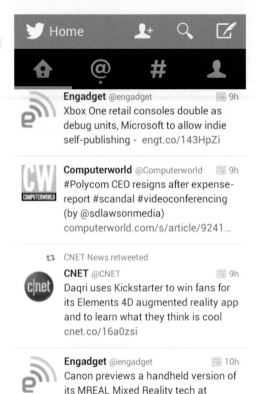

Twitter limits messages to 140 characters.

their main sites. Businesses use Twitter to announce anything from new products and services to daily discounts.

Twitter has become important for a variety of reasons. First, the short-form messages can be read quickly, allowing individuals to gather a wide range of information in a short amount of time. By scrolling down a few times, you can get a glimpse of today's headlines, information on new product releases, and thoughts from your close friends and favorite celebrities. Furthermore, because tweets can be written quickly, individuals are encouraged to report anything interesting that they see. This can include everything from eyewitness reports of an accident to viewers' thoughts and opinions on a live TV show. Because so many individuals post publically on Twitter, news organizations and businesses use the service to get a feel for how the public is reacting to an event. It is strongly recommended that you learn how to use Twitter, as it has become an indispensable tool for the transmission of information, thoughts, and ideas all over the world.

SPECIALTY SHARING

All the social media services that have been discussed so far allow users to contribute practically any type of information they desire. However, many services specialize in one particular type of media, focusing all of their energy in making one aspect of social sharing the best it can be. The following are some of these services.

VIDEOS

When it comes to social video, no service is as large or popular as YouTube. In a nutshell, YouTube provides a library of user-contributed videos to watch. The clips cover almost any topic you might think of, including snippets of TV shows, instructional videos, funny animals, and an endless variety of individuals

YouTube lets users upload, watch, and share a variety of videos.

talking or singing into a video camera. And speaking of singing, some musicians and artists use YouTube as the primary method for airing new songs or music videos. YouTube is also host to a rising number of business videos and original shows with a high production value.

Many people visit YouTube seeking a specific video or topic, and they can find them quickly by initiating a search. The service also provides lists of recommended and popular videos as determined by visitor ratings and a user's past viewing history. As with other forms of social media, YouTube lets users create a free account in order to upload content, provide comments on videos, and subscribe to the "channels" of their favorite users. With respect to sharing, YouTube allows videos to be embedded, or inserted, in many other websites such as blogs and social networks.

PHOTOS AND IMAGES

Some services specialize in the sharing of photographs. Although these sites often provide unique features for photo enthusiasts, part of their attraction lies in the omission of the excessive features found in larger social networking sites. At a minimum, these sites allow users to easily upload photos from their computers and mobile devices to create online albums at no cost. They can be kept privately in your account, or they can be shared with specific friends or even the general public. Once your photos shared, other users can comment on them. In addition, these services offer various tools to fix or enhance your photos with various effects. They can also be **tagged**, or marked, with keywords, faces, and your current location. Two of

Flickr lets you capture, share, and comment on photos.

the most popular services in this category are Instagram and Flickr.

A few other services offer unique features for sharing images. One of those is DeviantArt, which is the largest online social network for artists. From illustrations to professional photography, DeviantArt allows users to showcase their artwork, sell prints, and connect with other users and fans. Another popular service is Pinterest, which allows users to collect images and content from the web and organize them in a digital pin board. Any image gathered, along with your notes, is known as a pin. You then place related pins on a single board, which allows you to organize various things such as favorite recipes or a wish list of items. Pinterest encourages users to connect with others to share pins and spread good ideas.

NEWS AND LINKS

Social news sites, such as Reddit, encourage users to share links to news and other interesting content they find on the web. Users can comment and vote on the submissions of others, turning these sites into a sort of conversation about trending topics. The best submissions get voted up by users, making it easy to tell what content is hot at the moment. In addition to links, Reddit is also famous for hosting AMA (Ask Me Anything) sessions, where celebrities and politicians, including the president of the United States, answer questions from Reddit's users in a live session.

BOOKS AND DOCUMENTS

Reading has now become a social activity, thanks in part to sites such as Scribd. Authors of books, business documents, how-to guides, and even comic books can submit their work to Scribd for free or paid distribution. The site will rank what's hot based on how many users are reading or sharing that book. If you are a user, you can view and even download a significant amount of free content. However, some content must be purchased individually based on the author's selling price. If you plan to read a large number of documents and books that are not free, Scribd offers a premium subscription that includes many of these items for a single price.

WIKIS

A **wiki** is a collaborative information site that relies on the Internet community to both create and edit content. Wikis encourage people with subject knowledge to contribute at their convenience, adding to or fixing pages where information is missing or incorrect. The ongoing process of collaborative contributing and editing is designed to produce increasingly accurate and rich content over time.

Wikipedia is the most popular of these sites, offering millions of encyclopedia-style articles for free. In addition, you can find wikis all over the web that cover subjects such as video games, comic books, movies, finance, gardening, cooking, and much more. If, for example, you play a popular video game that has millions of users, you might find a fast-growing wiki that covers that particular game. Users will post articles that contain information about the game's characters and locations, along with guides and hints that help you complete the game.

The content on wikis can change rapidly based on current events. For example, if a country holds an election and new leader is elected, that leader's name will appear within minutes in the Wikipedia article for that country. In a traditional encyclopedia, that change would not have been made until next year's edition! Unfortunately, this benefit is also the curse of wiki-based sites. Because anyone (including those with bad intentions) can contribute and edit, you will find the occasional error or misleading information

Wikipedia contains millions of articles with photos, quick facts, and links to other content.

inside wiki articles. If this knowledge is crucial for your job or one of your classes, be sure to double-check that particular fact on another reliable site. We will discuss effective online research later in this chapter.

Electronic Commerce

The web has become a global vehicle for electronic commerce (**e-commerce**), creating new ways for businesses to interact with one another and their customers. E-commerce means doing business online, such as when a consumer buys a product over the web instead of going to a store to buy it. You can go online to buy a book, lease a car, shop for groceries, buy insurance, and rent movies. You can get pizza delivered to your door without picking up the phone and even check the status of your order while you wait.

These kinds of transactions are only a fraction of what e-commerce entails. In fact, the vast majority of e-commerce activities do not involve consumers. They are conducted among businesses, which have developed complex networking systems dedicated to processing orders, managing inventories, and handling payments. In this section, you will learn about many of the ways in which money, goods, and services are exchanged online.

Amazon sells just about everything, and it can make recommendations based on your interests.

BUSINESS TO CONSUMER (B2C)

Tens of thousands of online businesses cater to the needs of consumers. Online shopping is the process of buying a product or service through a website. These types of websites provide information about products, take orders, receive payments, and provide on-the-spot customer service. Even if you have never shopped online, you have probably heard of Amazon.com, the web's largest store. Amazon sells everything, from books and movies to groceries and kitchen appliances. In addition to goods, you can also purchase a variety of services all over the web. These range from weekly food delivery to legal consultation from a licensed attorney. Before choosing an online merchant, be sure to use a search engine to scan for the lowest online price for the specific product you are interested in purchasing.

THE SHOPPING EXPERIENCE

Most online retailers offer a detailed catalog of products and services, usually with various photos and lengthy descriptions. This is important because consumers don't have the luxury of holding the product or reading information on the box. In addition, many retailers offer consumer or expert reviews on the product, allowing you to make an informed decision. Whenever you are ready to purchase an item, you place it inside an electronic "shopping cart." This will keep track of every item you want while you continue to shop for other items. Shopping carts are easy

to modify, allowing you to remove items or change quantities with a few clicks. Once you are done shopping, you move to the checkout process where payment and shipping information must be entered. If you have already bought from this retailer before, it is likely that your payment and shipping information is already stored and the checkout can be completed with as little as one click.

PAYMENT AND SHIPPING

Most online merchants offer a variety of ways to pay for goods and services. Although electronic checks and debit cards are often accepted, it is always better to pay with a credit card that offers protection in case your computer or the merchant's site is compromised. Many argue that the best way to pay is by using an **online payment service** such as PayPal or Google Wallet. In a nutshell, you give these companies information about your bank and credit card accounts. You then use these services to pay for anything online or to transfer money to other individuals. This adds an extra layer of security and convenience for online payments. With respect to tax, you must check your state's law regarding online purchases. In many cases, online retailers in one state will not collect tax from consumers who are in a different state.

The last step of the purchase is making an arrangement for shipping. Many companies offer a variety of services, from next-day delivery to free shipping that uses a slower and more economical transit method.

An auction on eBay for a used iPad.

For websites that belong to a company with a physical presence in your city, you are often given the opportunity to pick up your items at the store. Regardless of shipping method, you can usually track the progress of your order and shipment online so that you know exactly when it will arrive. If your product is defective or otherwise unsatisfactory, most retailers will offer various ways to contact them such as email or online chats. Be sure to always read a company's return policy before making your purchase.

CONSUMER TO CONSUMER (C2C)

Many websites provide a variety of mechanisms that allow any individual to sell new or used goods to another individual. Amazon, for example, will often show you used versions of a product that you are currently viewing on the site. These are sold by other companies or individuals who are using Amazon as a way to reach millions of potential customers. Amazon keeps a small commission of every sale made through its site.

Auction sites offer a twist on the traditional shopping experience. A familiar example is eBay, a large and comprehensive auction site that allows buyers to bid and compete for an endless variety of new and used goods. Sellers post a starting price and a length of time to run the auction. Like Amazon, eBay will keep a small commission of the final selling price of the good or service. To help build trust between users of its service, eBay uses a feedback system for rating buyers and sellers. As transactions are completed, both the buyer and seller each enter a short description of the selling experience for others to see. Repeat buyers and sellers take their reputation seriously and generally strive to show that they are reliable. Many other online merchants, such as Amazon, use this feedback system whenever they allow individuals and smaller companies to sell goods on their site.

BUSINESS TO BUSINESS (B2B)

As its name implies, a business-to-business (B2B) transaction is one that takes place between companies; consumers are not involved. E-commerce has given companies an entirely different way to conduct business with each other. Using powerful websites and online databases, companies can track inventory, order products, send invoices, and receive payments. In addition, they can form online partnerships to collaborate on product designs, sales and marketing campaigns, and much more. The following are some examples of the sort of transactions companies can complete over the Internet:

- Auto repair shops can order parts from a wide range of suppliers.
- Stockbrokers and financial institutions can buy stocks and other commodities.
- Lenders can request a consumer's credit information from a credit-reporting agency.

ONLINE BANKING

The efficiency of online transactions has been an attractive way for banks to reduce costs and add services. With online banking, customers can securely

This website (Notebookcheck) contains relevant ads at the top (Acer) and on the right (Asus and Dell).

log into their bank's website and perform a variety of financial transactions. Users can pay bills, view monthly statements, and transfer money around the clock. A variety of companies, from cable TV providers to banks that issue car loans and credit cards, encourage their customers to establish regular automatic payments online. This allows these companies to automatically deduct each month's bill from the customer's bank account, eliminating the hassle of writing checks and possibly missing a payment deadline.

ADVERTISING

Advertising is one of the driving forces of both the Internet and many types of mobile software. Some advertising is done by online companies to promote their business or the products they offer. Other advertisements are created by traditional companies, from movie studios to car manufacturers. Either way, one of the top commodities that fuels advertising is consumer data, preferences, and trends. In a nutshell, advertising companies, search engines, and social media sites want to know more about their users and their Internet activities. These companies will look for patterns in a user's browsing habits so that they can deliver ads that the user will find appealing. The more these advertising agencies know about

consumers, the better they can represent the companies that hire them.

One of the most common ways in which to advertise is via email. Companies can create their own mailing lists from customers that have expressed interest or they can purchase lists of email addresses from a variety of sources. Another type of advertisement is a **banner ad**. These thin, rectangular ads are commonly placed across the top or on the sides of a web page. Once in a while, you may still stumble upon a "pop-up" ad that opens in a new window; however, since most browsers now have **pop-up blockers** built-in, few companies use this type of advertisement today.

The traditional practice of web advertising involved charging a certain amount of money for placement of the ad. However, many companies now prefer a model called **pay-per-click**, where advertisers pay for their ads only when a website visitor clicks on the ad to go to the advertiser's site. Google's AdWords is an example of the pay-per-click model. When a user of its search engine types a certain keyword or phrase, Google will display relevant advertisements along the side of the regular search results. Companies pay Google a certain amount of money per click based on the popularity of the keywords. Google also creates partnerships with many websites to display these ads, giving them a share of the profit when users click on them. Now that you know how popular pay-per-click can be, you may want to consider clicking on the ads of your favorite search engines, websites, or mobile apps; after all, it is the primary way in which you can support those who create and maintain these services.

Effective Online Research

Online research is an everyday activity, whether you're a student or you are looking for do-it-yourself tips for a home improvement project. Finding information on the web can often be a straightforward process thanks to powerful and intelligent search engines. However, on many occasions, users have trouble finding the information they need or they spend an excessive amount of time looking for it. Other times, a large number of sites claim to have the information, but your instincts tell you that the sites may be unreliable. In this section, we will explore some useful search tips and discuss how to properly cite websites for your schoolwork or professional research.

SEARCHING TECHNIQUES

Search engines have become quite good at figuring out what you are trying to ask and displaying information that is relevant to your search. However, if you are new to searching on the web or sometimes have trouble finding what you want, you may want to consider the following tips:

Reliable online sources can complement traditional resources.

- **Keyword quantity.** Type as few keywords as needed to express the topic you are looking for. Complete sentences are usually not necessary.
- **Common words and names.** If you are searching for the rock band known as Boston, you will likely get many results and maps for the city of Boston. Add words such as "band" to give the search engine a bit more information. For common names, add the city where the person is from or perhaps the type of work they do.

- **Search modifiers.** If you are still having trouble finding what you need, try using a few search modifiers. Placing quotes (" ") around a group of words will force the search engine to find pages where the words appear together. You can also type a minus sign (-) in front of any word that you do not want in the search results.

More **Online:** *Did you know that many search engines can solve math problems, convert units, and provide instant definitions? Visit the companion website to learn additional search engine tips and tricks.*

USING RELIABLE SITES

There are plenty of helpful and useful websites around the world, but there are also many sites that are designed to be misleading or are simply put together by someone with flawed information or a specific agenda. Furthermore, many users (intentionally or unintentionally) spread rumors and incorrect information via email and social networks. They will even provide a link to a site that contains that misinformation. Unfortunately, many web users believe that if the website and information *seem* reliable, then the information must be correct.

Although you might find experts disagreeing about the reliability of a few specific websites, you should consider some general criteria when judging a site's credibility. As a general rule, you should always try to use websites whose writers and publishers are expected to meet professional standards. When possible, use a site owned by an organization that you are familiar with or one that is cited often by other reliable sites. Avoid websites that have long domain names with many hyphens or a series of common search words; they are usually created just to rank highly on search engines and direct traffic to their site. (See Figure 4.6 for examples of what to watch for.) The following are a few categories of sites that are generally credible.

NEWS ORGANIZATIONS

Professional journalists are expected to meet standards for information gathering and fact checking. Many of them work for large news organizations that exist as TV networks, magazines, or local newspapers. Their sites are usually formal and complex with well-written and unbiased articles. They will have an "about" section that explains who they are and how long they have been in business. In general, avoid websites that appear to be heavily biased, are poorly designed or organized, and contain an excessive number of text-based advertisements.

ACADEMIC JOURNALS

Academic journals are written by professors and researchers in specific areas of study. These journals require that articles be reviewed by the researchers' peers. Ask your school's library or an instructor for

guidance about which journals in a particular field are highly respected. Articles in most academic journals are available online either directly or through database services.

GOVERNMENT SITES

Most of what the federal and state governments do these days is posted online. From laws to public records, you can find quite a bit of reliable information on government websites. In addition, government agencies hire experts in statistics and other fields to gather accurate data. The Census Bureau, NASA, and the Department of Energy are just a few of the agencies offering a wealth of reliable information online.

REFERENCE SITES

The major encyclopedias and dictionaries obtain their information from subject-matter experts. Although some can be searched online for free, others require a subscription. It is possible that your school offers access through your library. Ask your school's librarian for details, as well as advice on the best references sites in your field of interest.

IS WIKIPEDIA RELIABLE?

You have already learned that Wikipedia is an online encyclopedia that can be edited by anyone. Although many of the articles are written and edited by experts, you cannot be 100 percent certain that the specific information you need comes from a credible source. Because of this, it is not a good idea to use Wikipedia as a source for schoolwork or professional research. However, Wikipedia is a great starting point for gaining a general understanding of a topic. In addition, many parts of a Wikipedia article contain a citation to a reliable site. Follow that link to the original source, find the information you need, and then use this reliable website as a source in your paper.

CITATION AND PLAGIARISM

The web has such an abundance of useful information that it has created a great deal of temptation for students. With a simple mouse click, users can copy large chunks of text from a web page and paste it in their schoolwork. Obviously, such activity is highly unethical. Turning in the work of another as if it were your own or failing to cite the source of your work is known as **plagiarism**. It is considered a great offense

Figure 4.6 Searching for reliable sites.

in both school and professional writing. Many schools now use software, such as Turnitin, to scan students' papers for plagiarism and excessive copying from the web. If you are going to use facts and quotes from websites, always be sure to properly cite them using the method required by your instructor. If you need help creating a proper citation, you can use free sites such as EasyBib.com and BibMe.org.

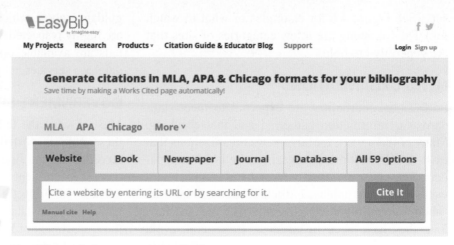

EasyBib can help you prepare citations.

KEY TERMS

ARPANET, 96
attachment, 102
backbone, 97
banner ad, 123
Bcc, 101
bits per second (bps), 106
blog, 117
bookmark, 109
broadband, 106
cache, 110
Cc, 101
cookie, 110
CSNET, 97
data plan, 107
dial-up, 106
domain name, 100
download, 104
e-commerce, 120
email, 100
emoticon, 102
extension, 111
forums, 115
forward, 101
hashtag, 115
history, 110
home page, 108
HTML, 99
HTTP, 99
HTTPS, 100
hyperlink, 98
instant messaging (IM), 103
Internet meme, 115
Internet service provider (ISP), 106
IP address, 97
learning management system (LMS), 105
massive open online course (MOOC), 105
microblogging, 117
MMORPG, 105
mobile hotspot, 107
modem, 106
news aggregator, 113
NSFNET, 97
online payment service, 121
pay-per-click, 123
peer-to-peer (P2P), 104
plagiarism, 125
plug-in, 111
podcast, 104
pop-up blocker, 123
protocol, 97
real-time communication, 103
reply, 101
residential gateway, 106
search engine, 112
social media, 115
social networking, 116
social news, 119
spam, 100
subdomain, 100
tabbed browsing, 109
tag, 119
TCP/IP, 97
tethering, 108
upload, 104
URL, 99
viral, 115
Voice over Internet Protocol (VoIP), 103
Web 2.0, 115
web browser, 108
web page, 99
web portal, 112
web server, 99
webcast, 104
website, 99
wiki, 120
World Wide Web, 98

Review Questions

MULTIPLE CHOICE

1. Which of the following networks, which began with just four universities, is the earliest ancestor of the Internet?
   a. NSFNET
   b. CSNET
   c. ARPANET
   d. TCP/IP

2. ________ translates analog voice signals into digital data and uses the Internet to transport the data.
   a. P2P
   b. Tethering
   c. VoIP
   d. Microblogging

3. The _____ language, which was used in the first web page, is still being used today alongside other languages.

   a. HTML
   b. HTTP
   c. TCP/IP
   d. BPS

4. Yahoo and MSN are both examples of:

   a. blogging sites
   b. e-commerce sites
   c. social networking
   d. web portals

5. When sending email to a large number of individuals, placing their addresses in the _____ field will prevent all those addresses from being seen by the recipients.

   a. CC
   b BCC
   c. HTTP
   d. HTTPS

6 Which part of a URL identifies a site and a brand on the web?

   a. Protocol
   b. Domain name
   c. Directory
   d. Backbone

7. Which of the following is NOT a high-speed Internet connection for homes?

   a. 4G
   b. DSL
   c. Cable
   d. Satellite

8. A(n) _____ is a huge, noncredit, online course that is offered for free by a variety of universities.

   a. blog
   b. LMS
   c. forum
   d. MOOC

9. A(n) _____ is a collaborative information site that relies on the Internet community to both create and edit content.

   a. wiki
   b. tag
   c. meme
   d. aggregator

10. Which of the following is NOT a web browser?

    a. Safari
    b. Skype
    c. Chrome
    d. Firefox

FILL IN THE BLANK

11. The _____ is the largest network in the world.

12. _____ file sharing uses a distributed network of individual users instead of a central server to transfer files.

13. To access the Internet from home you must connect to a(n) _____, which typically involves making monthly payments to a telecommunications company.

14. The _____ is a global system of linked, hypertext documents.

15. A(n) _____ is a discussion board where individuals can ask questions and reply to each other.

16. _____ sites, such as Reddit, encourage users to share links to news and other interesting content they find on the web.

17. Junk mail, or _____, is unsolicited email that is sent in bulk.

18. A(n) _____ is a web page or small website that contains a series of chronological posts and comments.

19. The term _____ is used to describe any digital data connection that can transmit information faster than standard dial-up by using a wider band of frequencies.

20. _____ is the act of having an online, text-based conversation with one or more individuals.

TRUE / FALSE

21. HTTP and HTTPS are the heart of Internet communication, setting rules for the transport and addressing of packets.

22. The asterisk symbol (*) is often used to mark keywords or topics in a social post or tweet.

23. 192.168.1.101 is an example of an IP address.

24. Google's Street View shows you almost any part of a map as if you were driving through a particular street.

25. No single person or group controls the Internet. It is a decentralized and cooperative community.

SHORT ANSWER

26. Contrast first-party cookies with third-party cookies. Which one of these raises privacy concerns for many individuals?

27. What are the differences between B2C, C2C, and B2B?

28. Describe three guidelines that should be followed for good email etiquette.

29. List and briefly define five navigation buttons found in most web browsers.

30. How are social networking sites different from professional networking sites?

31. List four categories of reliable sites and provide an example or brief description of each.

32. Describe three types (or models) of advertising on the web.

33. What are the differences between browser bookmarks, history, and cache?

34. Why has Twitter become such an important service? List three reasons.

35. What is the difference between a browser plug-in and a browser extension? Provide one example of each.

Research Exercises

Go beyond the book by performing research online to complete the exercises below.

1. How many email accounts do you currently use? Do you have a specific use or purpose for each of these? Provide details and examples.

2. Search for the following three things on both Google and Bing: (a) a local restaurant; (b) a famous athlete or celebrity; (c) any electronic product or appliance. List a few similarities and differences between the results. In addition, consider which results were personalized for you.

3. What is *net neutrality*? Do you believe that the U.S. government should enforce this principle? Should an ISP have the right to add surcharges for companies that generate a great deal of Internet traffic (e.g., Netflix) or desire higher priority for their data within the ISP's network? Provide examples and defend your answers.

4. How do you normally use social networking sites? What sort of content do you read? What do you post? What criteria do you consider when adding people to your friends list or circles?

5. If you do not have a Twitter account, create one. Add a few news organizations and any individuals you are interested in following. What do you think of this service? Do you find it useful? Do you ever see yourself posting any tweets? Defend your answers.

6. What do you think of the advertisements that you see on websites, social media, and apps? Do you pay attention to them? Do you ever click on them? Why or why not?

7. Using a search engine, perform a search for the following phrase: *United States economy*. Look through several pages of results and identify three reliable sites and three questionable sources. List the URLs of these sites and briefly explain why they are or are not reliable.

8. The popularity of community-based question and answer websites has been increasing over the years. Do you use services such as Yahoo Answers, Quora, Stack Exchange, and Answers.com? Why or why not? Are the answers provided on these sites reliable? Defend your answers and be sure to list the advantages and disadvantages of using these sites.

5

NETWORKING & SECURITY

- Researching media servers for the home and the benefits of a Windows Homegroup.
- Identifying the benefits of cloud-based office automation systems.
- Exploring the use of expert systems in industries such as health care.
- Discussing data mining practices by search engines, social media, and retailers.
- Configuring a wireless router in order to maximize security.
- Comparing weak and strong passwords.
- Comparing authentication categories such as passwords, access cards, and biometrics.
- Researching the effectiveness of various anti-malware products.

Chapter Overview

One of the most powerful aspects of computing is the capability to communicate and send information through networks. Whether it is a classroom, building, or the Internet, networks have changed the way individuals learn, work, run organizations, and stay in touch with each other. However, networks have also brought a variety of security concerns with them. To protect your information, it is important to understand networks and their risks.

PART 1:
Networking and Information Systems

As you learned in Chapter 1, a **network** allows users to communicate and share information between computers and various devices. For years, organizations have understood the importance of connecting computers. Homes also enjoy the benefits of networks, allowing families to transfer files between computers and share the Internet connection wirelessly throughout their home. And of course, networking equipment supports the entire Internet, facilitating the near-instant delivery of video, images, music, documents, and all types of information.

Networks go hand in hand with software systems to connect users and distribute computing power and storage. Together, the software and network hardware create information systems to properly serve both provider and user. Hospitals, for example, need to store, find, and retrieve information about their patients' records from every computer in the building. In addition, they also use complex information networks to manage employee data, inventories, and payment and billing records. In this chapter, you will learn about these types of information networks, as well as the hardware and software that support them.

Computer Networks

Computer networks are set up for a variety of reasons. They come in many forms and sizes, from a small home network to complex ones that connect multiple

A network can connect computers in offices, homes, and classrooms.

offices over a wide geographic area. Large networks can also connect smaller networks, as is the case with the Internet.

BENEFITS OF USING NETWORKS

Networks let multiple users access shared data, programs, and hardware devices almost instantly. For example, many organizations will purchase just one or two printers because they know that any user on the network will be able to print to them. It would cost that organization much more to purchase a separate printer for each individual.

Along with the ease of sharing devices, networks open up new ways to share data and applications that were not practical or possible in the past. In any business, several workers may need to use the same information at any given time. They might also need to simultaneously use a program that is installed on a server. This capability is important for many types of software, such as those that manage the entire company's customer service capabilities.

Communication is another key benefit of networks. In a company, employees can use internal messaging, mail, and videoconferencing systems to communicate with each other. They can also work together on documents that are stored on a server, making edits and placing comments on the work of a fellow employee. The other essential component to communication is access to the Internet. Whether you are at home, school, or the office, the power of networking can make it easy for you to communicate with almost anyone in the world. Without networks,

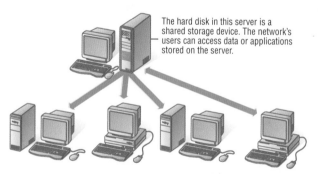

The hard disk in this server is a shared storage device. The network's users can access data or applications stored on the server.

A computer network lets users share access to data and applications.

the instant messages and photo sharing that we now take for granted would simply not be possible.

COMMON TYPES OF NETWORKS

To understand the different types of networks and how they operate, you need to know how networks are structured. The two main types of networks are local area networks (LANs) and wide area networks (WANs).

LOCAL AREA NETWORKS

A **local area network (LAN)** is a data communication system consisting of multiple devices that are relatively near each other and are physically connected using cables or wireless media. Any network that exists within a room, a single building, or even a group of adjacent buildings, is considered to be a LAN. It is often helpful to connect separate LANs so they can communicate and exchange data. Though a LAN can make a connection to other networks in the public environment (such as the Internet), that public connection itself is not part of the LAN.

WIDE AREA NETWORKS

A **wide area network (WAN)** is the connection of two or more central computers or LANs, generally across a wide geographical area. For example, a company may have its corporate headquarters and manufacturing plant in one city and its marketing office in another. Each site needs resources, data, and programs locally, but it also needs to share data with the other sites. To accomplish this feat of data communication, the company can attach devices that connect over public utilities to create a WAN. Though it is common for a WAN to be made up of interconnected LANs, it is not a requirement.

INTRANET AND EXTRANET

Some organizations offer an internal version of the Internet, called an **intranet**. An intranet uses the same software and service structure as the Internet, but it contains only the company's private information. It usually limits access to employees within the company. One common use of an intranet is the ability to manage and share company documents using a web application such as Microsoft's SharePoint.

Organizations can also create an **extranet** to share some of its intranet resources with people outside the organization. This can include selected contractors and partners that have ongoing business with the company. A company could also use an extranet to allow employees to access their intranet from another

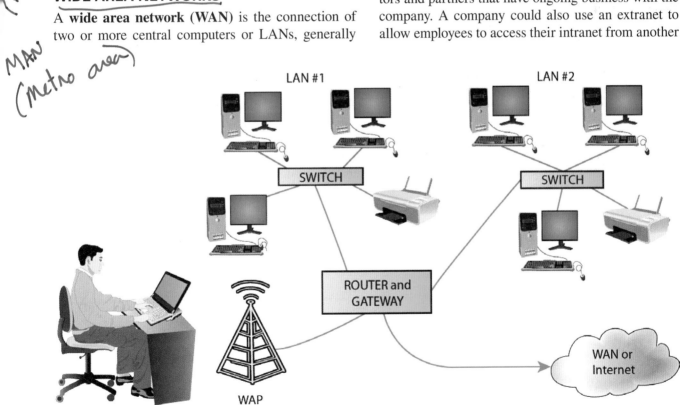

Networks are often complex, with wireless users, multiple LANs, and a connection to other buildings (WAN) and the Internet.

location. Access to an extranet is possible only if you have a valid username and password, and your identity determines which parts of the extranet you can view.

SPEED AND RELIABILITY

When comparing networks and the equipment used to create them, two factors are generally considered. The first is the maximum distance that data can reliably travel without **attenuation**, which is the loss of intensity and clarity of the data signal being transmitted. The second factor is **bandwidth**, which is the amount of data that can be transmitted over a given amount of time. For modern networks, bandwidth is measured in either megabits per second (Mbps) or gigabits per second (Gbps).

WIRED NETWORKS

The means used to link parts of a computer network are referred to as **network media**. The network uses the media to carry data from one **node**, or connection point, to another. This section will introduce the most common types of wires used as network media.

TWISTED-PAIR CABLE

Twisted-pair cable normally consists of four pairs of wires that are twisted around each other. Each copper wire is insulated in plastic, and all wires are collectively bound together in a layer of plastic that you would refer to as the network cable. Some cables are known as shielded twisted-pair (STP) because they contain a metal sheath that surrounds all the wires in order to reduce interference. However, most types of twisted-pair cables do not have this shielding and are therefore referred to as unshielded twisted-pair (UTP).

For wired networks, twisted-pair cable is by far the most common medium in use today for homes and businesses. Different wire specifications have been developed over the years. Currently, Category 5 (Cat5 or Cat5e) is the most common type of UTP cable. Category 6 (Cat6 and Cat6a) cables, designed to carry data at a higher frequency with less signal degradation between wires, is slowly gaining greater acceptance.

COAXIAL CABLE

Coaxial cable consists of a single copper wire that is surrounded by insulation and a wire mesh shield.

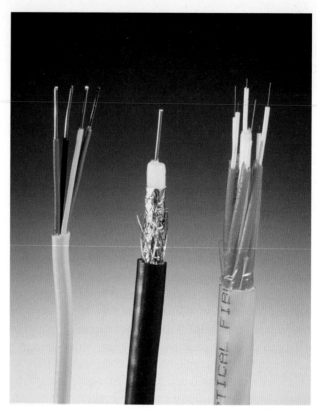

The most common types of wires for networks are (left to right) twisted-pair, coaxial, and fiber-optic cables.

All of these components are located inside a plastic sheath that looks like many cable TV wires. Coaxial cable's main advantage is that it is less susceptible to signal interference. Compared with twisted-pair wire, it allows for larger distances between the devices being connected.

FIBER-OPTIC CABLE

A **fiber-optic cable** consists of a thin strand of glass that transmits pulsating beams of light rather than electric current. Fiber-optic cable is immune to the electromagnetic interference that is a problem for copper wire, so distances between nodes can be greater than with coaxial or twisted-pair cables. Besides being extremely fast, fiber-optic cable can carry an enormous number of messages simultaneously and is a very secure transmission medium. However, it is much costlier than other cables and somewhat more vulnerable to damage in installation.

WIRELESS NETWORKS

Some types of networks do not require physical media for communication between nodes. **Wireless networks** use radio signals that travel through the air to transmit data. These signals operate on either the 2.4 GHz or 5 GHz bands. Practically all homes now use wireless technology for both networking and Internet access. Many businesses use it too, especially restaurants and cafes that offer Internet access, or hotspots, to their customers.

To create a wireless LAN, a **wireless access point (WAP)** is needed. All nodes connect to the device in order to communicate wirelessly. Mobile devices and laptops typically include wireless capabilities. However, most desktop computers require an internal or external **wireless adapter** to connect to a WAP.

A wireless access point.

WI-FI

The most popular standard for wireless networking is called 802.11 or **Wi-Fi**. This technology has gone through several revisions in order to increase its bandwidth and maximum range. As a general rule, Wi-Fi signals can reach about 100 to 200 feet indoors. However, that can be heavily affected by barriers such as the walls and floors of buildings. The following are the various specifications for Wi-Fi, which are essentially different letters added after 802.11:

- **802.11b:** up to 11 Mbps.
- **802.11g:** up to 54 Mbps.
- **802.11n:** up to 600 Mbps (most popular).
- **802.11ac:** can exceed 1 Gbps (>1000 Mbps).

PACKETS

Data moves though networks in structures known as **packets**, which are pieces of a message broken

A wireless USB adapter.

down into small units by the sending device and reassembled by the receiving device. Machines that communicate over a network must follow certain rules to ensure that the packets are sent, received, and interpreted properly, and that data integrity, or accuracy, is guaranteed. These rules are known as communication **protocols**. As you learned in Chapter 4, TCP/IP is currently the most popular protocol and the driving force behind the Internet.

Packets increase transmission efficiency and reduce the chances for a lost or broken transmission. Because a message's packets do not have to be received in any particular order, individual packets can be sent separately through whichever paths in the network are most efficient at the time of transmission. Different networks format packets in different ways, but most packets have two parts:

1. **Header.** This first part of a packet contains information needed by the network. It will have the address of the node that sent the packet (the source) and the address of the node that will receive the packet (the destination). The network reads each packet's header to determine where to send the packet and, in some cases, the best way to get it to its destination. The header also contains control data that helps the receiving node reassemble a message's packets in the right order.

2. **Payload.** The second part of a packet contains the actual data being transmitted between the two nodes.

NETWORK TOPOLOGIES

The **topology** of a network is the logical layout of the cables and devices that connect the nodes of the network. A network's topology aims to improve packet efficiency by reducing collisions, which occur when multiple nodes try to transmit data at the same time. If two packets collide, they are either discarded or returned to the sender to be retransmitted in a timed sequence.

Network designers consider several factors when deciding which topology or combination of topologies to use: the type of computers and cabling (if any) in place, the distance between computers, the degree of reliability needed, the speed at which data must travel around the network, and the cost of setting up the network. The following are some of the basic topologies that are used for computer networks (see Figure 5.1).

BUS TOPOLOGY

A network with a bus topology arranges the network nodes in a series, linking one node to the next via a single cable. A special device, called a *terminator,* is attached at the cable's start and end points to stop network signals so they do not bounce back down the

cable. This topology's main advantage is that it uses the least amount of cabling. However, extra circuitry and software are used to keep data packets from colliding with one another. Also, a broken connection can bring down all or part of the network.

STAR TOPOLOGY

With a star topology, all nodes are connected to a hub (a type of linking device, described in the next section) and communicate through it. Data packets travel through the hub and are sent to the attached nodes, eventually reaching their destinations. In a star topology, a broken connection between a node and the hub does not affect the rest of the network. If the hub is lost, however, all nodes connected to that hub are unable to communicate. The star topology is the most common type used today.

RING TOPOLOGY

The ring topology connects the network's nodes in a circular chain, with each node connected to the next. The last node connects to the first, completing the ring. Each node examines data as it travels through the ring. If the packet is not addressed to the node

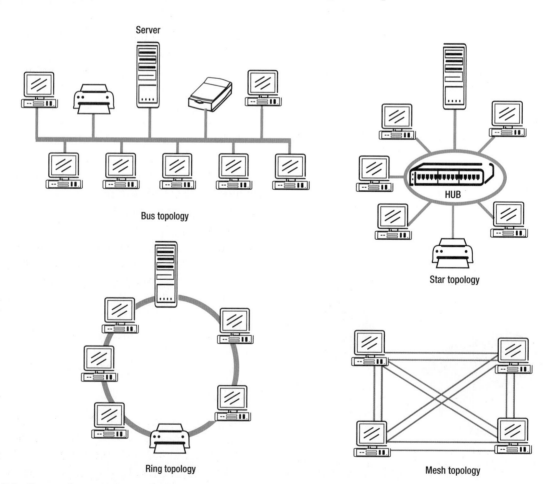

Figure 5.1 Types of network topologies.

examining it, that node passes it to the next node. If the ring is broken at or between nodes, the entire network may be unable to communicate.

MESH TOPOLOGY

In a mesh topology, a cable runs from every computer to every other computer. If you have four computers, you need six cables—three coming from each computer to the other computers. The big advantage to this arrangement is that data can never fail to be delivered. If one connection goes down, there are other ways to route the data to its destination. The downside to this topology is that all of these extra connections may end up being redundant, unused, or underused. The mesh topology is the least-used network topology and the most expensive to implement.

NETWORK HARDWARE

Transmission media are necessary to make a network, but wires alone are not enough. Hardware must be present at each node to translate, send, and receive the packets. The device at each node that performs translation and transmission is the **network interface card (NIC)**, which is also known as a network adapter card or network card. Historically, the NIC was a separate circuit board that was added to most computers. Today, the NIC hardware is integrated into a computer's motherboard and in network-ready printers. The NIC includes a port where data cables can be connected. In most networks, these data cables eventually lead to a variety of linking devices that can connect multiple nodes and ensure that data gets to the right place. These linking devices are described below.

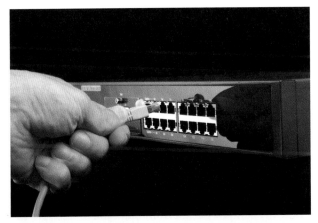

A switch can connect many computers in a LAN.

Many companies require large quantities of network hardware.

REPEATER

A **repeater** is used to prevent attenuation when packets are traveling long distances. It receives each packet, ensures that it is intact, and retransmits it down the line toward the next node at full-signal strength.

HUB

A **hub** provides multiple ports for connecting nodes. When it receives a packet from one port, it transmits the packet without modification to all the other nodes to which the hub is connected. Although all nodes receive the packet, they will ignore it; only the node that is the actual target of the packet will accept it.

SWITCH

A **switch** is similar to a hub, but it is aware of the exact address or identity of all the nodes attached to it. Because it can determine the identity of each node, it is able to send packets directly and only to the correct destination. Because it is not merely rebroadcasting in all directions like a hub would do, the chance for packet collisions and retransmission is greatly reduced. This increases the efficiency of the network. Switches can also allow multiple conversations between nodes to take place simultaneously. For example, two computers can deliver data to each other while two different computers send messages back and forth. This is possible because the switch can keep the packet flow of each conversation separate.

ROUTER

A **router** is a complex device that stores the routing information for networks. It looks at each packet's header to determine where the packet should go and then determines the best route for the packet to take toward its destination. Routers also provide increased security for the LAN they link. Because routers receive all packets and transmissions, they can detect and ignore attempts by unauthorized users to break into the local network. By refusing to acknowledge inquiries and attempts to access local computers, the router both prevents the attacks and provides no confirmation that the local computers even exist beyond the router.

Routers are usually connected to at least two networks. This is typically two LANs or WANs, or a LAN and the network of its Internet service provider. The wireless access points that are used in homes contain integrated routers, as do the devices that ISPs typically provide for Internet connectivity. In fact, many ISPs are now giving users a wireless broadband router that serves all the networking and Internet functions a home user needs. Most home routers also come with a built-in switch, which allows computers on a small, wired LAN to communicate without the need to buy a separate switch.

> More **Online:** *Visit the companion website to learn more about Cisco, a company that makes many of the routers used today.*

GATEWAY

In its simplest form, a **gateway** is a node on a network that serves as an entrance to another network. Gateways are needed because packets from different types of networks have different kinds of information in their headers, and the information can be in various formats. The gateway can take a packet from one type of network, read its header, and then add a second header that is understood by the second network (see Figure 5.2). The gateway also handles the configuration and maintenance of the various WAN or Internet addresses required to connect and relay information outside of the LAN. Each computer on the LAN can simply point to the gateway's network address without needing to know exactly where to find things on the Internet. In a small business or home network, the gateway is usually the router. That is why your ISP might refer to your broadband device as the "gateway" or "wireless gateway" device.

BRIDGE

A **bridge** is a device that connects two LANs or two segments of the same LAN. A bridge looks at the information in each packet header and forwards data traveling from one LAN to another. This is different from routers and gateways, which generally connect two different types of networks.

PUTTING IT ALL TOGETHER

Just as a network protocol sets a standard for the structure of the data to be transmitted, standards must exist for the hardware as well. This ensures that all the hardware—NICs, cables, linking devices—can all properly connect to each other. A number of physical transmission standards have been developed over the years. Of these, Ethernet is by far the most common.

Ethernet is a standard for local area networks. It provides a variety of specifications for the equipment and protocols used in a network. Most network installations use an Ethernet star topology with twisted-pair cables that plug into the RJ45 port located on many devices. However, Ethernet can also use fiber-optic cables, generally when communicating over longer distances. Originally, Ethernet was only capable of a 10 Mbps transmission speed. Now, Fast Ethernet can reach 100 Mbps, while Gigabit Ethernet transmits at 1 Gbps (1000 Mbps).

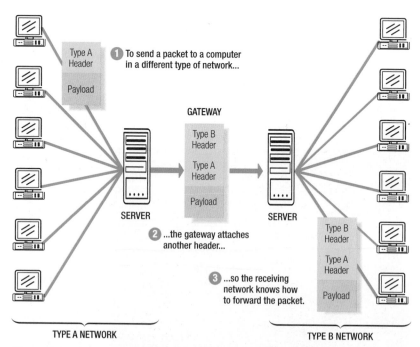

Figure 5.2 How a gateway sends a packet from one type of network to another.

Types of Information Systems

Network hardware and software provide an unparalleled vehicle for making connections between users, whether they are in the same room or around the world. Along with those connections, networks provide an ideal platform on which to build systems that actively collect, manage, and share information. An **information system (IS)** is a complex system for acquiring, storing, organizing, using, and sharing data and information. The basic purpose of any information system is to help its users get value from the information in the system, regardless of the type of information stored or the type of value desired. Information systems, therefore, can be designed to help people harness many kinds of information in countless ways. In this section, you will learn about the various types of information systems used today.

OFFICE AUTOMATION SYSTEMS

In organizations of any size, basic office work such as maintaining project schedules, keeping records of meetings, and handling correspondence can become extremely time-consuming and labor intensive. Collaborating with co-workers, serving customers, and dealing with suppliers require the sharing of accurate information as varied as phone numbers, meeting minutes, work schedules, and volumes of correspondence. If these types of information are scattered about the office on pieces of paper, it is easy to make mistakes, lose a key piece of information, or fall behind on recordkeeping or filing tasks.

For gathering, storing, and making available the kinds of information needed in an office environment, many organizations set up a type of information system known as an **office automation system**. This system uses computers and/or networks to perform various operations, such as word processing, accounting, document management, or communications. Office automation systems are designed to manage information and, more importantly, to help users handle certain information-related tasks more efficiently.

Using office automation tools frees workers at all levels from performing redundant and mundane tasks, allowing time for handling more mission-critical jobs such as planning, designing, and selling. Because office automation systems integrate different functions, information can be shared across applications such as a customer database, scheduling software, and a spreadsheet. This reduces the errors and time spent copying data from one program to another. While many companies use traditional office suite software for office automation, some have started to use cloud services such as Microsoft's Office 365 or Google Apps for Business.

Office automation systems allow sales employees to stay up to date on appointments and access important documents on the go.

TRANSACTION PROCESSING SYSTEMS

A transaction is a complete information operation. Transactions can be one-step events, such as adding a new piece of information to a database. They can also be more complex and require many steps, such as the process of selling a product online. The information system that handles the processing and tracking of transactions is called a **transaction processing system (TPS)**.

EXAMPLE OF A TRANSACTION

Consider the process of withdrawing cash at an automated teller machine (ATM). From your perspective, this involves a single transaction: you put in your card and take your money, with the understanding that the $60 in your hand has been removed from your account. However, this transaction is actually a series of smaller, linked transactions:

- Before any money is transferred, the ATM verifies your identity by reading your ATM card's magnetic stripe, requesting a PIN from you, passing that information to your financial institution, and receiving authorization to proceed.

- When you select an amount to withdraw, the ATM forwards that amount to your bank and requests authorization to dispense the cash. Your bank verifies the amount in your account and (assuming your balance is sufficient) places a hold on the funds in the amount of the withdrawal. It then authorizes the ATM to dispense the cash.

- The ATM counts out the requested cash, makes it available to you, and internally records its operation.

- The ATM notifies the bank that the cash was successfully distributed.

- The bank changes the hold on your funds to an actual debit, and the amount in your account is reduced.

THE IMPORTANCE OF TPS

What seemed like a single ATM transaction to you is actually broken down into this longer, behind-the-scenes list. This process allows the overall transaction (you getting your money) to be monitored and, in the event of an error, identifies precisely what went

Withdrawing money from an ATM triggers a series of behind-the-scenes transactions.

wrong and where. If the ATM's power goes out before it can dispense your cash, the bank will eventually release the hold on your funds because it will be able to determine that the ATM never gave it to you. If the ATM dispenses cash but its communication network crashes immediately afterward, the bank will be able to compare the ATM's log with the unfinished transaction and properly debit your account.

A transaction processing system is designed specifically to work with completing the basic transactions and monitoring the overall transaction for success and failure. Some transaction processing systems have sophisticated abilities to undo the unfinished parts of a failed transaction, correcting databases and performing other tasks to bring information back to the state it was in before the broken transaction began.

Management information systems analyze data to give managers information about company operations.

MANAGEMENT INFORMATION SYSTEMS

A **management information system (MIS)** is a set of software tools that enables managers to gather, organize, and evaluate information. This information might be limited to a particular group of employees or a single department, or it can cover the entire organization. Management information systems meet the needs of the different categories of managers by producing different kinds of reports drawn from the organization's database. An efficient MIS summarizes vast amounts of business data into information that is useful to each type of manager. Since different individuals have particular ways to express and understand information, a good MIS will allow the same data to be displayed in a variety of ways, such as columns of numbers, line graphs, and bar graphs. That allows digital thinkers to see the numbers, while 3D visual analysts can see a picture of how those numbers relate.

MIS EXAMPLES

Within any business, managers at different levels need access to the same type of information, but they may need to view the information in different ways. At a call center, for example, a supervisor may need to see a daily report detailing the number of calls received, the types of requests made, and the production levels of individual staff members. However, a mid-level manager, such as a branch manager, may need to see only a monthly summary of this information shown in comparison to previous months, with a running total or average.

Managers at different levels also need very different types of data. A senior manager, such as a chief financial officer, is responsible for a company's financial performance. This individual would view the company's financial information, in detail, on a regular basis. However, a front-line manager who oversees daily production may receive little or no financial data. This individual would need to access production data and summaries. Ultimately, the challenge in each scenario is the same: to get the right information to the right person at the right time, and in a format that is useful and appropriate.

Business managers often use decision support systems to access and analyze data.

DECISION SUPPORT SYSTEMS

A **decision support system (DSS)**, which is a special application that collects and reports certain types of data, can help managers make better decisions. Decision support systems are useful tools because they give managers highly tailored, highly structured data about specific issues. Many decision support systems are spreadsheet or database applications that have been customized for a certain business. These powerful systems can import and analyze data in various formats, such as flat database tables or spreadsheets, two-dimensional charts, or multidimensional "cubes" (meaning several types of data and their interrelationships can be graphically shown). They can quickly generate reports based on existing data and update those reports instantly as data change.

Decision support systems can combine and correlate information from multiple locations. Business managers often use decision support systems to access and analyze data in the company's transaction processing system. In addition, these systems can include or access other types of data, such as stock market reports or data about competitors. By compiling this kind of data, the decision support system can generate specific reports that managers can use in making mission-critical decisions.

DSS EXAMPLES

Some questions in business or management can be difficult to answer without some kind of assistance. Of the four colors of T-shirts that a shirt company produces, how many of each should be made in the latest production run? How many salmon should the local fishery controller allow fishers to catch before halting the season's activity? Without the proper information, answers to these questions are simply guesswork.

Decision support systems can help the shirt manufacturer collect and analyze buying trends, not only of its own T-shirts but also of the marketplace in general. It can also look for guidance when forecasting what current products will sell in the near future and what new product opportunities might be profitable. The fishery manager can collect data such as estimates of the current salmon population, historical population trends, the number of applications for fishing licenses, and so forth, in order to predict what level of fishing will be sustainable.

ACTIVE VERSUS PASSIVE

Decision support systems can be active or passive. A *passive* system simply collects and displays data in the format requested. An *active* system collects the data but also makes recommendations as to the best decision. Because few people are willing to blindly trust the recommendations of a program, active decision support systems are often used cooperatively, where users review the recommended decisions along with the data.

EXPERT SYSTEMS

An **expert system** is a type of information system that performs analytical tasks traditionally done by a human. It will typically ask a series of questions and then take specific actions based on the responses to those questions. To do this, an expert system requires a large collection of human expertise in a specific area. Detailed information is compiled from the human experts on:

- Ways that problems are considered.
- Steps that are taken to diagnose problems.
- Actions taken to find solutions.
- The reasoning for the actions.

HOW THEY WORK

The information gathered from human experts is entered into a highly detailed database, called a knowledge base. A program called an inference engine accepts information about the problem or question being analyzed and uses the knowledge base to select the most appropriate response or follow-up question.

Basic expert systems are typically little more than preset question and answer sequences, using simple yes or no answers to move along its list. Sophisticated expert systems may use new information to reevaluate the problem from the start. They also contain a feedback process that refines the data in the knowledge base. As users report success and failure during the diagnostic process, the expert system can learn more efficient diagnostic paths. For example, an expert system diagnosing network problems may, over time, discover that most of the faults involve malfunctioning network adapter cards in employees' personal computers. Based on the new data, the system changes its analysis path to focus first on testing those parts.

EXPERT SYSTEM EXAMPLES

Although expert systems mimic the routine decision-making process of experts, they cannot be as innovative as humans because they are simply machines following instructions. Consequently, expert systems are most useful in situations where a given set of circumstances always calls for the same kind of response. For example, an expert system can monitor the inventory levels for a grocery store chain. When the system determines that inventory of a product falls below a given level, it can automatically order a new shipment of the product from a supplier. In air traffic control, an expert system can be configured to issue a warning to ground controllers and pilots when two aircraft are on a collision course or flying too near one another. In education, expert systems are used to create adaptive exams or educational products that adjust the questions or material delivered based on a student's performance. McGraw-Hill's LearnSmart suite is one example of this new type of adaptive software.

Adaptive educational products, such as McGraw-Hill's LearnSmart Advantage, use extensive data and sophisticated programming to deliver a customized experience.

Supporting Information Systems

Many types of information systems, such as complex transaction processing systems, often need to be available without fail every moment of every day. They also require the storage and quick access of hundreds of terabytes of information. In this section, you will explore many of the requirements of information systems and both the hardware and software that support them.

REDUNDANT AND FAULT-TOLERANT HARDWARE

With a typical home or small business computer, most hardware failures cause the computer to crash. If the hard drive malfunctions or the CPU overheats after a cooling fan fails, the computer stops running. If network hardware such as a router breaks, network traffic is disrupted and the connection to the Internet will be lost. While these kinds of events are frustrating to homes and businesses, it isn't the end of the world for them. However, for certain types of organizations, any large-scale failure can result in catastrophic losses.

MISSION-CRITICAL SYSTEMS

Some types of organizations cannot afford to experience any type of extended systems malfunction. If computers running life-support systems at a hospital crashed, for example, many patients could lose their lives. Even small amounts of computer downtime at

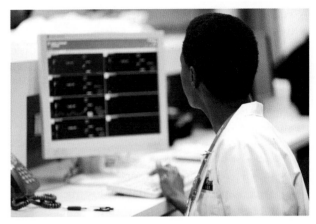

Many systems at hospitals are mission-critical. Their failure could be catastrophic.

a major stock exchange or in an air defense system could have dire consequences. These types of systems are called **mission-critical** because they must run without failure or with nearly instant recovery from failure.

It is simply not possible to construct computer hardware and software that can never fail. Therefore, mission-critical hardware and software systems have been designed to continue operating without interruption when components and programs fail. Such systems are known as **fault-tolerant** computers because they are able to continue their operation even when problems are present.

One of the ways fault tolerance is accomplished is via redundancy. **Redundant** computers have multiple hardware systems performing the same task at the same time. A fully redundant computer will have multiple system units, each with their own motherboard, CPU, memory, and hard drives. The computers execute software instructions in lockstep, meaning all CPUs and supporting hardware execute the same instruction at the same time. When one of the CPUs produces a different result (or no result, if it breaks), it is declared to have failed. The remaining hardware systems continue to operate without the failed unit until it can be fixed.

RAID

Even in computer systems that aren't mission-critical, extra disk drives are sometimes used as a way to provide a countermeasure against data loss.

A RAID offers redundancy by linking several disk drives.

A **redundant array of independent disks (RAID)** is a storage system that links any number of disk drives (a disk array) so that they act as a single disk. A RAID's capabilities are based on many different techniques, but there are three basic types:

- **Striping.** Also known as *RAID 0,* striping gives the user rapid access by spreading data across several disks. Striping alone, however, is used to boost data access performance and does not provide redundancy. If one of the disks in a striped array fails, the data is lost, because it's not being duplicated on any of the other disks.

- **Mirrored system.** Also known as *RAID 1,* this type writes data onto two or more disks simultaneously. This creates a complete copy of all the information on multiple drives, thereby preventing data loss if one drive fails.

- **Striping with parity.** Most commonly implemented as *RAID 5,* this strategy spreads data across several disks. However, it adds the safety of redundancy because the system stores parity information (a type of error-correcting code) that can be used to reconstruct data if a disk drive fails.

Scalable systems can be upgraded as an organization grows.

SCALABLE AND INTEROPERABLE SYSTEMS

Most businesses plan to expand over time, and computer systems need to be able to grow with the organization. Many company directors find it unacceptable to start from scratch with new computer and software systems every time the company outgrows its current system, and many information systems cannot practically be redesigned and replaced. Scalable systems address this issue because they can be incrementally expanded as the need arises. **Scalability** is the capacity to provide increasing amounts of computing power, storage, and/or software. Scalable systems allow organizations to buy affordable systems that meet their current computing needs and gradually increase their computing capability only as needed.

Many information systems need to interact with other systems. The efficiency of a tool manufacturer's accounting system, for example, can be greatly enhanced if it has access to the company's inventory and order-entry systems. **Interoperability** is the ability of each organization's information system to work with the other, sharing both data and services. Interoperability is also required by information systems that allow partnership and customer-vendor relationships between organizations. Though interoperability is often viewed at a software level, hardware interoperability is just as critical. When different types of computer systems are involved, a common interface is needed so that those systems can effectively communicate.

DATABASES

Most information systems attempt to organize data and information in ways that make it easier for users to find what they need. Databases are a fundamental building block for the storage, retrieval, and analysis of a company's data. This section will discuss some of the ways in which organizations manage large volumes of data for use in their information systems.

DATA WAREHOUSES

Many organizations keep track of large volumes of information. For a company such as Amazon, this will include details on every product sold, account information for all customers, and a detailed record of every order made on its website. Behind the scenes, the company would also need to keep records for all employees and suppliers. All of this information is generally stored or archived in a central repository known as a **data warehouse**. This enormous digital warehouse contains data gathered from multiple databases.

Data warehouses contain information from both the present and the past. Because it is an archive, businesses can access it to look for historical data that can be useful in creating a variety of graphs and reports. For example, Amazon's current database of products would naturally show the price of a product today. That price is displayed next to the product on the website. However, a data warehouse would contain that product's price at different points in time, which might be useful to a manager who is looking at Amazon's pricing when compared to that of its competitors. Another manager might use that data to analyze the correlation between the price of the product and the number of sales generated at different points in time. With such a large volume of correlated data, organizations can perform a great deal of analysis by using a data warehouse.

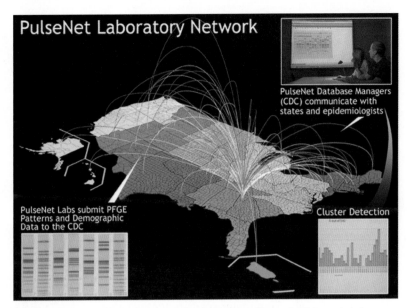

The Centers for Disease Control and Prevention uses large databases and tools to look for patterns that might signal a possible outbreak.

DATA MINING

Large databases that support information systems can provide an ideal environment for **data mining**, which is the discovery of new patterns or relationships between data. Businesses can tap into consumer and sales data to find trends, new sales opportunities, and signs of waning interest in their customers' behavior. Amazon.com, for example, uses data mining to predict what product a customer might like in order to feature it when the customer logs in and begins to browse. Governments can correlate and analyze data from many different areas to track needs and spending, look for possible disease outbreaks, and identify potential security threats. And as you learned in Chapter 4, advertising companies, search engines, and social media sites continuously look for patterns in the browsing habits of their users so that they can deliver ads that they will find appealing.

DATA VALIDATION

For information systems to be effective, the databases that support them must be as free of errors as possible. One method for checking and improving the reliability of data is called **data validation**. This is the process of safeguarding against erroneous or duplicate data by checking what is entered and, in some cases, placing restrictions on how the data is entered. Data validation is often accomplished by specifying format or range requirements at data entry. Zip code fields, for example, may require that the entry contain exactly five numeric characters. Email fields will look for required elements, such as the "@" sign, and ensure that the entire entry looks like a properly formatted email address. If an entry does not meet the rules enforced by the database, the entry will be rejected.

Data validation can also occur with information that has already been collected. For example, a government agency might want to make sure that a particular piece of information is spelled or formatted consistently throughout all its databases. It might also look for items that seem unusual. For example, if someone is listed as a felon in a criminal database, that person should not be listed in the database of active voters.

PART 2:
Security

You are aware that cars are stolen every day, so you probably take measures to reduce the risk of losing yours. These include locking the doors, parking in a well-lit area, and perhaps using a car alarm. In the same way, you should be aware of the various threats facing your computer and personal information. By taking precautionary steps, you can safeguard not only your hardware, software, and irreplaceable files, but also your privacy and safety.

Safeguarding data, computers, and information systems is crucial to both individuals and businesses. The first step to good computer security for everyone is awareness. Individuals and organizations should understand all of the dangers that threaten their systems and sensitive information. Only then can appropriate measures be taken to safeguard them. This section introduces you to some of the most common threats in the world of technology and shows you how to protect yourself from them.

Safeguarding data, computers, and information systems is crucial to both individuals and businesses.

Basic Security Concepts

Any discussion of computer security is likely to use terms such as threats, risks, and countermeasures. This section will explore many of these terms and how they affect the security of various systems.

THREATS AND VULNERABILITIES

The entire purpose of computer security is to eliminate or protect against threats. A **threat** is anything that can cause harm. In the context of computer security, threats can be as varied as a burglar, a computer virus, an earthquake, or a simple user error.

By itself, a threat is not harmful unless it exploits an existing vulnerability. A **vulnerability** is a weakness that has not been protected against threats, thereby making it open to harm. For instance, the presence of a car thief is a threat; however, if there are no cars on the street to steal, the threat is meaningless to those in the neighborhood. Similarly, a vulnerability is relevant only if a threat is likely to be present. Your expensive hat is vulnerable to being blown away by a gust of wind, but unless you are outdoors on a windy day, that vulnerability is not a concern.

UNDERSTANDING THREATS

We gauge the danger of a threat by a combination of factors:

- The probability of a threat.
- The degree of vulnerability.
- The penalty or injury that may occur if the threat succeeds in causing harm.

Threats that are very likely to cause harm, or threats that cause very negative consequences if unchecked, are much more likely to be guarded against. Most people wear a seat belt when driving their car, not because they are likely to crash every time they drive, but because the threat of severe injury in that unlikely event makes us cautious. Although a seat belt doesn't guarantee our safety 100 percent of the time, it is much better than ignoring the threat of harm because you believe it will never happen to you. This is true for computer systems just as much as it is for cars.

When people think of the ways their systems can be threatened, they may think only of damage to the hardware or the loss of some data. In reality, computer systems and those that use them can be harmed in many ways. Indeed, individuals themselves can suffer the consequence of poor security. Identity theft, humiliation, and even physical harm can result if individuals don't understand the threats to their security and privacy.

RISK ASSESSMENT

When protecting your computer system, it pays to think in the broadest possible terms about the types of harm that could affect you. This allows you to better assess the risk. A nasty virus or hacker can wipe out your programs as well as your data, but the risk may be greater than just that incident. If your PC is connected to a network, other systems on the network could suffer similar problems. Damages to your home or office from disasters such as a fire or flooding can easily extend to your computer, everything stored on it, and possibly even backup copies of data.

A practical and accurate **risk assessment**, where you identify and examine possible threats, is critical to being able to safeguard a system. Unfortunately, many individuals and businesses can err when assessing risks. For example, suppose that you always use your last name or date of birth as your password (a very bad idea). However, you are so fearful of an identity thief breaking into your computer that you install a complex security system in both your home and your computer. While that is not a bad idea, the risk of your password being discovered is higher from someone simply guessing it than it is from

Computer systems face many threats.

sophisticated break-ins. So, when companies ask that you create complex or strong passwords, they are simply helping you understand how risky an easily guessable password is.

Other times, solutions to problems can lead to greater problems. Requiring that your company's users change their passwords every few days might seem like a great idea. However, you may not notice that many employees are writing their ever-changing password on sticky notes in their office for fear of forgetting them. The risk of passwords being located in such a visible place is greater than the risk of letting employees use the same password for a longer period. When it's time to assess risks, consider as many factors as possible and try to be realistic about where the biggest threats lie.

COUNTERMEASURES

For any threat, there is some action or plan you can employ to guard yourself against the risk. Any step you take to ward off a threat is called a **countermeasure**. For example, regularly backing up your data is a countermeasure against the threat of data loss, much like an antivirus is a countermeasure against computer viruses. There are generally two classes of countermeasures:

- One type of safeguard protects the computer system from physical hazards such as theft, vandalism, power problems, and natural disasters.

- The other type of countermeasure is concerned with protecting data and software from threats such as viruses and hackers.

Network administrators must assess risks when configuring systems and creating security policies.

The remainder of this chapter will focus on introducing the various types of threats and the appropriate countermeasures that will help safeguard both your systems and precious data.

Safeguarding Hardware

Many threats can physically damage your computer or network equipment. Some of these are environmental in nature, such as those caused by power fluctuations, fire, and water damage. Others involve misuse by the individual operating the equipment or an unexpected breakdown of a faulty piece of hardware. And of course, a computer system can disappear if it is lost to theft. This section will explore these physical threats and the measures you can take to protect your computer hardware.

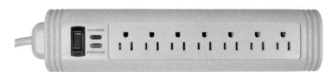

A surge protector offers necessary protection for your computer.

POWER PROBLEMS

The electricity supplied to computer hardware is critical to its operation. Problems such as power fluctuations and power failures can affect computers in a variety of ways. Let's take a closer look at these.

POWER FLUCTUATIONS

Power levels that rise and fall can produce unpredictable behavior in, or cause damage to, sensitive computer components. A computer's system unit has its own power supply that is designed to strictly regulate the power fed to the motherboard, CPU, and other internal parts. This makes the power supply especially vulnerable to problems with incoming electricity. When a system unit's power supply malfunctions due to an electrical surge, for example, it can simply shut off (causing a power failure) or it can go out with an eruption of electrical smoke and a massive power surge that ruins delicate components on the motherboard. Devices outside the computer, such as network hardware, printers, and external drives, may also be at risk from inconsistent power.

Power problems can arise for many reasons. People commonly think electrical storms are the primary cause of power interruptions, but storms are actually one of the least likely causes. A more likely source is the house or building itself. Disturbances from high-demand equipment such as air conditioners, space heaters, dryers, and copy machines can produce fluctuations. Old wiring in houses may also produce an inconsistent power feed.

POWER FAILURE

The complete loss of power, which can occur during a power outage in a particular neighborhood, may not cause component failure. However, it can cause the loss of unsaved work when the failure occurs. In addition, it can interrupt an important activity such as a videoconference with company executives or the ability to support customers that are contacting your business.

POSSIBLE COUNTERMEASURES

There are a couple of common countermeasures for the threat of lost or uneven power. For all hardware, a **surge protector** (or surge suppressor) is an inexpensive product that guards connected equipment against large power spikes or surges that may infrequently occur. This is an absolutely necessary piece of equipment, and every single one of your devices should be connected to a surge protector. This includes computers, monitors, printers, and even modern TVs and gaming consoles. Surge protectors are common products available at electronics and hardware stores. Check the packaging carefully to make sure you are actually buying a surge protector and not a many-to-one extension cord that looks the same but lacks protection against power surges.

Problems with both power fluctuations and power failure can be minimized by adding another kind of hardware known as an **uninterruptible power supply (UPS)**. A UPS contains both a surge protector and rechargeable battery, allowing it to handle any type of power issue for your computer. When the power fails, the battery contains enough power to run a computer system for a given amount of time. Depending on the size of the UPS and the needs of the user, this can range from a few minutes (good enough to save your work) to several hours if you need to keep your business operational. If you include a UPS unit for your network hardware, such as your router, you can maintain your connection to the Internet even when the lights go out.

THEFT AND ACCIDENTS

Both theft and vandalism can result in the total loss of the system and the data it contains. The financial loss may be high if you have to repair or replace many of your components. If you have stored sensitive information on the computer, the thief could use it to compromise your financial, professional, or personal safety. This fact makes it even more crucial that individuals take the proper precautions to protect their computers from intentionally destructive acts.

An uninterruptible power supply (UPS) can provide battery power in case of power failure.

THEFT COUNTERMEASURES

In principle, keeping hardware in a secure area can help to protect it from theft and vandalism. If it is difficult to get to the hardware or carry it off without being noticed, the computer hardware is safer. At home, keeping your home secure protects everything in your house including the computer. At work, you can use a variety of locks that help reduce the chance of hardware being stolen. One of the most popular types of locks, known as the Kensington lock, involves a steel cable and security device that attaches to a special oval slot on most laptop computers. By tying this steel cable around a desk, it makes it difficult for a thief to remove these lightweight portable computers. Locks can also be used to keep a tower's system unit from being opened, which guards against an office thief removing components such as hard drives and RAM modules.

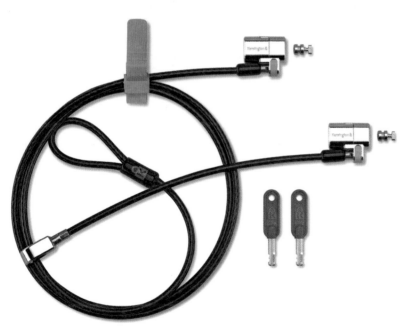

This Kensington lock uses a steel cable to help safeguard a laptop computer.

ACCIDENTS AND DISASTERS

Accidental harm is much harder to address, but it is no less of a threat. Dropping your laptop or mobile device can crack the screen or make the computer unusable. Other accidents, such as spilling liquids, can cause electrical damage to your system. If hardware gets wet, turn it off or unplug it immediately and leave it off until it is dry. Individuals and businesses must also consider natural disasters such as fires and earthquakes. Although there is little that can protect a system from major calamities, steps can be taken to protect valuable data. One of those involves making regular backups, which will be discussed later in this chapter.

More **Online:** *Do you have a mobile device that has a cracked screen or other type of damage? Visit the companion website to learn more about repairing these devices.*

ENVIRONMENTAL HAZARDS

Most individuals likely consider it obvious that water and extreme heat can damage electrical components. However, the environmental hazard that surprises many people is dust. This nuisance can clog cooling systems such as fans, which in turn may cause hardware to overheat. Fans are present in the system units of both tower and laptop computers, and they are often used to cool processors.

It is important to remove dust regularly from your system unit. With the computer unplugged, use a can of compressed air to whisk away dust from fans and anywhere else it has accumulated. Never use a vacuum cleaner to remove dust. Monitors can be gently dusted with a microfiber cloth or a manufacturer-approved

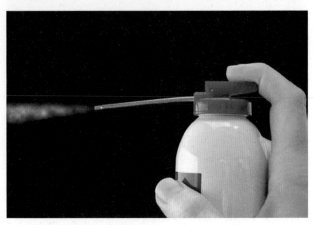
A can of compressed air helps keep fans and components free of dust.

cleaning solution, but never use glass cleaner or materials such as facial tissue or paper towels.

Safeguarding Data

When many individuals think of their computer, they likely think of that machine that contains their irreplaceable photos and documents. Organizations also think of their systems in this way, knowing that the precious data held by the computers is invaluable to their daily operations. Furthermore, many organizations, such as online stores and schools, hold large amounts of personal user information that simply cannot fall into the wrong hands. You have already learned that theft and other disasters can cause data loss. In this section, we will explore additional threats to computer data along with the countermeasures that can keep data safe.

MALWARE

As you learned in Chapter 3, **malware** refers to several types of malicious computer programs that are created to harm computer systems and their users. Malware is the most common threat to data and security. The exact goals of malware vary greatly, but most of the time it attempts to steal information, destroy data, harm the flow of data through a network, or take control of some of a computer's functions.

Malware is not always noticeable by the user. In fact, most forms of malware do not want to be recognized by you or your anti-malware utilities. The longer the activity can remain a secret, the more

A malware infection can cause all sorts of headaches for individuals and businesses.

damage it can do. The only time malware will make itself known is when it is designed to trick you into doing something more dangerous. For example, one popular scam is to issue an alert message warning users that they are infected or have committed some sort of crime. That message will then prompt users to install something that looks like a fix (it isn't) or pay for something they don't need. This type of scam is often referred to as **scareware** (or ransomware) because its goal is to scare the user into doing exactly what the thief wants.

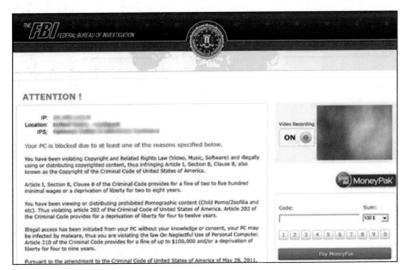

This "scareware" infection attempts to collect money from users by claiming to be the FBI.

VIRUS

A **virus** is a type of malware that is attached to a host file and has the ability to replicate, or copy, itself. A virus can be found in many types of files, from executable programs to Microsoft Office files. Users can unknowingly receive a computer virus via file-sharing services and email attachments, or when copying infected files from someone else's computer. When a recipient opens an infected file, the virus will activate itself and find more files to infect. It will also do the damage it was intended to do, which can be as extreme as making your operating system unusable.

WORM

A **worm** is a type of malware that self-replicates and spreads through computers and networks. Unlike a virus, a worm is a fully contained program that is not attached to a host file. Furthermore, a worm does not require that a user take an action such as opening a file. It can spread on its own rather quickly, usually by exploiting a vulnerability in an operating system or some other software. Some of the worst worms in history have infected millions of computers in a matter of hours.

TROJAN HORSE

A **Trojan horse** (or Trojan) is a program that disguises itself as an interesting, useful, or desirable program in order to gain access to your system. Users often download Trojans from a compromised website, file-sharing service, or even an email attachment. When the user installs this software, it will often work as intended so that the user will not suspect anything. However, the Trojan will do its damage behind the scenes by installing something sinister or changing the settings on your operating system.

SPYWARE

One type of malware that has rapidly grown in use is **spyware**, which is designed to report activity on your computer to another party. Spyware can record individual keystrokes (using *keyloggers*), visited websites, and other types of activities. It does this to obtain personal information such as passwords, account numbers, browsing history, and just about anything that might be useful to a thief or unethical marketing company. Once spyware has data to report, the program transmits the data back to its creator via the Internet. Most spyware is spread via Trojan horses or some other software that the user accidentally installed.

HACKING

In the early days of computing, a "hacker" was an individual who possessed advanced skills, often making a computer do something that it wasn't originally intended to do. Today, a **hacker** generally refers to an individual who uses a computer and/or network to commit a variety of crimes. Such crimes, from creating viruses to disrupting computer networks, are often referred to as **cybercrimes**. Hackers that commit these crimes are known as "black hat" hackers in order to distinguish them from non-criminal (or "white hat") forms of hacking.

Individuals engage in hacking for many reasons. One of those is curiosity. Many hackers break into networks and systems just to see if they can do it. Another reason is theft. Because so much personal and financial information is stored in computers, breaking into them can yield a bounty of credit card and social security numbers. **Hacktivism**, which has a social or political agenda behind it, has become a popular reason to hack in recent years.

No form of hacking is as dangerous as **cyberterrorism**, which is an attack that seeks to create large-scale chaos and damage to a country's infrastructure. At the moment, most hacking incidents between countries have focused on spying. However, experts believe that it is only a matter of time before major warfare begins to occur between Internet-connected systems. In fact, there has already been one incident where a foreign power was suspected of attacking the nuclear facility of another by creating a very specific type of worm.

These Air Force "cyber warriors" help defend the nation's infrastructure from attacks.

CONDUCTING ATTACKS

Hackers use a variety of tools and techniques to look for vulnerabilities that they can exploit. However, hackers rarely use their own computers to conduct attacks. They often use malware to open communication ports on the computers of thousands of users, making them available for control by the hacker.

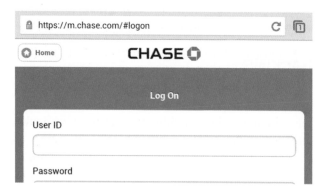

The HTTPS protocol secures your web activity from hackers who may be monitoring your communication.

Computers infected and compromised in this way are known as **zombies** because they are under external control. Massive networks of zombies, known as **botnets**, can be used by the hacker to spread malware, send spam, and conduct carefully orchestrated network attacks.

One popular type of network attack, known as a **distributed denial-of-service (DDoS)** attack, allows hackers to shut down or block access to websites and other network resources by overwhelming them with requests. And because the attacks come from millions of infected computers instead of the one owned by the hacker, it makes it difficult to know who was responsible. Unfortunately, users who are part of these botnets will usually have no idea that their computer has been compromised.

MONITORING COMMUNICATIONS

Sometimes hackers don't need to break into a system to get what they need. There are various ways hackers can "listen in" on unsecured network traffic to get valuable data. That is why, for example, many websites use the *https* protocol to encrypt communication that contains financial or personal information. It is also why many wireless routers ask that you set up a password.

One type of danger that you should be aware of is known as a **rogue hotspot**. Hackers will set up their own wireless access points at popular areas such as airports. When users turn on their mobile devices or laptops to look for a free hotspot, they may inadvertently connect to the hacker's hotspot. Once that happens, that hacker can intercept much of those users' communication. When at a location such as an airport, hotel, or coffee shop, always ask an employee for the name of that location's official wireless access point.

DATA THEFT

Many hacking incidents target the databases of large online businesses. Hackers are usually looking for user account data and credit card information. These companies will typically alert you if your account has been compromised, and most credit card companies will not hold you responsible for fraudulent charges that result from this incident. However, if hackers ever get a hold of additional information, such as your social security number and date of birth, they can do much more damage.

The worst type of data theft for an individual is known as **identity theft**. Hackers will essentially assume your identity and begin to open new bank accounts under your name. As you can imagine, this can create years of headaches for the individuals whose identity is stolen. Besides caution, one of the best countermeasures against identity theft is checking your credit report regularly. Since there are three credit reporting agencies and consumers are allowed one free report per year, it is recommended that you get one report from one company every four months.

> More **Online:** *Visit the companion website to learn how to get free annual credit reports from a trusted source.*

PASSWORD THEFT

Hackers often do their damage by figuring out a user's login and password for a specific account. Besides using spyware, a hacker can discover your password by attempting combinations that are used by many individuals. Studies have shown that a frightening number of users have easy-to-guess passwords such

The Federal Trade Commission (FTC) offers consumer information on scams and identity theft.

as "123456" or "password." We will discuss the creation of a strong password in the upcoming section on countermeasures.

Besides stealing your account information, hackers can do something equally dangerous if they gain access to your email account. They can send malware or a link to a compromised website to everyone in your address book. Because you are trusted by many of your friends and family members, they will let their guard down when they receive an email from you. They will likely download the infected file or visit the malicious website because they believe you are making a recommendation.

SOCIAL ENGINEERING

Social engineering is a form of hacking that focuses on deceiving individuals into giving away the information that the thief needs. Although technical expertise can be used, the most important skill needed is the ability to manipulate and trick other people. The following are two popular types of social engineering:

- **Pretexting** is gaining someone's trust by pretending you are someone else. Hackers have been able to gain valuable information over the phone or via instant message by pretending that they work for a bank or a company's tech support department.

- **Phishing** involves luring individuals into entering personal information into a website controlled by the hacker. This scam involves two steps. First, the hacker must make a website that looks like the login page of a popular site such as Facebook or PayPal. Second, the hacker will send an alarming email to millions of users asking them to sign into the site by following the bad link. Hundreds of thousands of individuals have fallen prey to this scam.

Hackers can use other tactics that require very little technical expertise. For example, going through the trash or simply looking at someone's desk can yield valuable information. Hackers also can gain quite a bit of information from what you post on social networks and online forums.

MALWARE AND HACKING COUNTERMEASURES

You have just learned many of the consequences of being infected by malware or having your personal information accessed by a hacker. Before we get to specific countermeasures, it is worth noting that nothing is more important than education and awareness. For example, there is nothing that you can install or configure that can protect you from a pretexting scam. However, being aware that the scam exists will allow you to be more vigilant and cautious about giving away account information to someone who is not verified. For other social engineering attacks, items such as a $20 paper shredder can go a long way to protecting you or your company. Let's now turn to some specific countermeasures against malware and hacking.

Classic countermeasures, such as a paper shredder, education, and awareness, can help prevent social engineering attacks.

SECURITY UTILITIES

In Chapter 3, you learned about various utility programs that can protect you and your computer. Below is a quick summary of what you learned in that section:

- **Anti-malware.** This software helps protect your computer from various types of malware.

- **Firewall.** This utility examines and blocks Internet traffic in order to protect your private network. Firewalls are present in most operating systems and many types of routers.

- **Encryption.** Many types of software and devices use encryption to scramble your data or communication, making it unreadable by anyone who doesn't have the proper key.

KEEPING SOFTWARE UP-TO-DATE

Both operating systems and application software issue updates to fix vulnerabilities and bugs in the programming. Whenever your operating system or browser issues an update, you should apply it immediately. Putting it off for weeks or even days can make your system susceptible to an attack. Remember, both malware and hackers often gain access to a system via security vulnerabilities.

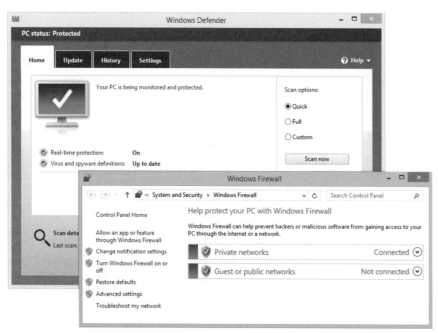

Windows 8 includes basic security utilities such as Windows Defender (anti-malware) and Windows Firewall.

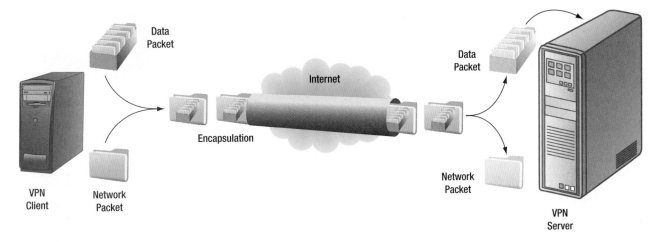

Figure 5.3 A VPN encapsulates packets for a more secure connection.

PROTECTING COMMUNICATION

You can protect your communication from being monitored by hackers. One method of protection involves the proper configuration of your wireless router. Always be sure to use *WPA2* encryption, which requires a password when connecting to your router and makes your wireless transmissions unreadable by hackers. When choosing a password, come up with something unique that you wouldn't mind sharing with a friend or family member. After all, they will likely want to connect to your wireless router when they come to your home.

A popular way for both individuals and businesses to increase the security of a network connection is by using a **virtual private network (VPN)**. A VPN employs a method called "tunneling" in which each packet from the sending computer is encapsulated within another packet before being sent over the Internet (see Figure 5.3). When you use a VPN, all of your activity will first pass through the secure connection between your computer and a VPN server before traveling to the Internet. This effectively shields your data traffic from nearby hackers who would otherwise be monitoring your unsecured communication. A VPN is often required for users who wish to access a company's private network (extranet) over an Internet connection.

PROPER AUTHENTICATION

Individuals and companies use two important principles to deter hackers and block the unauthorized access to

Access cards are often used for authentication.

information. The first is known as **authentication**, where an individual must confirm his or her identity. The second, known as **authorization**, gives individuals a certain level of access based on who they are. As you can imagine, a company's president is authorized to view much more information than a part-time mail room employee.

Three general strategies are used to authenticate individuals:

1. *What you know.* This typically refers to passwords or PINs that an individual must memorize.

2. *What you have.* In some cases, this can refer to a credit or debit card that allows individuals to access their money. For employees, it is often a special card or badge that is used to access certain systems or secure areas of a building.

3. *Who you are.* As you learned in Chapter 2, various parts of your body can be used as a biometric input device. Many systems are now authenticating individuals by scanning their unique fingerprint, iris, or face.

For most users, nothing is more important than having a **strong password** that is difficult to guess or crack by thieves. Strong passwords are long and use a mix of uppercase and lowercase letters, numbers, and at least one symbol such as a dash or period. In addition, you should never use the same password for multiple websites or devices. It is also very dangerous to leave your passwords in a visible location or to give them out to anyone. If you are fearful of forgetting all of your passwords, use a secure password management tool such as LastPass (see Chapter 3).

USE CAUTION ONLINE

As was stated before, nothing beats general awareness or common sense when it comes to protecting yourself and your data. Given the popularity of the web and social media sites, many thieves are turning to those services to look for useful information. Although there are many dangers on the Internet, a few general rules can help you avoid many problems:

- Avoid clicking suspicious links in email messages or social networking sites. If possible, always open a new browser window/tab and type the address yourself. This will help you avoid phishing attacks.

Exercise caution online, especially when it comes to your usernames and passwords.

- Never trust anyone that contacts you without warning and claims to be from tech support or customer service. Instead, ask for the telephone extension and call the toll-free number (or use the chat tool) for that business yourself.

- Avoid downloading software from file-sharing services. Many thieves use the temptation of free (illegal) software to lure individuals into downloading malware. Download software only from trusted sources, such as the websites of the companies that make the software or well-known companies such as Amazon.

BACKUPS

Very few countermeasures are as effective as making regular backups of data. No one truly knows when, or how, data may be lost. A simple disk error can do just as much damage as a hacker might do. And even the most experienced computer user occasionally deletes a file or folder by accident. When such events happen, information can be recovered quickly if data was backed up properly and regularly. In addition to data recovery, backups can also be used to access the previous version of a file.

There are many ways to create backups and archives of data. Large organizations have historically used a **tape library**, which is a large storage unit for magnetic tape drives. Many of these libraries are so vast, modern facilities use robotic arms to store and retrieve the tapes. Smaller businesses and individuals often turn to external hard drives and optical discs for their backup needs. However, nothing is more popular at the moment than cloud storage and backup services.

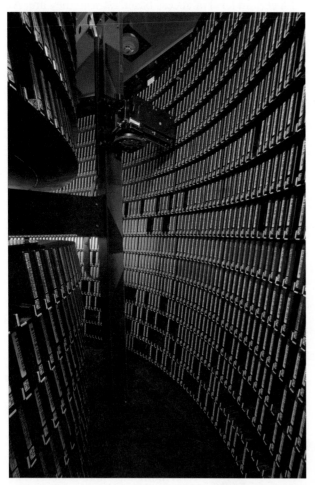

Fermi National Accelerator Laboratory, part of the U.S. Department of Energy, has a massive tape library.

As you learned in Chapter 3, cloud backups are immune from many of the problems that affect physical backups such as theft and damage. Furthermore, many cloud backup tools are incredibly easy to use. This makes them extremely attractive to both home users and businesses. Cloud storage accounts such as Google Drive, Microsoft OneDrive and Dropbox make a copy of your files the moment you save them in a specific folder in your computer. Cloud backup solutions such as Carbonite and CrashPlan also make things easy for users by performing continuous backups as the contents of a computer are changed. And of course, there is the added convenience of being able to access your backups from these services using any Internet-connected device.

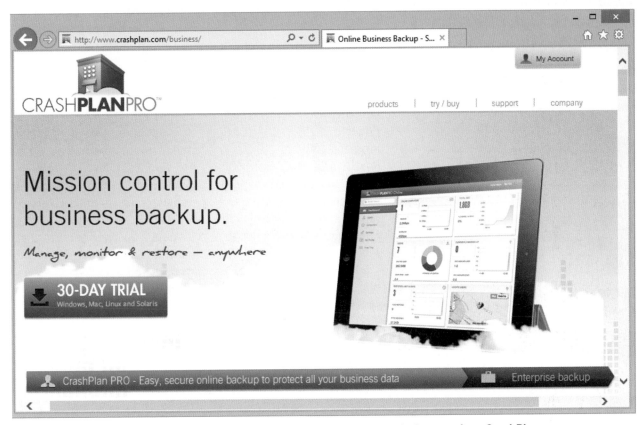

Individuals and businesses are increasingly turning to cloud backup solutions such as CrashPlan.

CHAPTER REVIEW

KEY TERMS

attenuation, 136
authentication, 157
authorization, 157
bandwidth, 136
botnet, 154
bridge, 140
coaxial cable, 136
countermeasure, 149
cybercrime, 153
cyberterrorism, 154
data mining, 147
data validation, 147
data warehouse, 147
decision support system (DSS), 143
distributed denial-of-service (DDoS), 154
Ethernet, 140
expert system, 144
extranet, 135
fault-tolerant, 145
fiber-optic cable, 136
gateway, 140
hacker, 153
hacktivism, 154
hub, 139
identity theft, 155
information system (IS), 141
interoperability, 146
intranet, 135
local area network (LAN), 135
malware, 152
management information system (MIS), 142
mission-critical, 145
network, 134
network interface card (NIC), 139
network media, 136
node, 136
office automation system, 141
packet, 137
phishing, 155
pretexting, 155
protocol, 137
RAID, 146
redundant, 145
repeater, 139
risk assessment, 149
rogue hotspot, 154
router, 139
scalability, 146
scareware, 153
social engineering, 155
spyware, 153
strong password, 157
surge protector, 150
switch, 139
tape library, 158
threat, 148
topology, 138
transaction processing system (TPS), 141
Trojan horse, 153
twisted-pair cable, 136
uninterruptible power supply (UPS), 150
virtual private network (VPN), 157
virus, 153
vulnerability, 148
wide area network (WAN), 135
Wi-Fi, 137
wireless access point (WAP), 137
wireless adapter, 137
wireless network, 137
worm, 153
zombie, 154

Review Questions

MULTIPLE CHOICE

1. The ______ topology, where nodes connect to a hub, is the most common type used today.
   a. bus
   b. star
   c. ring
   d. mesh

2. Which type of information system handles the processing and tracking of transactions?
   a. Office automation system
   b. MIS
   c. TPS
   d. DSS

3. Which of the following Wi-Fi standards is the fastest?
   a. ac
   b. b
   c. g
   d. n

4. Some organizations offer an internal version of the Internet, called a(n):
   a. intranet
   b. extranet
   c. botnet
   d. Ethernet

5. A(n) _____ is a storage system that links any number of disk drives so that they act as a single disk.

  a. NIC
  b. RAID
  c. WAP
  d. IS

6. Which type of malware is a fully contained program that self-replicates and spreads through networks?

  a. Spyware
  b. Trojan horse
  c. Virus
  d. Worm

7. _____ is the amount of data that can be transmitted over a given amount of time.

  a. Attenuation
  b. Bandwidth
  c. Topology
  d. Striping

8. A _____ is similar to a hub, but it is aware of the exact address or identity of all the nodes attached to it.

  a. repeater
  b. bridge
  c. router
  d. switch

9. Hackers often set up their own wireless access points in popular areas with the hope that users connect to them. These are known as:

  a. Trojan horses
  b. zombies
  c. botnets
  d. rogue hotpots

10. A(n) _____ cable consists of a thin strand of glass that transmits pulsating beams of light rather than electric current.

  a. fiber-optic
  b. twisted-pair
  c. coaxial
  d. Ethernet

FILL IN THE BLANK

11. In its simplest form, a(n) _____ is a node on a network that serves as an entrance to another network.

12. Networks must follow rules, known as communication _____, to ensure that data is sent, received, and interpreted properly.

13. A(n) _____ is a type of information system that performs analytical tasks traditionally done by a human.

14. Network media helps carry data from one _____, or connection point, to another.

15. The network standard known as _____ uses a star topology with twisted-pair cables that plug into the RJ45 port located on many devices.

16. A(n) _____ is a complex system for acquiring, storing, organizing, using, and sharing data and information.

17. Data moves through networks in structures known as _____, which are pieces of a message broken down into small units by the sending device and reassembled by the receiving device.

18. A(n) _____ employs a method called "tunneling" in which each packet from the sending computer is encapsulated within another packet before being sent over the Internet.

19. A(n) _____ is the device that all nodes connect to in order to communicate wirelessly.

20. _____ computers are ones that have multiple hardware systems performing the same task at the same time.

Review Questions (continued)

TRUE / FALSE

21. A decision support system can include or access other types of data, such as stock market reports or data about competitors.

22. Scalability is the ability of each organization's information system to work with the other, sharing both data and services.

23. A Kensington lock is an effective countermeasure against phishing threats.

24. Wireless networks use radio signals that travel through the air in order to transmit data.

25. For mission-critical systems, technology companies construct computer hardware and software that can never fail.

SHORT ANSWER

26. With respect to computer security, what is the difference between a threat and a vulnerability?

27. Define data warehouse and provide one example of how it can be used.

28. What is the difference between a surge protector and a UPS? In your response, be sure to indicate the types of threats they help minimize.

29. Describe the difference between a LAN and a WAN, and provide one example of each.

30. Define social engineering and provide two examples or techniques it employs.

31. What are the original and modern meanings of "hacker"? Are there different types of hackers? What is the most dangerous form of hacking?

32. List and describe three countermeasures (security utilities) against malware and hacking.

33. What are the three general strategies used to authenticate individuals? Include one example of each.

34. Define data mining and provide one example of how a retail company might use it.

35. What are zombies and botnets? What can hackers do with them?

Research Exercises

Go beyond the book by performing research online to complete the exercises below.

1. Suppose that you wanted to set up a media server in your home for wireless streaming to any other computer or mobile device. How would you go about doing this? What sort of hardware would you purchase? Is a Windows HomeGroup required?

2. Compare the cloud-based office automation systems of Microsoft and Google. What are some of their benefits? Which would you choose if you were a business? Defend your answers.

3. Explore the use of expert systems in the health-care industry. Provide at least two examples of how they are used and the benefits they offer.

4. Consider the data mining practices of search engines, social networking sites, and retailers. Do you agree with the way they gather, use, and share data? Why or why not?

5. Go to the configuration screen of your wireless router. What settings does it offer that help maximize security? Provide at least three examples. If you do not own a wireless router, find this information for any wireless router of your choosing.

6. Suppose that a website requires an eight-character password of your choosing. Provide at least three examples of weak passwords along with three examples of strong passwords. Explain the reasoning or evidence for your examples.

7. Evaluate the strengths and weakness of the following authentication categories: passwords, access cards, and biometrics. Then consider which one(s) you would use if you were in charge of security at a medium-size office with approximately 150 employees.

8. Name two reliable news sources or labs that test many of the anti-malware products on the market. What sort of tests do they run? Which paid and free products received the highest scores this year? Based on this research, which anti-malware utility would you install on your system? Defend your answer.

PART 1:
Legal and Ethical Issues

The advent of personal computing technology has undeniably taken the world by storm. In just a few short decades, personal and mobile computers have changed the way people interact almost everywhere on the planet. There was a time when our actions might have affected only a few dozen people around us. Today, our online behavior can either impact or be visible to thousands (or even millions) of individuals and businesses around the globe.

It is no surprise that the ethical use of computing technology is a pressing issue. The discussion of computing ethics should seem very familiar and serve as a reinforcement of lessons that were learned in childhood. Topics such as lying, stealing, and bullying are being revisited in the Information Age even though most individuals understand these behaviors outside of computing. In addition to these traditional topics, technology presents some new issues. This portion of the chapter will discuss and clarify some unethical

Many unethical behaviors, from gossiping to bullying, now affect online users.

computing practices that are common in the digital world, as well as some penalties that exist for violating computer-related laws.

Introduction to Ethics

Ethics is the philosophical study of morality. It is a rational analysis of the voluntary, moral choices that individuals make. When you study and apply ethics, you must provide a well-reasoned justification for why something is wrong. Stating that you did or didn't do something because a friend or family member told you so isn't sufficient justification. This is especially true of computer ethics. You cannot excuse the illegal downloading of music, for example, by stating that all of your friends do it too. If you believe that this activity is morally acceptable, you must provide rational justifications for it.

LEGAL CONSEQUENCES

Many activities that are unethical are also illegal. As you know there are laws for crimes such as stealing, cheating on taxes, and hurting other people. In the same manner, there are legal consequences for technology crimes such as hacking and sharing copyrighted files. Although it is useful to know the legal consequences of various actions, many individuals act ethically not because there is a law; rather, they do so because it is the right thing to do. Unfortunately, some individuals choose to act unethically if they believe they can get away with it.

EMPATHY

One of the factors that can significantly affect a person's ethical outlook and behavior is **empathy**, the ability to recognize, understand, and share the feelings of others. Empathy requires that we ask ourselves that age-old question that we've all heard many times: "How would you feel if that happened to you?" Applying this sort of question to ethical situations can help us see them more clearly and may even modify our behavior. Throughout this lesson, take time to not just understand the mechanical aspects of unethical behavior and the legal penalties, but also to practice being empathetic. Ethics can involve many gray areas and unanswered questions, but you may be surprised at how often a gray area resolves into clearer situations that seem right or wrong when you understand the perspective of others.

Piracy and Copyright Law

One of the most widespread forms of unethical computer use is piracy. In the world of computing, **piracy** means acquiring or exchanging copies of protected digital creations without payment to or permission from their creator. These creations often include software, photos, music, and movies. Piracy doesn't need to involve profit to be illegal. Sharing digital products without consent is considered piracy even if they are given away. Let's take a close look at the laws and ethics that govern piracy.

INTELLECTUAL PROPERTY

It can be a bit challenging to understand the products over which the piracy battle is being fought. It is much easier to picture the theft of a TV from a store than the theft of an MP3 music file. If someone makes a copy of a music file and shares it online, the original file is still in the same place. This makes it less obvious that a theft has occurred. Even so, legal concepts have been created and refined to help protect **intellectual property**, or products of the mind. While ideas, designs, and expressions of creativity may not have much (or any) physical form, they can be quite valuable.

The U.S. government fights piracy and protects intellectual property.

The Internet has increased the piracy of intellectual property such as music.

Centuries ago, individuals began to see the value of their ideas. While those ideas began as books and inventions, today they extend to music, photos, software, and many other creative works. Society rewards creative individuals and companies by protecting their works for a limited time. This grants them exclusive right to, among other things, sell their works and make a living off of them. If only one person bought a song, for example, and immediately made a copy for everyone on the Internet, that musician would be robbed of the opportunity to make money off her creative property. If society wants creative people to keep producing, it is in our interest to reward those individuals, not steal from them.

COPYRIGHT AND FAIR USE

One of the foundation blocks of intellectual property law is the **copyright**, a legal concept that grants rights and control to the owner of any published work. A creative product such as a book, song, or photograph is generally considered to be published when it is made available to the public for consumption. This includes retail releases, public performances, art exhibits, and even uploading to YouTube or a blog. Once that occurs, the author is protected and now has the exclusive right to sell, distribute, copy, and perform the work. It is through licensing, which you learned about in Chapter 3, that a copyright holder can grant usage or distribution rights to others.

Copyright protection lasts for a very long time, usually 70 years after the death of the author. Therefore, it is safe to assume that most of the things you see on the Internet are still under protection. This includes websites, photos, music, videos, and software. If, for example, you download a photo from a Google search result and place it on your business website, you will likely be guilty of copyright infringement. It is always safe to ask authors for their permission if you want to use their creative work somewhere else. The only exception is works that are in the **public domain**, which means that they can be downloaded and used without obtaining permission. Works go into the public domain when their copyright expires. They also include most works created by the government and any items that an author purposely released into the public domain.

FAIR USE

Copyright law contains an exception known as **fair use**, which provides for a limited set of circumstances where others can use portions of copyrighted material without first obtaining permission. Some of these circumstances include education, commentary, criticism, and parody. People can use small excerpts from a larger work in reviews and observations, so long as the review is genuine and not just a disguised means of unauthorized reproduction. Although determining fair use can sometimes be difficult, there are four questions that should be asked when considering whether it applies:

Many images that come from government websites are in the public domain.

1. *What is the nature of the use?* Educational use and commentary are more acceptable than a for-profit use.

2. *What is the nature of the work?* Copying from a news article (nonfiction) is more acceptable than a popular song or major network TV show (works of fiction).

3. *How much of the work is being copied?* Using only a few seconds of a song or video is more acceptable than copying the entire thing.

4. *How will the copy affect the market?* If you are claiming fair use just to avoid paying for a book, song, or movie, then fair use will likely not apply. Remember, the reason for the existence of copyright law is to protect authors and allow them to profit from their creations.

There is no easy formula to figure out if fair use applies. Mostly, it is a common sense review of the fair use criteria. For example, if you are a teacher who photocopies three pages of a 500-page book for your class, you are likely covered under fair use. But if you upload an entire song or movie to your blog and write a short comment for it, you will not be covered unless you have permission from the creator of the song or movie.

THE IMPACT OF PIRACY

Examples of piracy are common and varied. In most cases, it is everyday users that upload or distribute copyrighted works on the Internet. Popular songs are frequently exchanged via file-sharing services

Educators and students can often use portions of copyrighted material under the fair use provision.

such as BitTorrent. Software can often be found with modifications that disable **DRM (digital rights management)** technology such as copy protection and authenticity checks. Even TV shows and movies can be viewed at various websites that are not authorized to display or distribute them.

With piracy, both the provider and receiver are generally considered to be part of the crime. Individuals have been caught and prosecuted both for sharing material online and for copying it from a pirate site. Many services have also been prosecuted and shut down for facilitating copyright violations. Because so many computer users illegally engage in piracy, media companies report billions of dollars in annual revenue loss. The impact to artists, companies, and the economy is clearly substantial.

ALTERNATIVES TO PIRACY

There are many ways to enjoy your favorite songs, TV shows, and movies without resorting to piracy. Although many media companies need to modernize the way they distribute content, there have been major improvements over the years. The following are just some of the methods in which you can enjoy content in an affordable manner while still supporting your favorite artists.

PURCHASING ONLINE

You can purchase a digital copy of almost anything at various websites. Companies such as Apple, Amazon, and Google will sell you music, movies, books, and software that you can enjoy for as long as you wish. Songs cost about a dollar each, making it easy to own a permanent version of the music you love most. Furthermore, they can usually be copied and enjoyed on all of your devices such as laptops, tablets, and smartphones.

DIGITAL RENTALS

Instead of purchasing items such as movies, you can rent them for about two days. This is more convenient than driving to a video store to pick up the latest release. Apple, Amazon, and Vudu are popular services for renting movies and TV shows.

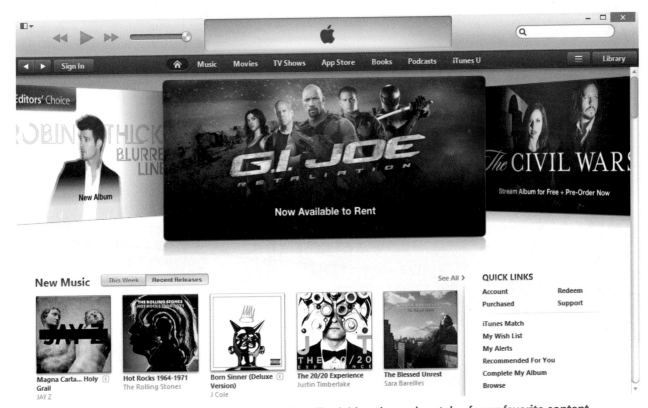

Apple's iTunes is just one of many services that offer affordable sales and rentals of your favorite content.

AD-SUPPORTED STREAMING

For music, many are turning to streaming services that are supported by advertisements. These companies, such as Pandora and Spotify, pay royalties to artists and music labels that are financed by the advertising companies. In a similar manner, video services such as Hulu use advertisements to support the free viewing of recent TV episodes. If using any type of mobile app that only uses banner ads, consider clicking them every now and then to support the creators of the app.

Streaming services such as Pandora often use ads to pay for music royalties.

SUBSCRIPTION SERVICES

Many of the free streaming services also offer a paid subscription option that eliminates advertisements or offers additional features. Your monthly payment to services such as Netflix, Hulu Plus, Amazon Prime, and Spotify Premium will help support the streaming company and your favorite artists. In addition, you get a variety of perks including faster shipping with Amazon and a larger catalog of TV shows with Hulu Plus.

CREATIVE COMMONS

A **Creative Commons** license allows authors to set conditions for the free use and distribution of their work. Most of these licenses require, at a minimum, that the user provide **attribution**, or credit, to the author wherever the work is used. For example, if you download an image that has a Creative Commons license, you can freely place it on your blog without paying for it. However, under the image, you need to write the name of the artist or photographer so that he or she receives full credit for the image. Other conditions that may be set by the author include preventing any modifications, derivative works, or commercial use.

> More **Online:** *Visit the companion website for links to Creative Commons websites.*

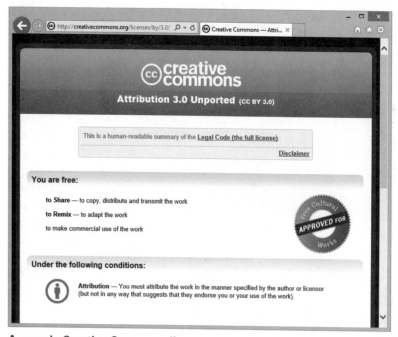

A sample Creative Commons license.

Personal Conduct

When we first begin to use computers and the Internet, we do not generally receive the same sort of guidance as we do at school, work, or even when growing up. Most people simply join in and participate, whatever their age, and either learn as they go or simply do whatever they want. That last approach, to do whatever one wants without regard for consequences, can cause a great deal of harm to your social, professional, and online reputation. It can also cause harm, inconvenience, and distress for others. While the Internet can accommodate many different styles of behavior and points of view, some actions are undeniably unethical and should be avoided without exception.

NETIQUETTE

The term **netiquette**, or Internet etiquette, refers to the set of online behaviors that are considered polite and proper. For the most part, the behaviors that find their way onto various netiquette lists are the same ones that we regard highly in our day-to-day interactions with others. Politeness, courtesy, and respect are highly prized, while abusive speech and rude behavior are discouraged. Interacting with others online may seem different because we do not always see the faces of other individuals. However, the consequences of our negative actions are still very real.

In Chapter 4, you learned a variety of rules and best practices for using email. Many of these also apply to various Internet activities such as posting on discussion forums and social networks. However, because online discussions tend to be more casual and often anonymous, many people engage in unacceptable behavior. The following are just a few examples.

POSTING AND SEARCHING

The user community has certain expectations when posting a question or message to a discussion forum. First, it is important to post your message in the correct forum of the website, as there are often several categories to choose from. In addition, each forum has many **threads**, which are essentially topics that contain related posts. Placing your message in the correct thread will maximize your chances of getting a reply. If creating your own thread, be sure to use a descriptive and informative subject. Most importantly, understand the general topics being discussed in a particular forum. Posting a message that

When it comes to online experiences, most individuals learn as they go.

is completely off topic or appears to be promoting something may be considered spam. And just like spam for email, this behavior is not welcomed and could get your account suspended on this website.

It is also important to search the forum thoroughly to check if your question has already been answered. Many websites also have **frequently asked questions (FAQ)** areas that should be checked for common questions and their responses. If you cannot find your question anywhere, go ahead and ask it; however, do not keep posting your question over and over. If it went unanswered, it means the user community likely does not know the answer.

ANGER, FLAMING, AND TROLLING

Anyone can get angry or frustrated on a forum or social network. The problem is that getting angry on the Internet is very different from yelling at someone in person. Angry words posted online will always outlive your anger because of the permanent nature of things written on the Internet. Even if you delete your message, there is a record of it somewhere. If you are skeptical, you may want to check how many celebrities and athletes have had to apologize for a message that they thought had been erased.

Online social interactions that exhibit anger and/or insults are known as **flaming**. You often see this type of behavior on forums or online games, where a user becomes enraged at another user. This is different from **trolling**, which is usually just the act of being annoying and antagonistic. Regardless of the type of nuisance, many feel that these behaviors occur because individuals forget that there is a human being on the other end, receiving the hateful message.

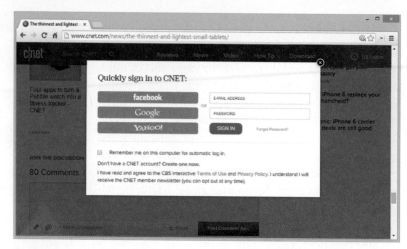

Sites that support discussions, such as CNET, often require users to log in or use their real name to reduce trolling.

CYBERBULLYING

Sometimes, anger and aggression can go too far on the Internet. Repeated hostile behavior with intent to harm another individual is known as **cyberbullying**. This can include actions such as intimidation and humiliation, often with the intention of ruining a person's reputation or causing psychological trauma. Children and teenagers are particularly vulnerable. In many cases, the bullying and taunting

that goes on in person might extend online, or vice versa.

Many teenagers have had to seek therapy because of cyberbullying and, in a few extreme cases, even committed suicide. Because of the prevalence of cyberbullying, many states have passed laws banning this type of online harassment. Whether or not it is illegal in your state, these actions are highly unethical and very harmful. Even a playful prank, such as posting an embarrassing photo or video against someone's wishes, can cause distress that you may not be able to predict.

USE OF HUMOR

Humor requires the right audience to be funny. Before you send or post a joke, make sure it will be appropriate for the readers and that the joke (especially if posted publically) will not come back to haunt you. This is equally true of photos, videos, and any other content posted under your real name or social networking account.

Sending email containing funny jokes to the people at work, for example, is more risky than it sounds. If the joke contains potentially offensive content, the sender's reputation in the company could suffer. Even if no one takes offense, the sender risks being reprimanded or fired for behavior that goes against acceptable use policies.

ACCEPTABLE USE POLICIES

An **acceptable use policy (AUP)** is a document containing an organization's policies for the ethical, secure, and appropriate use of computing resources.

Sending email containing potentially offensive jokes to the people at work can be inappropriate and risky.

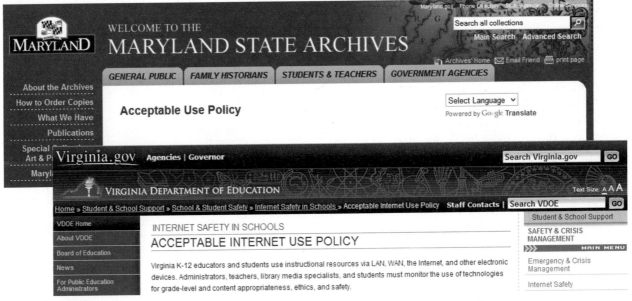

Most organizations, from government agencies to libraries, have an acceptable use policy.

They can be useful tools for protecting an organization and creating a legal framework for punishing wrongdoers. Some AUPs are simply a comprehensive statement of policy so that the institution's point of view is made clear. Others are framed as an agreement or contract that individuals are required to sign or agree to before being given access to computer-related resources. Although many different types of organizations use them, AUPs generally have a few common elements:

- Outlawing the use of computing resources to commit crimes, such as hacking and piracy.

- Restricting particular services, such as file-sharing, on their networks.

- Banning inappropriate and unethical behavior, and guidelines for the organization's netiquette.

- Stressing the importance of security, especially the creation of a strong password.

- Explaining the ownership and privacy of email, storage, and other resources that you have access to. Typically, companies reserve the right to monitor your email, web activity, and files stored on company equipment.

ACCEPTABLE USE AT SCHOOL

In addition to the above, your school might also add guidelines regarding the appropriate use of specific computers. What might be acceptable in the lab of a network security course might not be acceptable in the library's computers. Your school may also list the sort of online actions that are prohibited because they would constitute academic dishonesty.

ACCEPTABLE USE AT WORK

One of the most popular policies enforced by businesses is the ban on using computers for anything that isn't related to an employee's work. Many organizations understand the temptation of activities such as social networking and how they can hurt an employee's productivity. They use a variety of techniques, including monitoring, to ensure employees remain on task. We will discuss employee monitoring in the next section.

Acceptable use policies cover a variety of topics including the security of your account.

Privacy and Surveillance

One of the hottest topics in computer ethics pertains to the privacy of individuals in the Information Age. As you have already learned, many online companies routinely collect data from users for a variety of reasons. Advertisers are particularly interested in user habits and trends, as it will improve their marketing efforts. However, many other organizations are also interested in what you are doing on the computer. Businesses often monitor employees for productivity and security reasons. Governments also engage in surveillance to catch criminals and to look for suspicious activities that pose threats to national security.

Individuals often disagree when it comes to the need for privacy. Some people are naturally social and will post almost anything about their lives online. Others agree to exchange privacy for certain benefits, such as consenting to having their bags inspected in exchange for better airline security. On the flip side, many are often shocked when they learn what information is routinely collected about them and do everything in their power to retain their privacy or anonymity. In this section, you will learn about the variety of ways in which data is collected, so that you can decide for yourself what steps (if any) to take if you are interested in protecting your privacy.

More **Online:** *Visit the companion website for information about nonprofit organizations that fight for privacy rights and individual liberties.*

Is the Information Age threatening our privacy?

EMPLOYEE MONITORING

Most organizations feel that employees should focus solely on producing work and value for the business during the time they are being paid. With that in mind, it should not be surprising to discover that many employers are nervous about the negative impact that computers might have on worker productivity. The same Internet that can be used to access cloud-based business programs and shared documents can also be used to check Facebook activity, share copyrighted files, and view pornography. For employers, these activities can translate into reduced work output, security problems on the network, or even criminal liability.

As you already know, most companies use AUPs to inform employees about the behaviors and practices that are forbidden. A large number of companies

Companies often monitor their employees' online activity while at work.

will also use software that can either block particular Internet services or monitor what employees do on their computer. By checking **logs** (files that record activities and events) periodically, employers can determine whether there was inappropriate use by an employee. Organizations may also check the company-issued email account periodically if they suspect that an employee is violating the AUP or putting the company at risk.

ETHICS AND LEGALITY OF MONITORING

There is some debate as to whether employee monitoring has a positive outcome for a company. While cameras and monitoring software can force employees to remain productive, evidence shows that excessive surveillance lowers morale. Employees with low morale are less productive than those who are happy and motivated. Often, the chance to have a little fun with co-workers and discuss a recent sports game or fun weekend event can raise the spirits of an entire office. The difference today is that conversations that used to occur around a water cooler, for example, may now occur on a social networking site. Many have argued that as long as employees finish their work and remain productive, there is little harm in letting them unwind and stay in touch with the online world for a few minutes each day.

Everyone generally agrees about one aspect of monitoring: Employers should always inform employees about what kind of monitoring the company will engage in. This shows respect for the employee's privacy as no one will be caught off guard by monitoring devices. Also clear is the legality of monitoring.

Should employers treat conversations by the water cooler differently than those that occur online?

Various court cases have demonstrated that employers are generally within their rights to restrict Internet access at work and monitor employee use of the company's computing resources.

MONITORING ONLINE ACTIVITY

Many organizations do not restrict their monitoring to the workplace. They may check the public, online activity of their employees for anything that could harm the company. This includes statements that insult the company or executives, as well as those that may reveal company secrets. In addition, employee photos that can embarrass or hurt the reputation of a company are also deemed to be harmful. Many employees, from fast-food workers to corporate executives, have been fired for something they posted online because it made their company look negative or careless in the eyes of the public.

Organizations also check online activity before they hire employees. Your words, photos, and videos can say quite a bit about you. Anything you post online can affect your ability to get that initial interview. Many companies now specialize in gathering data about individuals on behalf of organizations such as businesses, universities, and government agencies.

GOVERNMENT SURVEILLANCE

Many government agencies such as the NSA and FBI monitor the Internet and mobile activities of individuals all over the world. They do this for national security purposes or as part of a criminal investigation. Laws such as the Patriot Act and the Foreign Intelligence Surveillance Act (FISA) give the government

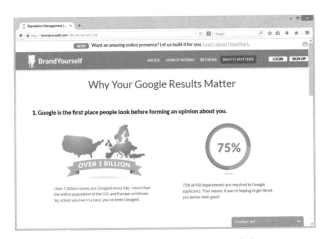

Since your online image could affect your job prospects, services such as BrandYourself help you manage it.

broad surveillance powers. In addition, law enforcement can request warrants and require that online companies turn over records including your email messages, search history, and social networking activity.

For hundreds of years, individuals in a society have had to trade some privacy for the purpose of security and enforcement of laws. What is being continually debated is how much of that privacy should be given up, especially by those who have committed no crime. Like many privacy-related debates, it often comes down to how much personal information you are willing to place on the Internet. In addition, you should keep in mind that you and your devices usually leave **digital footprints**, which is a trail of your data, activity, and even the locations where devices are used.

Agencies such as the NSA can monitor Internet and mobile activity.

ONLINE/SOCIAL RISKS

The most important thing to know about sharing anything online is this: Nothing posted to social media services or anywhere else on the Internet should be considered private. Many social media users feel that their right to privacy is being violated or abused by many online companies. Unfortunately, this is more of a misunderstanding on the part of the user than a legitimate concern. Although services such as Facebook allow users to control access to their personal information, you must remember that this data is stored on the systems owned by these companies. In addition, friends who can see your photos, videos, and status messages can copy, store, and forward that information to others.

Social media companies typically include conditions for using the service, in which each user grants permission to use the information in certain ways. Furthermore, automated programs run by social media companies and search engines can easily find, organize, and store the information that they find. This information can then be sent to marketing companies or partners who find usage patterns and trends very useful for their business. The more information they know about you or the users of a particular site, the more relevant the ads they can display to users.

ETHICS AND ONLINE COMPANIES

Most online companies have started to take privacy very seriously. Some companies, such as banks, are legally required to consider privacy. And when it comes to the privacy of children, various laws keep companies from taking advantage of them. However, many companies fear backlash from their users or the news media if they engage in actions that violate privacy. For this reason, online companies typically have a **privacy policy** on their websites that clearly states what information is collected from users and what is done with that information.

Many companies have taken steps to allow users to control various privacy settings on their services. Google, for example, allows users to view and control all their data with a tool known

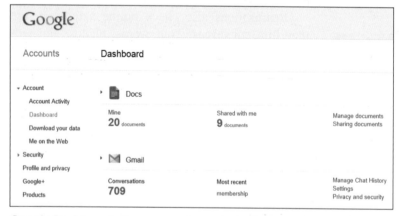

Google Dashboard allows users to control privacy settings and manage their data on Google's various services.

as Google Dashboard. Here, users can see everything from email messages to their YouTube and search activity. Online services also allow users to delete their personal information and accounts. However, even if you were to delete everything on your social media accounts, there is no assurance that this information is completely gone. Remember, anyone from your friends to search engines that gather public posts could still have some content that you thought was gone forever. Therefore, the only means for truly keeping information private is to not share it at all.

ETHICS OF SHARING

You have already read about how your words or photos can come back to haunt you later, both personally and in your career. It is also important to realize that anything you share online can hurt the individuals you care about. Compromising photographs, such as those showing a group of friends at a wild party, should not be posted to social media sites if they could be embarrassing or devastating to the lives of others. If you really want to post it, ask the individuals in the photo for permission.

PRIVACY TOOLS

In most cases, you can safeguard your privacy by following the advice in this chapter and using the security tools discussed in Chapter 5. However, when

When sharing photos and videos, always be considerate of those who appear in them.

it comes to leaving digital footprints, you should be aware of a few additional tools.

- **Private browsing** is a feature of all modern browsers that will delete your history, cache, and cookies the moment you close the private window. This is ideal if you are using a computer that is not yours.

- **Do not track** is a browser feature that attempts to stop websites from automatically sharing details about your visit with other companies. However, this is simply a request and websites are not obligated to obey it.

- **Anonymity software**, such as Tor and Anonymizer, will help mask your IP address from websites. This can help protect your privacy when visiting a website that does not have a privacy policy, as it will not allow that particular company to keep your real IP address in its records.

For regular browsing, you can control your desired privacy through various settings, such as keeping history for only a certain number of days. Browsers also include a feature that will delete all of your browsing history with a single click.

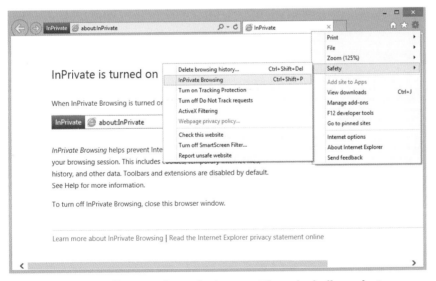

Internet Explorer offers a variety of privacy settings, including private browsing.

Global and Environmental Issues

Many of the ethical issues discussed in the previous section focused on actions that individuals and organizations should avoid in order to be ethical. However, ethics involves more than those things we shouldn't do. Ethics also tells us those things that we ought to do in order to help other people and even our planet. The following section will offer many examples of how individuals and organizations are using technology to change our world for the better.

SOCIAL AND POLITICAL CHANGE

In the last few years, technology has become an important tool for revolution and social action. Uprisings against governments have been started by and chronicled with Twitter updates and YouTube video clips. Rebels have used mobile devices and social media to coordinate their actions and receive information to aid their cause. Oppressive governments have been caught by surprise by how quickly socially sensitive information can spread through these channels. In fact, some leaders have been so terrified by the power of the Internet that they have shut it off during times of turmoil.

In the United States, most politicians now have social media accounts and often engage their constituents through them. They will also use the Internet for

Mobile devices and social media have been used in various political demonstrations and uprisings.

raising money and campaigning. The White House even has a petition form on its website, promising to address any issue from citizens if it receives enough signatures online. Social media also receives extensive use by individuals, groups, and organizations that want to advance a social or political agenda. On several occasions, unpopular proposals in Congress have been withdrawn due to the coordinated outrage shown on social media.

THE DIGITAL DIVIDE

The **digital divide** refers to the technology gap that exists between different social and economic classes. Many experts believe that without access to technology such as computers and the Internet, certain groups may fall behind when it comes to education and the ability to find a job. Because technology has become so important, many U.S. cities offer public access to computers in libraries and schools. In addition, various charities collect used computers that can be donated to homes that do not have one. One particular organization, One Laptop Per Child (OLPC), is taking this idea further by placing affordable, durable laptops in the hands of children all over the world. It is hoped that these laptops can engage students in both education and communication with others, empowering them to improve themselves and the lives of those in their community.

One Laptop Per Child (OLPC) places these laptops in the hands of children around the world.

WHISTLEBLOWING

Whistleblowing is the act of alerting the public about harmful activities that are being hidden by an organization. These activities can range from the production of harmful chemicals to deceiving the U.S. government or its people. Since most companies keep electronic records of just about anything, evidence is often easy for potential whistleblowers to find. However, before someone can ethically blow the whistle and turn against their organization, a few questions should be considered:

- Have I alerted my supervisor and, if needed, the top-level managers of the organization?

- Is the activity in question illegal or likely to cause harm to the public?

- Do I have documented proof of the activities that will cause this alleged harm?

Many state and federal governments have laws that protect the job and safety of whistleblowers, preventing them from being fired for identifying illegal or unethical behavior within the company. Even so, retaliatory action is often a real consequence for the whistleblower, whether it manifests itself as reassignments to lower-priority roles in the company or isolation from co-workers who no longer wish to associate with the whistleblower.

WHISTLEBLOWING CONTROVERSY

The Internet has given whistleblowers a new forum for alerting the public of misconduct. WikiLeaks is

WikiLeaks, which offers whistleblowers an anonymous way to submit evidence of wrongdoing, has received significant media attention due to high-profile leaks.

a global, online organization that offers whistleblowers an anonymous way of posting information and submitting evidence. It has become a very polarizing service, with some singing its praises while others criticize its decision to release many private documents and communications belonging to various countries.

Blowing the whistle may not always be the ethical thing to do. Some have argued that recent whistleblowers against the U.S. government have put lives in danger and hurt the standing of their country in the eyes of others. While the debate rages as to whether they should or shouldn't have blown the whistle, it is important for potential whistleblowers to look at the big picture. They must consider whether the outcome of their actions might be worse than the harm they were trying to prevent. In addition, they must explore all possible options for addressing the harm being done by an organization before making details of the problem public.

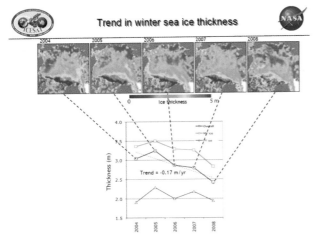

NASA uses satellite imagery and software to track sea ice thickness and look for trends in climate change.

ENVIRONMENTAL PROBLEMS AND SOLUTIONS

As the years pass, our society finds itself increasingly concerned with the effect we have on the global environment. Technological advances have accelerated our use of resources and contributed to various global problems such as pollution. However, technology has also helped us to better understand a variety of issues facing the planet.

Satellites orbiting Earth are providing us with a wealth of data about air and water pollution. Data stations on the planet's surface as well as in orbit allow us to measure changes in climate and global temperature with unprecedented precision. Computers now provide sophisticated simulations to test "what-if" climate change scenarios, along with heavy-duty data analysis that aids scientists in developing solutions. Technology also helps us create or improve environmentally friendly energy solutions such as solar and wind power.

Green computing follows the reduce, reuse, and recycle model.

GREEN COMPUTING

Green computing concentrates on reducing the environmental impact of computers and their widespread use. Many computers consume a great deal of electricity to operate. And like other metal and plastic creations, they do not disappear very quickly in a landfill. As billions of people put computers or other devices into use, the cost to the global environment becomes significant. To help lower that impact, green computing follows the "reduce, reuse, recycle" model that has been promoted for decades in environmental initiatives. Let's take a closer look at what this model entails.

REDUCING ENVIRONMENTAL IMPACT

Green computing has emerged as a new way to consider the manufacture and operation of computers to reduce their environmental impact. Designs that

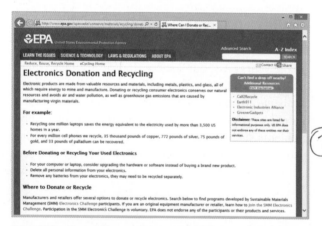

The EPA offers information on recycling and donating electronic devices.

yield even a fractional reduction in a computer's power consumption can cause a substantial reduction in the global demand for electricity. Computers and their components, such as CPUs and monitors, are being developed to run on less power. Operating systems use **power management** utilities to place computers and devices in low-power states when they are not being used. These states include:

- **Sleep**, which uses only enough electricity to keep the contents of your RAM active.

- **Hibernate**, which saves more electricity by copying the contents of RAM to your hard drive. RAM can now be powered off since the hard drive does not require power to remember its content.

Companies that use heavy computing resources also strive to reduce their environmental impact. In fact, it is common for the websites of many large organizations to promote their environmental initiatives. These range from recycling programs to the improved management of their large servers and networks. Many organizations have reduced the amount of technology purchased and used because of the increased reliance on shared, cloud computing resources.

WASTE & RECYCLING

Some local and international programs collect old computers to be refurbished and redistributed to individuals or schools that do not have access to computers. Most population centers now have a municipal or private program that encourages the recycling of old and broken computers and peripherals. Those centers can resell working parts and strip gold or other useful metals from components for recycling. In addition, many retailers offer recycling programs for computers, mobile devices, and printer cartridges, often offering discounts if you trade something in.

One of the most significant activities that helps reduce waste is going **paperless**. Both companies and individuals are using technology to lower their consumption and reliance on paper. Throughout this book, you have learned of the countless benefits offered by technology. As time goes on, you will find many types of organizations, including schools and hospitals, eliminating paper from their facilities.

PART 2:
Changes at Work

As the computer revolution began decades ago, people often wondered if their job might someday require computer expertise. Given the explosion in the use of technology, individuals are no longer asking themselves this question; instead, they are finding themselves using computers on a daily basis. In fact, the more appropriate question for today's graduates and job applicants to ponder is what sort of hardware and software they should master in order to do their job.

This section will focus on more than the use of technology in various types of businesses. You will learn how technology has changed not just the way we work, but also what type of work we do and where we can do it. You will also learn about the growing fields of robotics and artificial intelligence, and the ways they are changing many aspects of business and education. Lastly, you will explore the various computing careers that are responsible for developing and supporting most of the technology used today.

Telecommuting allows individuals to work away from the office.

Workplace Changes

In Chapter 1, you learned about the various ways in which organizations use computers. From health care to law enforcement, technology allows workers to do their jobs quickly and effectively. However, technology has also allowed organizations to engage in certain activities that were practically impossible before the advent of powerful computers and networks. This section will introduce some of these activities and discuss their advantages and disadvantages.

TELECOMMUTING

Telecommuting is the process of working for a company without being physically present at the company's office. The term describes a wide variety of remote work practices, from working at home occasionally to living in a different country than the company you work for. Powerful home computers, mobile devices, and high-speed Internet have made telecommuting possible for millions of individuals.

To be effective as a telecommuter, a worker must become self-disciplined enough to complete work efficiently and avoid distractions. Telecommuters also

need to have the computer hardware, software, and connectivity required to get the job done properly. Employers will often provide some of this technology and a VPN so that the remote worker can access the company's network securely. In addition, video-conferencing applications can make it easy for that employee to have conversations with supervisors and join in on team meetings.

ADVANTAGES OF TELECOMMUTING

When a particular job is capable of being completed from home, employees often jump at the chance. Companies should also be excited by some of the advantages that telecommuting offers. These include:

- The ability to hire or keep workers whose schedule or location would make it impossible for them to work at the company's offices.
- Reduced costs for office space and utilities.
- Improved employee morale, which can boost productivity and loyalty.

DISADVANTAGES OF TELECOMMUTING

Although telecommuting can seem like an exciting idea, some employees just don't have the self-discipline or a distraction-free home. On the flip side, some companies or managers are not ready or capable of having employees away from the main office. The disadvantages of telecommuting for both employees and organizations include:

- Clients and managers that prefer traditional face-to-face interactions will not be able to have them with remote workers.

- Sensitive information is now located at the employee's home, which may be less secure.

- Employees who are not at the office may receive inferior wages or opportunities for promotion.

- Employees may find themselves working more hours, especially if their supervisor feels as if they are always "on the clock."

EMPLOYEE AVAILABILITY

The last point made in the previous section marks a growing problem for many employees, not just

Distractions at home may cause problems for telecommuters.

remote ones. A large number of office workers and executives now have mobile devices that are capable of retrieving company email and receiving instant messages. This creates an expectation of being available at all times, ready to read a message or answer a quick question. Technology has made work easier in many ways, but it also has individuals working more hours than ever.

OUTSOURCING

In addition to allowing employees to work from home, technology has made it possible for companies to outsource many of their functions or services. **Outsourcing** occurs when an organization transfers some aspect of its business to a third party. For example, many companies choose not to have an accounting department; instead, they hire an outside accounting firm to handle their finances. With networking technology, such as extranets, it is very simple for this firm to access the company's sales and expense figures as if they were in the same office.

OFFSHORING

When companies outsource functions to another country, it is referred to as **offshoring**. Some of the most popular uses of offshoring are the call centers and live support tools that handle customer service for an organization. With high-speed networks, an employee located in India, for example, can access customer data and support files that may be located in the United States. In addition to customer

High-speed networks allow call centers to be located anywhere.

support, many companies outsource manufacturing for various devices and components. Most of the mobile devices used today are manufactured in China, with some components coming from Japan or South Korea. Computing and communication technology make many aspects of the global economy possible.

Automation and Emerging Technologies

You have already learned various ways in which technology has changed the way we work. Perhaps none has had a more significant impact than automation. Computers and robots are now performing many jobs that used to be performed by humans. However, these tools, along with other emerging technologies, are creating new jobs and helping organizations all over the world tackle some of the biggest issues facing us today. This section will explore automation and many of these emerging technologies.

AUTOMATION

Automation occurs when computers or machines can perform the work that was once done by a human. In some cases, the machine completely replaces a human worker. For example, large robotic arms now handle many aspects of a car's assembly, a process that used to take several people to complete. In other cases, the automation can help individuals complete their work faster or free them to do other tasks. This is especially true for small-business owners, who can enjoy more free time with the help of systems

Automated checkout systems are being used at many stores.

that manage inventory and other business functions automatically.

Automated systems offer many benefits to organizations and individuals. However, sometimes the advantages for a company can result in lost jobs or job shifts. For example, a large number of Americans were employed in manufacturing 60 years ago. Today, very few people are needed for those types of jobs. More people are now working in service industries and in the creation or support of those automated systems.

USES FOR AUTOMATION

Both computers and automated machines are used in a variety of roles. Often, they increase an organization's productivity. Others can be used to save people's lives. The following are some examples of where you will find these types of systems today:

- Areas where pinpoint accuracy is required, such as in the manufacture of microprocessors.

- Tasks that require long hours of physical work or extreme strength.

- Activities or locations that are too dangerous for humans, such as cleanup efforts in a toxic area or search and rescue operations in a catastrophe.

- Activities that involve fixed or predictable transactions, such as checkout lines and course registration.

ROBOTICS

During early robotic research, machines were limited to performing a single and specific task with consistency and precision. Robotic arms, for example,

These robotic arms bring automation to manufacturing.

could be taught to position themselves over an object, grasp that object, move it to a new location, and set the object down. While that accomplishment may not seem like much in retrospect, it required the development of machinery that could be programmed and manipulated in precise ways. As you have learned, companies such as car manufacturers found these specific and repetitive tasks quite useful.

The complexity and sophistication of robots has increased dramatically over the years. This has coincided with an improvement in computing technology such as faster processors and more sophisticated programming. Their ability to understand their environment has greatly improved, as evidenced by affordable robots that can vacuum your home. As time goes on, you will see improvements in both their intelligence and range of motion.

HUMANOID ROBOTS

Humanoid robots are those that are created to imitate the appearance or capabilities of humans. New technology in robot construction is exploring ways to simulate a variety of human movements, such as running or shaking someone's hand. In addition, various sensors can perform functions similar to our eyes and ears. Some humanoid robots, like Honda's ASIMO, can already perform a variety of activities that require a great deal of balance and range of motion. It can jog, climb stairs, and even kick a ball. Furthermore, it can recognize stationary and moving objects, and understand certain kinds of human input such as spoken words and gestures.

Honda's ASIMO humanoid robot displays human-like movement.

There are many applications for humanoid robots. They may be used to perform a variety of activities that are too risky for humans, such as traveling in space for long periods and exploring the surface of other planets. We can also use these robots as caretakers for elderly or disabled individuals, providing 24/7 oversight for those who wish to stay in their homes instead of moving to assisted-living facilities. And because these robots continue to look and act more like humans, it makes it easier, psychologically, for individuals to relate to them.

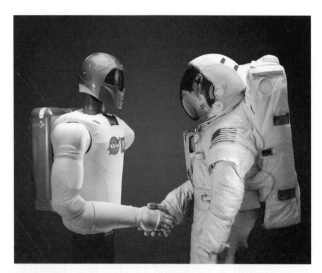

NASA Robonaut 2 can work alongside astronauts or perform tasks that are too dangerous for humans.

> More **Online:** *Visit the companion website to learn more about robots, including some that you can build or program yourself.*

ARTIFICIAL INTELLIGENCE

Artificial intelligence (AI) involves the development of intelligent systems. These systems can include anything from sophisticated programs that answer questions to futuristic robots that can think and act like humans. Though the sciences of AI and robotics are very different, some of the futuristic products and accomplishments we envision involve contributions from both of them.

WHAT IS INTELLIGENCE?

Superficially, intelligence can be defined as the processes used in learning, problem solving, and communication. However, not everyone agrees on an exact definition. Philosophers, scientists, psychologists, programmers, and many others have struggled to create a precise and comprehensive definition of intelligence. And even if a standard model for human intelligence were created, the model might not cover the behavior of other species that are normally considered to be intelligent.

Equally ambiguous is the notion of when a machine can be classified as being intelligent. One popular test of a machine's ability to think is known as the **Turing test**. It was developed by Alan Turing, who was a very influential figure in the development of computer science as a discipline. In his test, a computer would be said to exhibit intelligence if it could imitate humans and deceive an interrogator in the way it responded to a variety of questions. Although no system has exhibited this type of intelligence yet, various supercomputers such as IBM's Watson now have an astounding capability to understand complex questions and quickly find the answers using large databases of information.

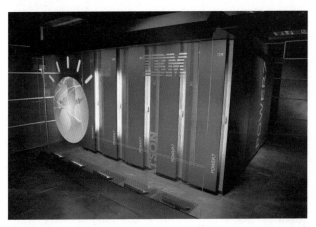

IBM's Watson system displays remarkable intelligence when it comes to research.

AI APPLICATIONS

Many types of programs attempt to imitate a certain type of human intelligence. One system may act as a personal sales consultant that can make recommendations based on what it knows about you (e.g., Amazon.com). Another might focus on understanding human languages and the way we ask questions (e.g., Apple's Siri and Google's Voice Search). Expert systems, which you learned about in Chapter 5, are often regarded as intelligent for their ability to provide expert answers to specific types of questions.

As stated earlier, AI and robotics can often come together to produce fascinating results. If robots are to act as caretakers, companions, and explorers, they must possess enough intelligence to handle a variety of tasks on their own. Furthermore, they must be able to "think outside the box" when an unexpected situation occurs. The good news is that we already have software and devices that can recognize our faces, follow verbal commands, and provide personalized recommendations. Little by little, these abilities will be integrated into robots that have a wide range of motion and can be made to look like us. Many feel that it is just a matter of time before a truly intelligent, humanoid robot is developed.

EMERGING TECHNOLOGIES

It would be an impossible task to list all the technology being developed and researched today. Most areas of study and activity,

Many robots are being made to look like humans (Einstein, in this case) and imitate many of our facial expressions.

from sports to space exploration, are continually being improved and aided by emerging technologies. To make our task easier, let's focus on just a few areas where emerging technologies are aiming to improve the lives of humans.

BIOTECHNOLOGY

Biotechnology is an application of biology that uses living organisms to manufacture new products or improve existing ones. Computing technology is being used by researchers in this field to develop new medications, map human genes, and increase crop yields. There are many exciting areas of research in biotechnology, some of which aim to cure a variety of diseases or engineer organisms that help fight pollution.

NANOTECHNOLOGY

Nanotechnology involves the creation or manipulation of matter at the smallest possible scale. Researchers from a variety of fields are creating new types of materials, devices, and even computer circuits by working directly with molecules and atoms. At the moment, nanotechnology is being used to develop effective drug delivery systems that can better target problem areas while reducing side effects. Many dream of a day when tiny, nanoscale robots can be injected into the body to repair damaged tissue or deliver compounds directly into human cells. Others eagerly await the arrival of the *quantum* computer, which will be millions of times faster than today's

Researchers use DNA sequencing technology to find genes that may cause cancer.

devices. This is because their atoms can represent data in states beyond the two bits (0's and 1's) of today.

HUMAN ENHANCEMENT

Technology can be integrated with biological systems in various ways to repair or improve human functions. For those who have lost a limb, engineers have developed robotic prosthetics that can perform a variety of movements by simply projecting a thought to them. Others act as a sort of exoskeleton that can help paralyzed individuals walk again using motorized leg attachments. Researchers have also discovered ways to make computer chips interact with various areas of the body and brain to help those who suffer from conditions such as Parkinson's or blindness. Some chips are even able to record new memories, helping those who have suffered damage to parts of the brain or have early-stage memory loss.

It is just a matter of time before technology begins to be used in healthy individuals who wish to enhance one or more parts of their body. A variety of implants could be used to give someone superhuman strength, vision, and even brain function. Biotechnology will one day be able to modify a person's genes before they are born, allowing parents to "customize" their child, so to speak. Some futurists even believe that human memories can one day be copied and stored into a computer, allowing that person to achieve a sort of immortality. Ethicists are already debating many of these topics, feeling that some of these developments are not far away.

Advanced technology is allowing amputees to control a robotic arm as if it were their natural one.

Computer Careers

As you have learned throughout this book, many types of computing technology support organizations today. This technology changes rapidly, with new hardware, software, and Internet features being released continuously. This has created a strong demand for professionals who can develop and maintain these systems. The following section will introduce you to various careers and positions in the information technology field.

Software engineers create diagrams in order to visualize systems.

> More **Online:** *Visit the companion website for up-to-date information on computer careers and salaries.*

SOFTWARE ENGINEER

A **software engineer** is responsible for the development of computer software. Some of these engineers take on the role of a **systems analyst**, who specializes in developing plans and recommendations that meet the software and system needs of an organization. Regardless of their role, these individuals are experts in one or more computer programming languages and have a good understanding of the software that runs on (or manages) various computer systems. In addition to designing and developing software, those with computer programming skills may find careers in specific areas such as:

- **Game development.** Today's video games are quite complex and require programming for user interaction, realistic motion and physics, and even intelligent character behavior.

Web developers are often responsible for the programming and graphics of today's websites.

- **Mobile app development.** Different considerations go into making apps for mobile users, such as ensuring that a program works well with a smaller, touchscreen interface.

DATABASE ADMINISTRATOR

A **database administrator (DBA)** is responsible for configuring, maintaining, and securing an organization's database. Given the explosion in data storage and analysis, this field is growing rapidly. Some of the duties of a DBA include:

- Developing and designing a database.
- Installing and configuring a database server.
- Optimizing a database for maximum performance and security.
- Creating backups of data and restoring those backups when necessary.

WEB DEVELOPER

A **web developer** creates and maintains websites for organizations. Web developers are trained in web programming languages and are often responsible for connecting the company's website to a database. Because websites have become such a crucial component of an organization's marketing efforts, many developers have added skills or branched out into additional areas of specialization. Some of these include:

- **Search engine optimization (SEO)** involves improving the ranking of a website when users enter relevant keywords in a search engine.

- **Graphic design** skills, such as editing photos and designing layouts, have become an important skill for creating websites.
- Many positions, such as **social media strategist**, are being created for experts in sales and marketing using the web and various social media tools.

NETWORK ADMINISTRATOR

A **network administrator** is responsible for configuring and maintaining networks and communication systems. In addition, they are responsible for securing a company's infrastructure from internal and external threats. Some of their duties include:

- Installing and updating network software.
- Managing network hardware.
- Creating and configuring user accounts.
- Configuring and securing Internet, intranet, and extranet connections.

SUPPORT SPECIALIST

A **computer support specialist** excels when it comes to installing, configuring, and supporting computer systems. Most companies have the need for a **help desk** department that can quickly repair and troubleshoot systems, as well as provide technical support to employees. Some of a support specialist's duties include:

- Installing and configuring new computer hardware.
- Troubleshooting and repairing hardware of all types.

Network administrators are in charge of the configuration and security of an organization's network.

- Troubleshooting problems with the operating system and other company software.
- Providing support to employees or customers.

INFORMATION SYSTEMS MANAGER

Information systems managers are responsible for managing a diverse team of IT professionals that include programmers, network administrators, and many others. In addition to overseeing employees, they make top-level decisions regarding the purchasing of software and hardware for an organization. These individuals often possess a wide range of knowledge in information technology fields, along with experience or a degree related to business and management.

Information systems managers supervise other IT personnel and make top-level decisions.

KEY TERMS

acceptable use policy
   (AUP), 172
anonymity software, 177
artificial intelligence (AI), 184
attribution, 170
automation, 183
biotechnology, 186
computer support
   specialist, 188
copyright, 167
Creative Commons, 170
cyberbullying, 172
database administrator
   (DBA), 187
digital divide, 178
digital footprints, 176
digital rights management
   (DRM), 169
do not track, 177

empathy, 166
ethics, 166
fair use, 168
flaming, 172
frequently asked questions
   (FAQ), 171
graphic design, 188
green computing, 180
help desk, 188
hibernate, 180
humanoid robot, 184
information systems
   manager, 188
intellectual property, 167
log, 175
nanotechnology, 186
netiquette, 171
network administrator, 188
offshoring, 182

outsourcing, 182
paperless, 180
piracy, 167
power management, 180
privacy policy, 176
private browsing, 177
public domain, 168
search engine optimization
   (SEO), 187
sleep, 180
social media strategist, 188
software engineer, 187
systems analyst, 187
telecommuting, 181
thread, 171
trolling, 172
Turing test, 185
web developer, 187
whistleblowing, 179

Review Questions

MULTIPLE CHOICE

1. A(n) _____ license allows authors to set conditions for the free use and distribution of their work.

  a. public domain

  b. acceptable use

  c. DRM

  d. Creative Commons

2. _____ is a feature of all modern browsers that will delete your history, cache, and cookies the moment you close the browser.

  a. Do not track

  b. Intellectual property

  c. Green computing

  d. Private browsing

3. One of the foundation blocks of intellectual property law is the _____, a legal concept that grants rights and control to the owner of any published work.

  a. copyright

  b. attribution

  c. netiquette

  d. acceptable use policy

4. Which of the following fields involves the creation or manipulation of matter at the smallest possible scale?

  a. Biotechnology

  b. Nanotechnology

  c. Artificial intelligence

  d. Robotics

5. _____ is the act of being annoying and antagonistic in areas such as online forums.

   a. Piracy
   b. Whistleblowing
   c. Flaming
   d. Trolling ✓

6. _____ occurs when computers or machines can perform the work that was once done by a human.

   a. Automation ✓
   b. Outsourcing
   c. Offshoring
   d. Green computing

7. _____ involves the development of intelligent systems.

   a. AI ✓
   b. DRM
   c. SEO
   d. DBA

8. _____ is the act of alerting the public about harmful activities that are being hidden by an organization.

   a. Outsourcing
   b. Whistleblowing ✓
   c. Green computing
   d. Turing

9. Many websites have _____ areas that should be checked for common questions and their responses.

   a. DRM
   b. AUP
   c. SEO
   d. FAQ ✓

10. In the world of computing, _____ means acquiring or exchanging copies of protected digital creations without payment to or permission from their creator.

    a. trolling
    b. flaming
    c. piracy ✓
    d. attribution

FILL IN THE BLANK

11. The term _Netiquette_ refers to the set of online behaviors that are considered polite and proper.

12. Online companies typically have a(n) _privacy policy_ on their websites that clearly state what information is collected from users and what is done with that information.

13. _empathy_ is the ability to recognize, understand, and share the feelings of others.

14. The _digital divide_ refers to the technology gap that exists between different social and economic classes.

15. You might find a computer support specialist at a company's _help desk_, troubleshooting systems and providing technical support to employees.

16. _____ is the philosophical study of morality.

17. A(n) _Database administrator_ is responsible for configuring, maintaining, and securing an organization's database.

18. Repeated hostile behavior with intent to harm another individual is known as ___Cyberbulling___

19. Legal concepts have been created and refined to help protect _Intellectual Property_, which are essentially products of the mind.

20. ___Green computing___ concentrates on reducing the environmental impact of computers and their widespread use.

TRUE / FALSE

21. If a company hires an outside organization to handle its accounting, it is engaged in outsourcing.

22. It is illegal for social networking companies to share profile and usage information with marketing companies they are partnered with.

23. Copyright protection lasts for approximately 15 years after the author applies for it.

24. For a computer, "sleep" mode uses less electricity than "hibernate" mode.

25. Some humanoid robots can already jog, climb stairs, recognize objects, and understand human speech.

SHORT ANSWER

26. List five elements that are typically found in acceptable use policies.

27. How can your online activity affect your ability to find or maintain employment?

28. Briefly describe the four factors that must be considered for "fair use."

29. What sort of Internet surveillance does the U.S. government engage in? Name two laws that give government agencies broad surveillance powers.

30. Describe at least three ways in which you can recycle and reduce computing-related waste.

31. Suppose that you wanted to watch a Hollywood movie or the entire season of a TV show. List four legal ways in which you could view this content.

32. List three advantages of telecommuting.

33. Describe three ways in which social media have been used to help bring about political or social change.

34. Is it legal for a company to monitor employees while they work? Is it ethical? Defend your answers.

35. List four ways in which technology can be integrated with biological systems to repair or improve human functions.

Research Exercises

Go beyond the book by performing research online to complete the exercises below.

1. Find YouTube's policies or guidelines on uploading music and videos protected by copyright law. What does YouTube it say? What does YouTube do when a copyright violation is reported?

2. Perform additional research on the government's use of sophisticated computers to monitor communications. What did you find? Do you agree with this type of surveillance? Defend your answers.

3. Name two nonprofit organizations that support privacy rights. What are some of the issues they are currently fighting? Describe at least three of these issues.

4. Find at least three local organizations and/or retailers near you that can recycle or reuse your unwanted devices. Describe the services they provide and consider which one(s) you will use in the future.

5. Find an organization that can analyze your DNA and generate reports on your health risks and ancestry. Would you use this service? Why or why not?

6. Do you believe it is ethical for researchers to create intelligent robots? Discuss some of the pros and cons of the development of these machines.

7. Consider the implications of using a smartphone for work. What are some of the advantages and disadvantages? Is it ethical for employees to be contacted outside of work hours? Defend your answers.

8. Perform research on any emerging technology (such as biotech) that can improve or enhance human lives. Describe one example of a technology that is already in place and another example of a technology that is in development. Do you support such research? Is there a line that shouldn't be crossed with respect to improving or modifying humans that are otherwise healthy? Defend your answers.

Buying Guide

Many people feel lost or overwhelmed during the computer buying process. There are many categories of computers for individuals, from desktops and laptops to tablets and smartphones. And within each category are countless devices with a wide range of specifications and prices. Unfortunately, no one-size-fits-all recommendation can apply to everyone. And to make matters more complicated, specifications and prices change rapidly in this industry as new hardware and devices are continually released.

This buying guide contains recommendations for the typical student. It assumes that you are still in school and are interested in using a computer wherever you go, including at home and on campus. As you read the list below, please note that it is arranged *in order of priority*. In other words, the first category is the most important, followed by the second, and so on. If you are interested in more up-to-date information, check the companion website for this book.

1. All-Purpose Laptop

The best device to meet all of your computing needs is an all-purpose laptop. It is small enough to take to school, but powerful enough to be your primary computer at home. If you plan on using it extensively at home, you should consider connecting it to a TV or external monitor for comfort. Many individuals also buy a larger keyboard and external mouse. The following are some of the specifications and prices you should be looking for in a Windows-based system:

- **Price:** $450 to $750
- **CPU:** Intel Core i3 or i5; AMD A-Series
- **RAM:** 4 GB to 8 GB
- **Hard drive:** 500 GB to 750 GB
- **Monitor:** 15 to 17 inches, touchscreen preferable for Windows 8

ALTERNATIVE: CONVERTIBLE ULTRABOOK

Choose this option if you need two specific things: a very lightweight laptop and a tablet computer. These laptops will either convert to a tablet or will allow you to detach the screen for use as a tablet. Expect the following differences:

- **Price:** $800+
- **Monitor:** 11 to 13 inches, touchscreen
- **Weight:** 2.5 to 3.5 pounds

2. Smartphone

Choosing a smartphone starts with your budget. If you are interested in the lowest possible price, your wireless carrier likely offers several Android, iOS, and Windows devices for free (or close to free) with a two-year wireless contract. These phones are slightly older models, yet still excellent smartphones that are capable of running any app.

If you are willing to pay more to get the latest and greatest, expect to pay around $200 (with a two-year contract). You can choose from the best devices offered by manufacturers, running the latest mobile operating systems. When choosing between mobile OS, be aware that Apple and Android devices have more available apps than those running Windows. In addition, be sure to compare some of the following specifications:

- **Camera quality:** Megapixels can guide you, but be sure to check the web for reviews on the camera's overall performance. Consider color accuracy, image sharpness, and low-light performance.
- **Screen size:** Newer smartphones are coming out with bigger screens, with some getting close to six inches. Consider how well it fits in your hand and whether a large screen is useful for your smartphone activities.
- **PPI:** The number of pixels-per-inch will indicate how sharp or crisp objects appear on your screen.
- **Battery life:** Find out how long the battery is expected to last on a single charge.
- **Storage:** If you plan to install many apps and store large numbers of photos and music, you should consider 16 GB to 32 GB. Also check if the phone allows you to add an external SD card. Lastly, remember that many of your files can be stored in the cloud, reducing the need for high storage amounts.

3. Tablets

Tablets are very hot at the moment. That being said, purchase one only if you absolutely need one. Consider what activities would be significantly easier or convenient with a tablet. Keep in mind that quality tablets with larger screens can be pricey, and many of their functions can be performed by your laptop or smartphone. If you do decide to purchase one, consider the same specifications as smartphones but with a few differences:

- **Screen size:** This ranges from 7 to 10 inches. The bigger the screen, the pricier the tablet.
- **Price:** Expect to pay around $200 for smaller tablets and $400 to $500 for larger ones.
- **Operating system:** It is often best to choose the same OS as your smartphone, as you will not need to buy the apps all over again.

4. Desktop (All-In-One)

Desktops, which were once the standard computers for the home, are losing popularity quite quickly. Laptops and mobile devices are now preferred, and users often have little motivation to sit down in one place and use desktop computers for extended periods. That being said, if you want to have a family computer that many can share or you desire maximum comfort when using a computer, a desktop may be desirable. Consider the following specifications for your all-in-one desktop computer:

- **Price:** $600 to $900
- **CPU:** Intel Pentium-based or Core i3/i5
- **RAM:** 4 GB to 8 GB
- **Hard Drive:** 500 GB to 1 TB
- **Monitor:** 20- to 24-inch touchscreen

Macs and Chromebooks

The prices given for both laptops and desktops have assumed the purchase of a Windows-based computer. Apple's Mac computers are generally more expensive than their Windows counterparts. As you have learned in this textbook, Apple makes excellent computers that are powerful, reliable, and user-friendly. Choose a Mac only if you can afford it or wish to be part of the Apple "ecosystem" along with your smartphone and/or tablet. With respect to Chromebooks, they are typically the most affordable category of laptops. However, they are best suited as a secondary device unless your computing needs are very light and limited mostly to online activities.

3D modeling software Used by professional artists and animators who need to create three dimensional graphics and characters for advertisements, video games, cartoons, and movies.

3D printer A printer that can create a three-dimensional object made of various materials.

A

Acceptable use policy (AUP) A document containing an organization's policies for the ethical, secure, and appropriate use of computing resources.

Algorithm A series of steps that describe exactly what each portion of a program is supposed to do.

All-in-one computer Computers that have all of the hardware integrated with the monitor.

Anonymity software Software that helps mask your IP address from websites.

Application software Software that allows individuals to complete a variety of work and school-related tasks. Entertainment software and most mobile apps are also in this category.

ARPANET A predecessor to the Internet, this government-funded network connected four U.S. universities in 1969.

Artificial intelligence (AI) Involves the development of intelligent systems or machines that possess capabilities such as learning, problem solving, and communication.

Attachment A file attached to an email message.

Attenuation The loss of intensity and clarity of a transmitted data signal.

Attribution Credit to the author of a work wherever it is used.

Augmented reality An experience where the real-world is supplemented with computer-generated information.

Authentication A security measure used to confirm an individual's identity.

Authorization A security measure used to give individuals a certain level of access based on who they are.

Automation The use of computers or machines to perform the work that was once done by a human.

B

Backbone Refers to the connections that carry most of the Internet's traffic.

Backup A copy of one of more files (or entire storage devices) that is made in case the originals become lost or damaged.

Bandwidth In networks, it refers to the amount of data that can be transmitted over a given amount of time.

Banner ad A thin, rectangular advertisement that is commonly placed across the top or on the sides of a web page.

Bcc Stands for "blind carbon copy," and is used to send a copy of an email to recipients who will remain invisible to other recipients of the message.

Beta version An early version of a computer program used to test the software in real-world conditions.

Biometrics The measurement of patterns or characteristics found in the human body.

Biotechnology An application of biology that uses living organisms to manufacture new products or improve existing ones.

Bit A fundamental unit of computing that is represented as an on (1) or off (0) value.

Bitmap graphic A type of image that is represented by individual pixels.

Bits per second (bps) A unit of measurement used to track the speed at which data travels to and from the ISP.

Blade server A thin unit that can slide in and out of a rack that holds many of its companion servers.

Blog A web page or small website that contains a series of chronological posts and comments.

Bluetooth A short-range wireless technology used in devices such as hands-free systems.

Blu-ray disc (BD) The latest optical storage technology, which typically stores 25 or 50 GB of data.

Bookmarks A list of favorite websites or pages.

Boot process The start-up process of a computer, which includes loading the operating system from the disk.

Botnets Massive networks of zombies that can be used by a hacker to spread malware, send spam, and conduct carefully orchestrated network attacks.

Bridge A device that connects two LANs or two segments of the same LAN; looks at the information in each packet header and forwards data traveling from one LAN to another.

Broadband Any digital data connection that can transmit information faster than standard dial-up by using a wider band of frequencies.

Bugs Errors in a software program.

Byte The unit of memory or storage that represents eight bits. It is the amount of space required to store a single character, such as a letter or number.

C

Cache (browser) Also known as temporary Internet files, the browser cache stores every single page, image, and video for all the web pages you have recently retrieved.

Cache (memory) A form of high-speed memory that stores a small, frequently used set of instructions and data. It is located inside modern CPUs.

Cc Stands for "carbon copy," and is used to send a copy of your message to individuals other than your primary recipient.

Central processing unit (CPU) The main processor of a computer. It is responsible for organizing and carrying out instructions to produce a desired output.

Chipset A part of a motherboard that acts as a traffic director for data.

Chromebook A line of lightweight laptops that run Google's Chrome operating system.

Clipboard A temporary holding space in the computer's memory for data that is being copied or moved.

Clock rate The frequency or speed at which CPUs process instructions.

Cloud backup Utility software that creates automated backups to an online account.

Cloud collaboration The ability to view, edit, and share documents online.

Cloud computing The ability to store your files and use various applications in an online account.

Cloud storage The ability to store your files online and access them from any Internet-connected device.

Coaxial cable A cable that consists of a single copper wire that is surrounded by insulation and a wire mesh shield.

Coding The process of converting algorithms and flowcharts into an actual computer program.

Command-line interface A way to interact with computers that requires users to memorize and type a series of commands.

Compact disc (CD) A type of optical storage technology that is capable of storing 700 MB of data.

Compatible The condition whereby two computers can use the same software because they run the same operating system.

Compiler A program that translates a specific programming language into a machine language that can be processed by the CPU.

Computer A device that accepts input, processes data, and can output or store the result of its actions.

Computer aided design (CAD) Software that aids architects, engineers, and many others who need to create a digital model of an object.

Computer program A set of instructions that directs the computer to perform a variety of tasks.

Computer support specialist An individual who is responsible for installing, configuring, and supporting computer systems.

Contrast ratio Measures how close the monitor can get to the brightest white and the darkest black.

Convertible laptop Lightweight laptop computers that allow users to swivel or detach the touchscreen monitor.

Cookie A small data file created by a web browser that remembers your preferences for a specific website.

Copy A command that places a copy of the selected object (or objects) into the clipboard.

Copyright A legal concept that grants rights and control to the owner of any published work.

Copyright law A federal law that gives software creators a variety of rights and privileges over their creative work.

Core An individual processor inside a chip.

Countermeasure Any step you take to ward off a threat.

Creative Commons A license that allows an author to set conditions for the free use and distribution of their work.

Crowdsourcing The gathering of information from a large group of people.

CRT monitors Rarely used today, these large and bulky displays used cathode-ray tube (CRT) technology.

CSNET An early computer network created in 1981 to bring together researchers in the field of computer science.

Cursor A mark on the screen indicating where the characters you type will be entered; also known as "insertion point."

Customer relationship management (CRM) Software that allows sales departments to manage call centers, support customers, and keep track of sales commissions.

Cut A command that removes the selected object (or objects) from their current location and places them into the clipboard.

Cybercrime The use of a computer and/or network to commit a variety of crimes, such as creating viruses or disrupting networks.

Cyberbullying An online form of aggression that involves repeated hostile behavior with intent to harm another individual.

Cyberterrorism A dangerous form of hacking that seeks to create large-scale chaos and damage to a country's infrastructure.

D

Data Individual facts or pieces of information.

Database An organized method for storing information.

Database administrator (DBA) An individual who is responsible for configuring, maintaining, and securing an organization's database.

Database management system (DBMS) Software that allows users to create and manage complex databases.

Data mining The discovery of new patterns or relationships between data.

Data plan A subscription that allows individuals to connect to the Internet using a cellular network.

Data validation A method for checking and improving the reliability of data.

Data warehouse A central repository where records from multiple databases are stored.

Decision support system (DSS) A special application that collects and reports certain types of data, thus helping managers make better decisions.

Delete A command that removes a file from your drive.

Desktop The traditional starting area on GUI-based operating systems.

Desktop computer A personal computer that has been traditionally found on the desks in many offices and homes. Most are in the form of a tower.

Device driver Programs that allow operating systems to communicate with hardware.

Dial-up An older type of Internet connection that uses analog signals over a phone line.

Digital camera Portable devices that electronically capture and store still images and video.

Digital divide The technology gap that exists between different social and economic classes.

Digital footprints A trail of your data, activity, and the locations where devices are used.

Digital literacy A broad understanding of computer and information technology, and the ability to use it well.

Digital projector A device that projects digital images and video onto a large screen where they can be viewed by an audience.

Digital rights management (DRM) Technologies used to protect copyrighted material.

Digital versatile disc (DVD) A type of optical storage technology that is capable of storing 4.7 or 8.5 GB of data.

Digital video recorder (DVR) A device that allows you to record television shows for future playback.

Disk cleanup A utility that clears out temporary files that take up space on your hard drive.

Disk defragmentation An optimization utility that will reorganize files and fragments to place related ones nearer to each other.

Distributed denial-of-service (DDoS) A network attack that attempts to shut down or block access to websites or other network resources by overwhelming them with requests.

Do not track A browser feature that attempts to stop websites from automatically sharing details about your visit with other companies.

Document feeder A tray that allows you to scan several sheets of paper automatically.

Domain name The portion of a URL that uniquely identifies a site and a brand on the web.

Dot matrix printer A printer that creates output by striking an inked ribbon against paper using metal pins.

Dots per inch (DPI) A measurement of image quality for printers.

Download To receive data.

Drive A computer's storage devices.

Duplexing The ability to automatically print to both sides of a piece of paper.

Dye-sublimation printer A printer that uses a process where colored dyes are heated and then diffuse on specialty paper or other materials.

E

E-book reader A device that makes it convenient for individuals to store and read many electronic books.

E-commerce Doing business online.

Electronic book Digital book that is stored on a computing device.

Email A system for exchanging messages through a computer network.

Embedded system Limited computers that are placed inside devices that require specific computing functions.

Emoticon A symbol that represents an emotion in casual messages.

Empathy The ability to recognize, understand, and share the feelings of others.

Encryption The process of scrambling your data or storage devices to make them unreadable by anyone who doesn't have the proper key.

End-user license agreement (EULA) The typical license that a user must agree to before installing software.

Enterprise resource planning (ERP) A system that brings together many types of business functions into one software solution.

Ergonomic keyboard A keyboard that's designed to be comfortable and tailored for the human body, with keys that are angled and a palm rest at the base in order to keep your wrists straight.

Ethernet The most common physical standard for local area networks.

Ethics The philosophical study of morality.

Executable file A file that can be run by the operating system on a user's computer.

Expansion card Add-on circuit boards that improve the performance of a system's video or sound.

Expert system A type of information system that performs analytical tasks traditionally done by a human, using sequences of questions to ask and actions to take based on the responses to those questions.

Extension A program used to add a variety of useful features to the web browser.

Extranet A service that allows organizations to share some of its intranet resources with people outside the organization.

F

Facial recognition A biometric technology that looks for unique measurements in an individual's face.

Fair use An exception to copyright law that provides for a limited set of circumstances where others can use copyrighted material without first obtaining permission.

Fault-tolerant Systems that are able to continue their operation even when problems are present.

Fiber-optic cable A high-speed cable that consists of a thin strand of glass that transmits pulsating beams of light rather than electric current.

File The most fundamental component of storage that users interact with. A file can contain the instructions of a computer program or the data that you care to store.

File compression The process of making a file smaller than its original size.

File extension A short, unique sequence of characters located after a file's name that indicate the file type.

File hierarchy The way a computer organizes files, consisting of drives, folders, and files.

File system The way in which the operating system views and manages the space on a storage device.

Fingerprint scanner A biometric technology that can detect the unique patterns and swirls of an individual's finger.

Firewall A software utility dedicated to examining and blocking Internet traffic.

Firmware Instructions placed on a chip that contain device-specific information.

Flaming Online social interactions that exhibit anger and/or insults.

Flowchart A chart that uses special symbols to trace the steps of a program's development.

Folder A container that can store files or other folders. Also known as a directory.

Formatting The process of preparing a storage device for use by an operating system.

Forums Discussion boards where individuals can ask questions and reply to each other.

Forward To re-send an email after its initial transmission.

Freeware Any software that is free to use without any specified time restrictions.

Frequently asked questions (FAQ) A list of common questions and their responses on a website.

G

Game controller An input device for a computer game.

Gaming consoles Complete entertainment systems that offer Internet connectivity, movie rentals, photo storage, and many other services in addition to video games.

Gateway A node on a network that serves as an entrance to another network. It helps one network understand the packet headers from another network.

Gesture A type of finger movement that can accomplish various tasks on specialized input devices.

Graphic design The art or skill of editing photos and designing layouts.

Graphical user interface (GUI) A type of operating system interface that allows users to communicate with the computer via graphical elements on the screen.

Graphics processing unit (GPU) A video card's microprocessor.

Graphics tablet A tool that offers extra-sensitive touch surfaces that translate an artist's motions into drawings on the computer screen.

Green computing The principle of reducing the environmental impact of computers.

H

Hacker In the negative sense, this term refers to an individual who uses a computer and/or network to commit a variety of crimes, such as creating viruses and disrupting computer networks.

Hacktivism Hacking with a social or political agenda.

Hands-free computing The ability to communicate with a device without using your hands.

Haptic feedback The communication of vibration, motion, or physical resistance to a user; also called "haptics."

Hardware The physical devices that make up a computer system.

Hard drive The primary storage device of a personal computer.

Hashtag A symbol (#) to mark keywords or topics in a message.

Help desk A department at a company that can repair and troubleshoot systems, as well as provide technical support to employees.

Hibernate A computer state that saves electricity by copying the contents of RAM to your hard drive.

History A list of every website you have visited, kept by your web browser.

Home automation The technology that allows various household activities to be automated or controlled from a distance.

Home page The starting page for a web browser.

HTML Hypertext markup language. It is used to create web pages.

HTTP Hypertext transfer protocol. It helps web servers deliver a requested page to a user's computer.

HTTPS A secure, encrypted version of HTTP.

Hub A basic network device that provides multiple ports for connecting nodes.

Humanoid robot A robot that is created to imitate the appearance or capabilities of humans.

Hyperlink A word or picture users can click on to immediately jump to another location within the same document or to a different web page.

I

Icon A graphical representation of a file, folder, or drive.

Identity theft A type of crime in which criminals essentially assume your identity and begin to open new bank accounts under your name.

Information processing cycle The series of steps the computer follows to receive input, process the data according to instructions from a program, display the resulting output to the user, and store the results.

Information system (IS) A complex system for acquiring, storing, organizing, using, and sharing data and information.

Information systems manager A person responsible for managing a diverse team of IT professionals that include programmers, network administrators, and many others.

Inkjet printer A type of printer that creates an image directly on the paper by spraying ink through tiny nozzles.

Input User entries or activities that tell the computer what to do.

Install The process of having software set up by the operating system so that it can be used.

Instant messaging (IM) The act of having an online, text-based conversation with one or more individuals.

Integrated development environment (IDE) Software that helps developers build their computer programs.

Intellectual property Products of the mind such as ideas, designs, and expressions of creativity that may not have any physical form.

Interactive whiteboard A large screen that allows a user to interact with the images projected on it.

Internet The largest network in the world, it connects billions of people and organizations throughout the planet.

Internet meme Online content that has become very popular and widespread over time.

Internet service provider (ISP) Telecommunications companies that offer Internet access to homes and businesses.

Interoperability The ability of each organization's information system to work with the other, sharing data and services.

Intranet An internal version of the Internet containing information that is restricted to a particular company's employees.

IP address A unique set of numbers and/or letters that uniquely identifies every computer or device on the Internet.

K

Keyboard shortcuts Keystrokes that can quickly perform an operation within software.

L

Laptop computer A portable computer that contains all of the components of a desktop computer in a single, integrated unit. It is also known as a notebook computer.

Laser printer A fast, high-quality printer that creates output by using a laser that is aimed at a rotating drum.

LCD monitor A common type of flat-panel monitor that contains a light source and a screen of special crystals placed in the monitor between the user and the light source.

Learning management system (LMS) A system that offers students the ability to complete exams, turn in work, and communicate with their instructor and classmates.

LED monitor A thinner, lighter, and more energy-efficient type of LCD monitor that is lit by a grid of tiny electronic lights called light emitting diodes.

Live tile A graphical element on the Windows 8 Start screen that can display real-time information such as the current weather, news, or social media updates.

Local area network (LAN) A data communication system consisting of multiple devices that are relatively near each other and are connected using cables or wireless media.

Location-based services (LBS) Services that can give you certain information based on where you are physically located.

Lock screen The start screen of a mobile device that allows the user to set a variety of security measures.

Log A file that records activities and events.

M

Mainframe computer Very large and powerful systems used in organizations where a heavy amount of processing and user requests need to be handled.

Malware A generic term to describe various kinds of malicious programs created to harm a computer or steal valuable information.

Management information system (MIS) A set of software tools that enables managers to gather, organize, and evaluate information.

Massive open online course (MOOC) Huge online courses offered for free by a variety of universities.

Media The physical locations, such as discs, where things are stored.

Media player An application that allows you to listen to music and play videos.

Megapixel A unit of graphic ???resolution equivalent to one million pixels.

Memory General term for electronic chips that store data and program instructions that can be accessed quickly by the CPU.

Memory card A type of solid state storage used to store data in tablets, smartphones, and other electronic devices.

Microblogging A short-form blog where users share brief thoughts, links, and multimedia.

Mission-critical Systems that must run without failure or with nearly instant recovery from failure.

MMORPG Stands for "massively multiplayer online role-playing game" and lets millions of players connect to various servers to team up with other players in very large virtual worlds.

Mobile device Lightweight, handheld computers that offer a variety of software and communication services for mobile users.

Mobile hotspot A device that can connect to a mobile network and offer Internet access to multiple devices near it.

Modem A device that can convert digital information from a computer into the analog sound waves that can be transmitted over phone lines.

Motherboard The largest circuit board in a personal computer. It contains a variety of slots, connectors, and plugs for hooking up all the other parts of a computer.

Multifunction printer A device that combines either inkjet or laser printing capabilities with scanning, photocopying, and faxing capabilities.

Multimedia The capacity of a computer to input and output sound, music, images, and video.

Multimedia Messaging Service A service offered by wireless companies that allows cell phone users to attach and send a variety of media to other users.

Multitasking The ability to run multiple programs at the same time.

Multiuser computer A computer that's designed to work with many people at the same time.

N

Nanotechnology The creation or manipulation of matter at the smallest possible scale.

Netbook A small and inexpensive laptop that has reduced processing power and lacks a DVD drive.

Netiquette The set of online behaviors that are considered polite and proper.

Network A connection between computers that allows users to communicate and share information.

Network administrator A person responsible for configuring and maintaining networks and communication systems.

Network interface card (NIC) A computer component that translates and transmits network packets.

Network media The means used to link parts of a computer network.

Network server A powerful computer with special software and equipment that enables it to function as the primary computer in the network.

News aggregator An app that allows you to pick a variety of news sources and read them in a magazine-style interface.

NFC A wireless technology (near field communication) that lets your mobile device communicate over very short distances, such as when paying for goods on wireless payment devices.

Node A connection point within a network.

NSFNET A high-speed network created by the National Science Foundation in 1986 that established connections to smaller regional networks, other agencies' networks, CSNET, and ARPANET.

O

Office automation system A type of information system that is designed to manage information in an office environment and help users handle certain information-related tasks more efficiently.

Office suite A bundle of programs that help businesses efficiently carry out tasks such as writing letters, analyzing sales figures, and scheduling meetings.

Offshoring A company's outsourcing of certain business functions to another country.

Online payment service A company that offers a secure and convenient way to pay for online goods and services.

Open source A type of software license that permits the source code to be freely distributed and modified.

Operating system Software that manages the flow of data between hardware components and allows the user to communicate with the computer.

Optical character recognition (OCR) Technology that can translate a scanned document image into text that can be edited and formatted.

Optical mouse The most common pointing device for desktop computers, it includes a left and right button, a scroll wheel in the middle, and a light-emitting mechanism at the bottom to sense movement.

Output The processed results that a computer sends to you.

Outsourcing An organization's transfer of some aspect of its business to a third party.

P

Packet Pieces of a message broken down into small units by the sending device and reassembled by the receiving device in a network.

Pages per minute (PPM) A measure of printer speed.

Paperless The use of technology by companies and individuals to lower their consumption and reliance on paper.

Parental control Utilities that allow parents to set a variety of limits on their children's Internet usage.

Partitioning Dividing a hard drive into multiple sections.

Paste A command that places the contents of the clipboard into the location where this command is issued.

Path A complete address that describes the exact location of a file.

Pay-per-click Payment model where advertisers pay for their ads only when a website visitor clicks on the ad to go to the advertiser's website.

Peer-to-peer (P2P) A file transfer method that uses a distributed network of individual users instead of a central server to transfer files.

Personal computer A computer that is meant to be used by only one person at a time; also called "microcomputer."

Personal information manager (PIM) Software that is designed to keep individuals organized via the management of contacts, appointments, to-do lists, and email.

Phablet A mix of the terms "phone" and "tablet," this term is given to very large smartphones.

Phishing Luring individuals into entering personal information into a website controlled by a hacker.

Piracy Acquiring or exchanging copies of protected digital creations without payment to or permission from their creator.

Pixel Tiny dots on a display screen, each with its own unique address, that the computer uses to locate it and control its appearance.

Plagiarism Turning in the work of another as if it were your own or failing to cite the source of your work.

Plug-in A separate program that allows your web browser to play several types of multimedia content.

Podcast A type of prerecorded webcast that users typically subscribe to for future streaming or automatic downloading.

Pop-up blocker A browser feature that automatically blocks advertisements that attempt to open in a new, "pop-up" window.

Port A plug on a computer that is used to connect external devices.

Power management The ability to place computers and devices in low-power states when they are not being used.

Presentation software A category of software that enables users to create electronic slideshows that are used to present information.

Pretexting Gaining someone's trust by pretending you are someone else.

Privacy policy A website's written statement that clearly states what information is collected from users and what is done with that information.

Private browsing A feature of all modern browsers that will delete your history, cache, and cookies the moment you close the private window.

Processing The ability of a computer to perform actions based on instructions from the user or a program.

Project management A sophisticated plan used by businesses to track and achieve a variety of goals.

Protocol A set of rules or standards that must be followed by computers that wish to communicate over a network.

Public domain A term that refers to creative works whose copyright has expired or never existed in the first place. These works can be freely used without permission.

Q

QR code A scannable product code, which appears as a square filled with patterns of dots and lines, that typically directs users to a website.

R

RAID A storage system that links any number of disk drives (a disk array) so that they act as a single disk.

Random access memory (RAM) A type of memory that temporarily stores the data and programs that a computer is currently using.

Read-only memory (ROM) A small chip that contains device-specific information and handles a computer's basic functions when it is powered on.

Real-time communication When messages and conversations between two or more people occur instantaneously.

Real-time information Any information that is delivered to you immediately after it is created.

Redundant Computers that have multiple hardware systems performing the same task at the same time.

Remote wipe The ability to completely erase a mobile device if it is lost or stolen.

Repeater A network device used to prevent attenuation when packets are traveling long distances.

Reply Abbreviated "re" in the subject line of emails, this indicates that the message is a reply, or response.

Residential gateway A device that connects your home's network to the Internet.

Resolution The number of pixels that are displayed on the screen.

Response time The amount of time in milliseconds that it takes for a pixel to change from black to white.

RFID tag A tiny chip or label containing electronically stored data that can be accessed wirelessly.

Risk assessment Identifying and examining possible threats to a computer system.

Rogue hotspot A wireless access point set up by a hacker in a public area to intercept users' communication.

Root directory The location on a drive that is outside of any folders or directories.

Router A complex device that stores the routing information for networks. It looks at each packet's header to determine where the packet should go, then determines the best route for the packet to take toward its destination.

S

Scanner A device that uses optical technology to convert objects that it analyzes into a digital format.

Scareware A type of scam whose goal is to scare the user into doing exactly what the thief wants.

Scalability The capacity to provide increasing amounts of computing power, storage, and/or software.

Search engine optimization (SEO) The process of improving the ranking of a website when users enter relevant keywords in a search engine.

Search engine A sophisticated combination of hardware and software that stores the URL of millions of web pages and most of the content on those pages. When users type specific keywords into the search engine, they will receive an organized list of matching sites, images, and articles that contain those keywords.

Security software Programs that help keep you, your computer, and your personal information safe from a variety of threats.

Security suite A bundle of programs that accomplish a variety of security-related tasks.

Shareware Software that is free to download and install, but will stop working after a trial period unless the user purchases the software.

Short Message Service (SMS) A service offered by wireless companies that allows cell phone users to send text messages of 160 characters to any other user.

Sleep A computer state that uses only enough electricity to keep the contents of your RAM active.

Smartphone A device that combines the functions of a mobile phone and a handheld computer.

Smart TV A TV that offers connectivity to a variety of online services to let you watch movies and listen to music. Many also connect to other computing devices in your home.

Social engineering A form of hacking that focuses on deceiving individuals into giving away the information that the thief needs.

Social media A variety of websites and services that allow individuals to share photos, news, and thoughts with other individuals.

Social media strategist An expert in sales and marketing who uses the web and various social media tools.

Social Networking Websites that are used to create connections between friends, family members, and organizations, thereby allowing individuals to share information and receive updates from those in their social circles.

Social news Websites that encourage users to share links to news and other interesting content they find on the web.

Software One or more computer programs that are packaged together for a unified purpose.

Software development life cycle (SDLC) A series of steps that take programmers from the idea and planning stages through the actual programming, testing, and maintenance of software.

Software engineer A person responsible for the development of computer software.

Software license A contract from the software creator that specifies the rules for using this software.

Software updates Software patches used to fix errors and security vulnerabilities.

Solid state drive (SSD) A small and fast type of hard drive that uses flash memory instead of the more traditional magnetic technology.

Sound card A circuit board that converts sound from analog to digital form and vice versa for recording or playback.

Spam Unsolicited email that is sent in bulk.

Speech recognition A computer's ability to recognize human speech.

Spreadsheet software Software used for entering, calculating, and analyzing sets of numbers. This software is also used for creating charts.

Spyware Malware that reports activity on your computer to another party.

Start screen The new default screen in Windows 8, it can run mobile-style apps and display live tiles that show real-time information.

Storage The ability of a computer to hold or remember the information it processes.

Streaming media Music and movies that are delivered on demand from an online source.

Streaming player A small, affordable device that allows you to stream videos and music using your TV and wireless home network.

Strong password A password that is difficult for thieves to guess or crack.

Stylus A pen-like tool used to input information directly into a variety of touchscreen devices.

Subdomain A portion of a URL that usually indicates a specific subdivision or server within a large site.

Subscription model A payment method for software that has users pay a fixed amount of money per month in order to use the software.

Supercomputer The largest and most powerful type of computer in the world, they are ideal for handling large and highly complex problems that require extreme calculating power.

Surge protector An inexpensive product that guards connected equipment against large power spikes or surges that may infrequently occur.

Switch A network device that is similar to a hub, but it is aware of the exact address or identity of all the nodes attached to it, thereby increasing the efficiency of the network.

Systems analyst A person who specializes in developing plans and recommendations that meet the software and system needs of an organization.

System software Any program created for the operation, maintenance, and security of a computer.

System unit The case that houses the computer's critical parts, such as its processing and storage devices.

T

Tabbed browsing An interface that allows you to have multiple web pages open in one browser window.

Tablet computer A mobile device that typically ranges from 7 to 10 inches in size.

Tag Data attached to a photo, such as keywords, faces, and the location where it was taken.

Tape drive A storage device that uses magnetic tape to back up or archive large amounts of data.

Tape library A large storage unit that houses multiple tape drives.

TCP/IP The protocols at the heart of Internet communication.

Telecommuting The process of working for a company without being physically present at the company's office.

Tethering A feature that makes a phone act as a wireless access point.

Thermal printer A printer that applies heat to special thermal paper, turning select areas black to produce text and basic graphics.

Thread In a forum, a topic that contains related posts.

Threat Anything that can cause harm.

Topology The logical layout of the cables and devices that connect the nodes of the network.

Touchpad A stationary, rectangular pointing surface that is typically found on laptop computers.

Touchscreen A technology found on monitors and mobile devices that accepts input by allowing the user to perform a variety of finger taps and gestures directly on the screen.

Trackball A pointing device that works like an upside-down mouse.

Transaction processing system (TPS) A type of information system that handles the processing and tracking of transactions.

Trojan horse A program that disguises itself as an interesting, useful, or desirable program in order to gain access to your system.

Trolling A type of social interaction where a user acts in an annoying and antagonistic manner.

Turing test A test for artificial intelligence that measures a system's ability to hold a human-like conversation.

TV tuner A device that can capture television signals for viewing on a computer.

Twisted-pair cable A cable that consists of four pairs of wires that are twisted around each other. Each copper wire is insulated in plastic, and all wires are collectively bound together in a layer of plastic.

U

Ultraportable computer A thin, lightweight laptop that possesses strong processing power.

Uninterruptible power supply (UPS) A device that contains both a surge protector and rechargeable battery, allowing your computer system to run for a limited amount of time during a power failure.

Upload To send data.

URL A standard addressing system that allows web pages to be located on the Internet.

USB flash drive A small, solid state storage device that plugs into a USB port.

USB port A small, rectangular port which is used to connect almost all of today's external devices.

Utilities Programs that enhance or extend the operating system's capabilities or offer new features not provided by the operating system itself.

V

Vector graphic A type of image that relies on mathematics, which allows users to increase or decrease the size of the image without any distortion.

Vertical market software Software that is created for a specific industry such as health care or insurance.

Video card An intermediary device between the CPU and the monitor that contains a processor, video-dedicated memory, and other circuitry.

Videoconferencing Voice and video communication that allows multiple individuals to hold meetings and converse over a network.

Viral When funny or fascinating content is shared again and again over a short period.

Virtual machine A special environment that allows users to run an operating system on top of another operating system.

Virtual memory A portion of your hard drive that is being used as RAM.

Virtual private network (VPN) A type of connection that increases the security of network communication by employing a method called "tunneling," whereby each packet from the sending computer is encapsulated within another packet.

Virtual reality An experience where humans can interact with realistic environments that are simulated by computers.

Virtualization software The software that allows you to run a virtual machine.

Virus A type of malware that is attached to a host file and has the ability to replicate, or copy, itself.

Voice over Internet Protocol (VoIP) Translates analog voice signals into digital data and uses the Internet to transport the data; can connect to telephone networks and digital sources such as PCs.

Volume license A license that allows companies to install software on multiple machines.

Vulnerability A weakness that has not been protected against threats, thereby making it open to harm.

W

Wearable technology Computing devices that are worn on various parts of the body.

Web 2.0 A term that refers to a new way to use the web, whereby any user can create and share content, as well as provide opinions on existing content.

Web browser Software that helps you find and retrieve a web page that you are interested in viewing.

Web developer A person who creates and maintains websites for organizations.

Web page A web-based document.

Web portal A website that provides a variety of useful information and services to visitors.

Web server A server that hosts websites.

Web-based application A program that runs directly on your web browser.

Webcam A small video camera, typically attached to a monitor, that is commonly used for online video chats or conversations.

Webcast The broadcast of various types of media over the web.

Website Several related web pages that connect to each other.

Whistleblowing The act of alerting the public about harmful activities that are being hidden by an organization.

Wide area network (WAN) The connection of two or more central computers or LANs, generally across a wide geographical area.

Widget A small screen element that provides automatically updating information without the need to open an app.

Wi-Fi The most popular standard for wireless networking; also called "802.11."

Wiki A collaborative information site, such as Wikipedia, that relies on the Internet community to both create and edit content.

Wireless access point (WAP) Connects single or multiple PCs in the wireless environment.

Wireless adapter A piece of hardware that is plugged into a desktop computer to gain Wi-Fi access.

Wireless network A type of connection whereby communication takes place using radio waves.

Word processing software Software that provides tools for creating, editing, and formatting all kinds of text-based documents.

World Wide Web A global system of linked, hypertext documents known as web pages.

Worm A type of malware that self-replicates and spreads through computers and networks without the need to attach to a host file.

Z

Zombie An infected and compromised computer that is under the external control of a hacker, usually without the knowledge of the computer's owner.

Front Matter

Page x (top center): Google; p. x (top left): Source: Facebook; p. x (top right): Source: Twitter; p. x (bottom right): Source: Evernote; p. xi (top): Source: Microsoft; p. xi (bottom right): Google; p. xii: Source: AVG.

Chapter 1

Page 2: Gandee Vasan/Stone/Getty Images; p. 4: Rubberball/Punch-stock; p. 5 (bottom left): ERproductions Ltd/Blend Images ; p. 5 (top right): JLP/Sylvia Torres/Flame/Corbis; p. 6: David R. Frazier Photolibrary, Inc.; p. 7: Michael Spence/Alamy; p. 8 (bottom left): Ian McKinnell/Photographer's Choice/Getty Images; p. 8 (top right): Digital Vision/Getty Images; p. 9 (top right): David Caudery/Official Windows Magazine via Getty Images; p. 9 (bottom left): Image Source/Getty Images; p. 10 (bottom left): John Kershaw/Alamy; p. 10 (top right): AP Images/Julie Jacobson; p. 11 (top right): NASA; p. 11 (bottom left): Jan Woitas/dpa/picture-alliance/Newscom; p. 12 (top right): Future Publishing/Getty Images; p. 12 (bottom left): Simon Dawson/Bloomberg/Getty Images; p. 13 (top right): Source: Comcast; p. 13 (top left): Patrick T. Fallon/Bloomberg via Getty Images; p. 14 (bottom left): Jacek Lasa/Alamy; p. 14 (top right): Stacy Walsh Rosen-stock/Alamy; p. 15 (top left): AP Images/Mark Lennihan; p. 15 (top right): Krista Kennell/ABACAUSA/Newscom; p. 16: Daniel Acker/Bloomberg/Getty Images; p. 17 (top right): Steve Carroll/Alamy; p. 17 (bottom left): Source: Android; p. 17 (bottom left): Source: Android; p. 18 (bottom right): Juice Images/Alamy; p. 18 (top center): mage 100/PunchStock; p. 19 (bottom left): Thomas Northcut/Riser/Getty Images; p. 19 (top right): Ingram Publishing; p. 20 (bottom left): Source: Waze; p. 20 (bottom left): Source: Waze; p. 20 (top right): Source: Yelp; p. 21 (bottom left): Source: Google; p. 21 (top right): Courtesy of SquareUp. Photo By Dwight Eschliman; p. 22 (bottom left): Source of interface image: Instagram; Source of photo: NASA; p. 22 (bottom left): Source: Instagram; p. 22 (top right): Snapchat; p. 23 (top right): Source: iheart-radio; p. 23 (bottom left): Source: Hulu; p. 24 (top right): Source: Healthtap; p. 24 (bottom left): Source: Accupedo; p. 24 (bottom left): Source: Sleepbot; p. 25 (bottom): Kim Kulish/Corbis News/Corbis; p. 25 (top right): Gavin Roberts/Tap Magazine /Getty Images; p. 26: Source: Microsoft; p. 27: Source: Google.

Chapter 2

Page 32: Victor Habbick Visions/Science Photo Library/Corbis; p. 34 (bottom left): AP Images; p. 34 (top right): Kitch Bain/age fotostock; p. 35 (bottom left): Ludovit Repko/Alamy; p. 35 (top right): Alamy; p. 36 (top right): AP Images/Paul Sakuma; p. 36 (bottom left): © Keith Eng 2007 /McGraw-Hill Companies; p. 37: Simon Belcher/Alamy; p. 39 (bottom left): AP Images/Itsuo Inouye; p. 39 (top right): Digital Stock/Corbis; p. 40 (bottom left): © McGraw-Hill Education; p. 40 (top right): Maciej Latałło/Alamy; p. 40 (center): © Keith Eng 2007 / McGraw-Hill Companies; p. 41 (top right): Gavin Roberts/Official Windows Magazine via Getty Images; p. 41 (bottom left): JG Photog-raphy/Alamy; p. 42: Erkan Mehmet/Alamy; p. 43 (bottom left): goldy/Getty Images; p. 43 (top right): Photodisc/Getty Images; p. 43 (top right): Source: Microsoft; p. 44 (top right): Thinkstock/Getty Images; p. 44 (bottom left): Creative Crop/Digital Vision/Getty Images; p. 45 (bottom left): Epson; p. 45 (bottom right): Epson; p. 45 (top right): Digital Stock/Corbis; p. 46 (bottom left): Source: Google; p. 46 (top right): Don Farrall/Getty Images; p. 47 (top right): Joby Sessions/Digi-tal Camera Magazine /Getty Images; p. 47 (bottom left): Photodisc/Getty Images; p. 48 (top right): AP Images/ Al Powers/Invision/AP,

File; p. 48 (bottom left): Source: Google; p. 49 (bottom left): Seth Joel/Photographer's Choice RF/Getty Images ; p. 49 (top right): © iStock-photo.com/Signature/rustemgurler; p. 049 (inset)(bottom left): NASA; p. 50 (bottom left): AP Images/PRNewsFoto/NVIDIA Corporation; p. 50 (top left): Roy Wylam/Alamy; p. 50 (top center): David Cook/Alamy; p. 50 (top right): Ingram Publishing /Alamy; p. 51 (top right): Zoonar/Vladimir Blinov/Alamy; p. 51 (bottom left): HANDOUT/KRT/Newscom; p. 52 (top right): Source: Microsoft; p. 52 (bottom left): ermingu/Getty Images; p. 53 (bottom left): Stephen VanHorn/Alamy; p. 53 (top right): Ryan McVay/Getty Images; p. 54 (top right): AWM concepts/Alamy; p. 54 (bottom): AP Images/GLOBE NEWSWIRE; p. 54 (top left): evolis; p. 55 (bottom): NASA; p. 55 (top right): Smart Technologies.

Chapter 3

Page 60: Jorg Greuel/Photodisc/Getty Images; p. 62: NASA; p. 63 (bc): Linux; p. 63 (top right): Ivan Voras/Wikimedia; p. 64: Source: Microsoft; p. 65: Source: Apple; p. 66: Source: Ubuntu; p. 67 (top right): AP Images/Google; p. 67 (bottom left): David Paul Morris/Bloomberg/Getty Images; p. 68 (bottom): Source: Microsoft; p. 68 (bottom right): Nokia; p. 69 (top right): Source: Norton Security; p. 69 (bottom left): Source: Microsoft; p. 70 (top right): Source: Star-bucks; p. 70 (top right): Source: LastPass; p. 70 (bottom left): Source: Ubnuntu; p. 71: Source of interface image: Microsoft; Source of logo: Hewlett-Packard; p. 72 (top right): Source: Microsoft; p. 73 (top right): Source: Apple; p. 73 (bottom left): Google; p. 74 (top right): Source: Microsoft; p. 74 (top right): Source: NASA; p. 75 (bottom): Source: Apple; p. 75 (bottom left): Source: Microsoft; p. 76 (bottom right): Source: Apple; p. 76: Source: Microsoft; p. 77: Source: WinRAR; p. 78: Source: Microsoft; p. 79 (top): Source: AccuWeather; p. 79 (top right): Source: Weather Channel; p. 80 (top right): Source: LibreOffice; p. 80 (bottom): Source: Microsoft; p. 81, p. 82: Source: Microsoft; p. 83: Google; p. 84 (top right): Source: Adobe; p. 84 (bottom left): Source: Apple; p. 85: Source: Autodesk; p. 86 (center left): EVE-VR; p. 86 (center right): EVE-VR/Oculus VR; p. 88: Source: Microsoft.

Chapter 4

Page 94: David Malan/Photographer's Choice RF/Getty Images; p. 96: Dieter Spannknebel/Photodisc/Getty Images; p. 97: Donna Cox and Robert Patterson, courtesy of the National Center for Supercomputing Applications (NCSA) and the Board of Trustees of the University of Illinois; p. 98: Copyright 2002 The Regents of the University of Cali-fornia; p. 99: EPA (Environmental Protection Agency); p. 100: 1and1.com; p. 101: Google; p. 102: Source: Microsoft; p. 103: Skype; p. 104 (bottom left): BitTorrent; p. 104 (top right): Whitehouse.gov; p. 105: Coursera; p. 106 (bottom right): ©iStockphoto.com/rbouwman; p. 106 (top right): Mark A. Ibele/lao.ca.gov; p. 107: Source: AT&T; p. 108: AP Images/AT&T; p. 109: Google; p. 110 (top right): Source: Google; p. 110 (bottom): Source: UPS; p. 111: Source: Google; p. 112: Source: Bing; p. 113 (bottom left): Source: Flipboard; p. 113 (inset)(top right): AP Images/Brian Snyder, Pool; p. 113 (main)(top right): © 2014 Yahoo. YAHOO! and the YAHOO! logo are registered trademarks of Yahoo.; p. 114: Google; p. 115: Source: BusinessUSA; p. 116: Google; p. 117: Source: Tumblr; p. 118 (top center): Source: Twitter; p. 118 (bottom left): Source: Youtube; p. 119: Source: Flickr; p. 120: Wiki-pedia; p. 121: Top Sites/Alamy; p. 122: "These materials have been reproduced with the permission of eBay Inc." © 2014 EBAY INC. ALL RIGHTS RESERVED; p. 123: Notebookcheck http://www.note-bookcheck.com/; p. 124: Larry Williams/Jay Newman/Getty Images; p. 125: Source: Google; p. 126: Source: EasyBib.

Chapter 5

Page 132: Tetra Images/Getty Images; p. 134: Colorblind/Cardinal/ Corbis; p. 136: Phil Degginger/The Image Bank/Getty Images; p. 137 (top right): Sheval/Alamy; p. 137 (bottom left): vetkit/YAY Media AS/Alamy; p. 139 (top right): Arthur Kwiatkowski/Getty Images; p. 139 (bottom left): Jacus/Getty Images; p. 141: Paul Bradbury/OJO Images/Getty Images; p. 142 (top right): Jetta Productions/Iconica/ Getty Images; p. 142 (bottom left): Duncan Smith/Photodisc/Getty Images; p. 143: Steve Cole/Getty Images; p. 144 (main): McGraw-Hill Education; p. 144 (inset): FilippoBacci/Getty Images; p. 145 (bottom left): Sehenswerk/Alamy; p. 145 (top right): PhotoAlto/Odilon Dimier/ Getty Images; p. 146: Andrew Holt/Photographer's Choice RF/Getty Images; p. 147: CDC; p. 148: Martin Poole/Getty Images; p. 149 (top right): Image Source/Getty Images; p. 149 (bottom left): Erik Isakson/ Getty Images; p. 150: Amos Morgan/Jupiter Images; p. 151 (bottom left): Handout/MCT/Newscom; p. 151 (top right): Schneider Electric; p. 152 (top right): Rob Wilkinson/Alamy; p. 152 (bottom left): Jose Luis Pelaez Inc/Blend Images/Getty Images; p. 153: Federal Bureau of Investigation; p. 154 (bottom left): Source: Chase; p. 154 (top right): Air Force; p. 155: Federal Trade Commission; p. 156 (bottom left): Source: Microsoft; p. 156 (top right): CMCD/Getty Images; p. 157: Brand X Pictures/Jupiterimages; p. 158 (bottom left): Fermi National Accelerator Laboratory; p. 158 (top right): James Lauritz/Digital Vision/Getty Images; p. 159: CrashPlan.

Chapter 6

Page 164: Bloomimage/Corbis; p. 166: SW Productions/Getty Images; p. 167 (top right): Federal Bureau Of Investigation; p. 167 (bottom left): Comstock Images/Getty Images; p. 168 (bottom left): Andersen Ross/Digital Vision/Getty Images; p. 168 (top right): NASA; p. 170 (bottom left): Creative Commons; p. 170 (top right): Source: Pandora; p. 171: Somos/Veer/Getty Images; p. 172 (top right): Source: CNET; p. 172 (bottom left): Allison Michael Orenstein/The Image Bank/Getty Images; p. 173 (top): Maryland State Archives; p. 173 (bottom right): Comstock/Jupiterimages; p. 173 (top): © 2014 by the Commonwealth of Virginia Department of Education. All rights reserved. Reproduced by permission.; p. 174 (top right): Paul Bradbury/The Image Bank/Getty Images; p. 174 (bottom left): Image Source/Getty Images; p. 175 (bottom left): Brand Yourself; p. 175 (top right): Comstock/PunchStock ; p. 176 (bottom left): Google; p. 176 (top right): National Security Agency; p. 177 (bottom left): Source: Microsoft; p. 177 (top right): Stockbyte/Getty Images; p. 178 (top right): Sallie Pisch/Demotix/Demotix/Demotix/Corbis News/Corbis; p. 178 (bottom left): VAN CAKENBERGHE TO/SIPA/Newscom; p. 179 (bottom left): NASA; p. 179 (top right): WikiLeaks; p. 180 (top center): Tanja Niesen/Westernd61/Corbis; p. 180 (bottom left): EPA (Environmental Protection Agency); p. 181: Klaus Vedfelt/ The Image Bank/Getty Images; p. 182 (bottom left): Plush Studios/DH Kong/Blend Images/Getty Images; p. 182 (top right): BananaStock/ Jupiterimages; p. 183 (top right): AP Images/Roland Weihrauch/ picture-alliance/dpa; p. 183 (bottom left): Aaron Roeth Photography/ McGraw-Hill; p. 184 (top right): Jason Kempin/WireImage/Getty Images; p. 184 (bottom left): NASA; p. 185 (top right): Ben Hider/ Stringer/Getty Images; p. 185 (bottom left): Hanson Robotics; p. 186 (bottom left): © 2014 The Johns Hopkins University/Applied Physics Laboratory. All Rights Reserved. For permission to use, modify, or reproduce, contact the Office of Technology Transfer at JHU/APL.; p. 186 (top right): National Cancer Institute; p. 187 (bottom left): Simion Marian/Alamy; p. 187 (top right): nullplus/Getty Images; p. 188 (bottom left): Stockbyte/Gettyimages; p. 188 (top right): Purestock/ SuperStock.

Privacy policy, 176
Privacy tools, 177
Private browsing, 177
Processing, 7
Professional networking, 117
Programming languages, 87
Project management, 86
Projector, 55
Protocol, 97, 137
Public domain, 168
Python, 87

Q

QR code, 45
Quantum computer, 186
QuarkXPress, 85
QuickBooks, 83
Quicken, 83
QWERTY, 41

R

RAID, 146
RAID 0, 146
RAID 1, 146
RAID 5, 146
RAM. *See* Random access memory (RAM)
Random access memory (RAM), 37
Ransomware, 153
RAR, 72
Read-only memory (ROM), 37
Read/write head, 39
Real-time communication, 103
Real-time information, 20
Record, 81
Recovery utility, 73
Recycle Bin, 76
Recycling, 180
Red Hat, 64
Reddit, 119
Redundant array of independent disks (RAID), 146
Redundant computer, 145
Reference sites, 125
Relationships, 81
Remote wipe, 17
Repeater, 139
Reply, 101
Research, 124–126
Residential gateway, 106
Resistive touchscreen, 44
Resolution
    monitor, 49
    printer, 52
Response time, 49
RFID scanner, 46
RFID tag, 46
Right-clicking, 43
Ring topology, 138–139
Risk assessment, 149
Robotic arms, 183–184
Robotics, 183–184
Rogue hotspot, 154–155
rogue hotspot, 154–155
Roku, 12, 13
ROM. *See* Read-only memory (ROM)
ROMs, 68
Root directory, 74
Rosetta Stone, 86
RottenTomatoes.com, 114
Router, 139–140
RunKeeper, 24

S

Safeguarding data, 152–159. *See also* Security
Safeguarding hardware, 150–152
Sage 50 Accounting, 83
Samsung Chromebook, 67
Samsung Galaxy Note, 15
Scalability, 146
Scalable system, 146
Scanadu Scout, 25

Scanner, 45–46
Scanner apps, 46
Scareware, 153
Scribd, 119–120
Scrolling, 43
SD. *See* Secure Digital (SD)
SDLC. *See* Software development life cycle (SDLC)
Search engine, 112, 124
Search engine optimization (SEO), 187
Search modifiers, 124
Searching for files, 76
Secure Digital (SD), 40
Security, 148–159
    accidents and disasters, 151–152
    authentication/authorization, 157
    backup, 158–159
    countermeasures, 149–150, 156
    data theft, 155
    environmental hazards, 152
    hacking, 153–154
    identity theft, 155
    malware, 152–153
    password, 157–158
    password theft, 155
    phishing, 155–156
    power problems, 150–151
    pretexting, 155
    risk assessment, 149
    rogue hotspot, 154–155
    safeguarding data, 152–159
    safeguarding hardware, 150–152
    scareware, 153
    security utilities, 156
    social engineering, 155–156
    spyware, 153
    theft, 151
    threats and vulnerabilities, 148–149
    tips/pointers, 158
    Trojan horse, 153
    up-to-date software, 156
    vandalism, 151
    virus, 153
    VPN, 157
    worm, 153
    WPA2 encryption, 157
    zombies/botnets, 154
Security software, 69
Security suite, 69
Security utilities, 69–70, 156
Server farm, 11
Server operating system, 63–64
SharePoint, 135
Shareware, 78
Sharing. *See* Specialty sharing
Sharing photos and videos, 177
Shielded twisted-pair (STP) cable, 136
Shopping, 121. *See also* Buying guide
Shopping cart, 121
Short-duration messaging, 22
Short message service (SMS), 21
Siri, 16, 46, 67, 185
Skype, 22, 103
Sleep, 180
Sleepbot, 24
Smart Search, 76
Smart TV, 12
Smart watch, 15
Smartphone, 14–15, 193. *See also* Mobile devices
SMS. *See* Short message service (SMS)
Snapchat, 22
Social engineering, 155–156
Social media, 8, 115. *See also* Social web
    Facebook, 116
    friends and circles, 116
    Google+, 116
    LinkedIn, 117
    privacy, 176
    social and political change, 178
    Tumblr, 117
    Twitter, 118
Social networking, 22. *See also* Social media
Social news sites, 119
Social web, 115–120
    blogging, 117
    commenting and rating, 115
    friends and circles, 116

    microblogging, 117–118
    professional networking, 117
    social media. *See* Social media
    specialty sharing, 118–120
Software, 60–92
    application. *See* Application software
    defined, 7
    how developed, 87–88
    system. *See* System software
    updates, 156
Software acquisition and installation, 77–79
Software development, 87–88
Software development life cycle
    (SDLC), 87
Software engineer, 187
Software license, 77
Software update, 88
Solid state drive (SSD), 40
Solid state storage, 40
Songza, 23
Sony PlayStation 4 (PS4), 12
Sound card, 51
Sound editing programs, 51
Sound system, 51
Spam, 100
Speakers, 51
Specialty sharing, 118–120
    books and documents, 119–120
    news and links, 119
    photos and images, 119
    videos, 118–119
Speech recognition, 46
Spotify, 23, 170
Spotify Premium, 170
Spotlight, 76
Spreadsheet software, 81
Spyware, 153
SSD. *See* Solid state drive (SSD)
Star topology, 138
Start screen, 64
Storage, 7, 38–40
Storage optimization, 71–73
Streaming media, 22–23, 104
Streaming player, 12
Streaming services, 170
Street View, 114
Striping, 146
Striping with parity, 146
Strong password, 157
Stylus, 44
Subdomain, 100
Subfolder, 74
Subscription model, 78
Subscription services, 170
Subwoofer, 51
Supercomputer, 11
Support specialist, 188
Surface tablet, 68
Surge protector, 150
Surround sound speaker system, 51
Switch, 139
System and GUI keys, 42
System Restore, 72
System software, 62–76
    defined, 62
    file management, 74–76
    operating system, 62–68
    utilities, 69–73
System unit, 34–35
Systems analyst, 187

T

Tabbed browsing, 109
Tablet computer, 14, 194
Tag, 119
Tape drive, 39
Tape library, 158
Tax preparation software, 83
TB. *See* Terabyte (TB)
TCP/IP, 97
Telecommuting, 181–182
Terabyte (TB), 38
Terminator, 138
Terminology (glossary), 195–204